Counseling
Employment Bound
Youth

By

Edwin L. Herr, Ed.D.
Distinguished Professor of Education and
Associate Dean for Academic Programs and Research
The Pennsylvania State University
University Park, PA 16802-3206

ERIC Counseling and Student Services Clearinghouse
School of Education
University of North Carolina at Greensboro
Greensboro, North Carolina 27412-5001

1-800-414-9769

ERIC/CASS Publications
School of Education
University of North Carolina at Greensboro
Greensboro, NC 27412
1-800 414-9769

ISBN 1-56109-061-1

This publication was funded by the U.S. Department of
Education, Office of Educational Research and Improvement,
Contract no. RR93002004. Opinions expressed in this
publication do not necessarily reflect the positions of the
U.S. Department of Education, OERI, or ERIC/CASS.

Dedication

To:

Pat, Alicia, Amber, and *Christopher* for providing the
support, time, and love to make writing
Counseling Employment-Bound Youth
a positive experience.

To:

Beverly M. King for providing the clerical excellence,
follow through, and loyalty that has sustained
the writing process and made the
final product complete.

To:

Garry Walz for his invitation to write this book
and for his consistent encouragement
and positive feedback through the process.

Edwin L. Herr is Distinguished Professor of Education (Counselor Education and Counseling Psychology) and Associate Dean for Academic Programs and Research, College of Education, The Pennsylvania State University. Previously, Dr. Herr served as Head of the Department of Counselor Education, Counseling Psychology, and Rehabilitation Services Education or earlier department iterations for 24 years. During this time, he also served as University Director of Vocational Teacher Education and Director of the Center for Professional Personnel Development in Vocational Education.

A former business teacher, school counselor, and director of guidance, Dr. Herr previously served as the first director of the Bureaus of Guidance Services and the Bureau of Pupil Personnel Services, Pennsylvania Department of Education (1966-68). He has been visiting professor, researcher or coordinator of international conferences in some 20 European universities as well as in Africa, Canada, Japan and Taiwan.

Among his many prestigious professional awards, in 1984 he was appointed an Honorary Member of the Swedish National Labor Market Board for his research and conceptual work in career development. In 1990, he received the Professional Development Award of the American Association for sustained national and international influence on theory, research, and practice in career behavior. In 1990, he received the Professional Development Award of the American Association for Counseling and Development for national and international scholarship and research on systems of counseling and the 50th Anniversary Professional Leadership Award of the Association for Counselor Education and Supervision for his scholarship and leadership in counselor preparation. For his scholarship and leadership in Vocational Education, he was chosen the Visiting Scholar of the University Council of Vocational for 1990-1991. In 1993, he received a Government Relations Award for outstanding achievement in legislation and public policy in behalf of the counseling profession from the National Employment Counselors Association and the American Counseling Association, and he was chosen the Distinguished Scholar for 1993 by Chi Sigma Iota, the Counseling Academic and Professional Honor Society International.

Dr. Herr is past president of the American Association for Counseling and Development, past president of the National Vocational Guidance Association, and past president of the Association for Counselor Education and Supervision. He is author or co-author of over 275 articles and some twenty-eight books and monographs, *A Handbook for Career Centers in Colleges and Universities; Counseling in a Dynamic Society: Opportunities and Challenges* and *Career Guidance and Counseling Through the Life Span*. He is the current editor of the *Journal of Counseling and Development* and a member of several other editorial boards, including the *British Journal of Guidance and Counseling.*

Herr is a National Certified Counselor, a National Certified Career Counselor, and a licensed psychologist in Pennsylvania. He has a part-time practice in career counseling, and he has consulted widely in the United States and abroad with government agencies, schools, universities and corporations.

Introduction

At long last, we have the monograph which so many persons have needed and sought out for such a long period of time—*Counseling Employment Bound Youth*. Employment bound youth, a large and vital segment of our population (20 million plus) and future labor force, have largely been ignored in the literature on careers and on counseling and guidance. This neglect has clearly been to the great detriment not only of the young people themselves but to our country's vitality and competitiveness in the rapidly expanding global economy. In many ways, their future is our future. Among the major industrialized countries of the world, the United States alone has ignored the needs of employment bound youth; we as a nation shall therefore suffer the consequences.

In masterful writing that offers a broad and comprehensive overview of the challenges faced as well as specific recommendations for how school, business, and communities can and should respond, Dr. Herr has produced a thoughtful, yet eminently practical, book. Persons concerned about the future of the United States and the role that youth will play will find resources needed to plan and take action to initiate change in how localities respond to employment bound youth. The compelling and rewarding monograph is directed towards counselors, career specialists, teachers, administrators, policy makers, and community members who are concerned about the direction of their schools. Dr. Herr resists the temptation to trivialize the challenge that employment bound youth present and avoids suggesting band-aid treatments or the interventions of a single helping group. Perhaps most of all, the book is an urgent wake-up call to us all that we have overslept, and it is imperative that we act immediately. Fortunately, as we emerge blurry-eyed from our sleep, he provides clear choices and steps we can take to respond *now* to this ever growing challenge.

It is extremely doubtful that many, if anyone else, could have written a book of such high quality. Dr. Herr is an eminent scholar, researcher, and professional leader who has repeatedly won the highest awards that education and counseling can bestow. He is known for his cogent insight into contemporary life and his ability to synthesize massive bodies of literature into digestible bites that counseling and career practitioners and educators can use to initiate helpful programs and practices. In short, this truly is a masterful book that will stimulate, excite, and motivate the reader to confront a major local and national problem—our neglected employment bound youth.

Garry R. Walz, *Director*
ERIC/CASS

TABLE OF CONTENTS

Chapter One

Chapter Two

Chapter Three

Chapter Four

Chapter Five

Chapter Six

Chapter Seven

Chapter One

Work-Bound Youth: Diversity in Characteristics, Opportunities, and Support

The Meaning of the Term

There are several terms that are used to describe the population about whom this book is most concerned. The term "employment-bound" has been chosen as the key descriptor although it would be equally appropriate to use terms such as job-bound, work-bound, or, as Hoyt (1965) suggested almost 30 years ago, "the Specialty Oriented." As the use of these terms typically occurs, they can be seen as essentially interchangeable or, perhaps more accurately, they portray different segments of the adolescent and young adult populations. While it is true that virtually all youth and young adults regardless of educational level are, in some sense, employment-bound, we use the term here to refer to those whose primary work/educational goal at the end of high school is to go to work. There are also other terms that are frequently used to describe the population of concern here. They include the Non-College-Bound or the "Forgotten Half" (W. T. Grant Foundation, 1988). While both of these terms are useful, they tend to be used in a pejorative way that evinces suggestions of inferiority or sympathy. The stance taken here is that employment-bound youth, those whose prime educational motivation is to acquire an occupational skill or set of skills so that they can enter the labor market, who intend to go directly into employment, into a job, following high school are assets to the nation, not deficits. But, their special needs for the exploration of, preparation for, choice of and adjustment to work, in whatever institutional or self-employed form it takes, must be examined comprehensively, reflected in national policy, and incorporated in the training and practice of educators, counselors, and other persons of significance (e.g., employers) in the facilitation of their career development and employment.

It is important to acknowledge in both the definitions of employment-bound or job-bound youth and in counseling or educational responses to this population that the students or young adults included are not homogeneous or static or even well-defined. Employment-bound youth, as well as any other sub-population of persons that can be identified, are diverse in their characteristics, and such diversity across social and economic levels, gender, geography, racial and ethnic backgrounds, intellectual ability, and physical status must be acknowledged in the provision of educational or training programs, in counseling, and in other initiatives.

For the purposes of this book, employment-bound youth are those who aspire to enter the labor force, to acquire a job, usually full-time, immediately upon graduation from high school. Included in this population would be early school-leavers, those who do not persist in school attendance until high school graduation, but who tend to "drop out" in order to focus on paid work of some form or in the case of many females to become parents. They may ultimately pursue a General Educational Diploma (G.E.D.) or other form of high school equivalency credential. However, their inclusion in the population described here is based on their primary motivation to seek paid, typically full-time employment, not to seek post-secondary education. Similarly, the larger portion of employment-bound youth, who do graduate from high school and immediately enter the labor force, may, and in increasing numbers probably will, enter some form of post secondary education, including college, at some future time in their life, but that is not the primary goal they seek at the conclusion of high school.

The potential pool of employment-bound youth, then, incorporates at least 50 percent of the students who graduate from most school districts in the nation. While there are community and regional variations in these numbers across the nation, when one subtracts the number of students who primarily aspire to college and actually attend immediately following high school graduation, a description of an average of 50 percent of students as employment-bound is reasonable, although it probably understates the total population of concern. When those who begin postsecondary education, but do not complete a baccalaureate degree, are included, and students who drop out of high school before graduating are incorporated, the number of youth involved is a large portion, perhaps as much as 75 percent, of each adolescent cohort. Of these numbers, almost 80 percent are White, 12 percent are African-American and 9 percent are Hispanic (Whitman, 1989).

There are several reasons for avoiding use of the term "non-college bound" to describe this population. For one, many young people who are employment-bound at the end of high school are likely to attend community or four-year colleges at some point in their working life. They may do so following a period of military service from which they accrue significant educational benefits. They may do so because an employer or a union agreement provides financial and psychological support to continue their education. They may do so because when they were in high school, they were quite unclear about why they would go to college or what they would study and after a period of employment such goals became clearer.

Perhaps the more important reason to avoid use of the term "non-college bound" is to avoid the simplistic notion that there are two clearly defined, static strata of youth—those college-bound and those not—with the second group considered to be less capable, less motivated, and less qualified then those who say that they plan to go to college. Such assumptions are not accurate. Although employment-bound youth are more likely to be from lower socioeconomic levels with fewer financial resources and college-oriented role models, and to have different aspirations and goals than do students whose primary motivation following high school graduation is to attend college, many of these youth are the intellectual equal of "college-bound" students. As a group, employment-bound students are less likely to be in the highest academic or socioeconomic quartiles of the adolescent population, but this does not imply that employment-bound students are incapable of academically superior work or of completing baccalaureate degrees or beyond. Many adolescents, originally classified as employment-bound youth, do ultimately attend college or enter intellectually rigorous technical occupations. Thus, these subpopulations of adolescents are fluid, not rigidly stratified, and comprised of many persons in each category of comparable academic and intellectual ability.

The Importance of Employment-Bound Youth

It is true that, because of elitist attitudes in the society at large that tend to favor college attendance and provide financial investment for college-bound at twice the level provided to students not going directly to college (W. T. Grant Foundation, 1988), employment-bound youth may feel forgotten or disaffected. Or, such social attitudes may encourage some youth to say that they are going to college although they have little motivation to do so. Such attitudes may cause some youths to plan for college even though their true career aspirations may be in fields that require technical or other specialized sub-baccalaureate education. Such attitudes, however, do not reflect the importance of the contribution of employment-bound students to the economic viability of their nation now or in the future. At one level, this reality is epitomized by continuing projection that in the future the majority of jobs in the American economy will not require baccalaureate degrees even though the trend is to suggest that new jobs coming into the occupational structure will require some post-secondary education, not necessarily collegiate in nature (Hudson Institute, 1987). According to projections by the U. S. Department of Labor (1989), by the year 2000 only 23.4 percent of U. S. jobs are predicted to require a four-year college or university degree even though some 40 percent of high school graduates are going to college. For these reasons and others, Kutscher (1987) has predicted that the surplus of college graduates in the U. S. that began in the early 1970s is expected to continue through the year 2000. Whether or not a college degree is a necessity for more than 25 percent of youth in the future, with a general rise in educational level required to participate in many of the emerging occupations spawned by a global economy in the late 1990s, educational reform policies are assuming that the substance of education for work at all levels of manufacturing and service will, in the future, require greater concentration of mathematics, science, and communications skills as well as other general employability skills for employment-bound youth. Such trends will be described more fully in subsequent parts of the book.

At another level, it is becoming clear, in view of the diverse challenges of international economic competition, that no nation can sustain its economic viability with only a highly educated elite. Rather, workers in all sections of production, distribution, transportation, financial services and other industries must be prepared with the basic academic skills, the teachability and flexibility, the commitment to life-long learning that permits them to rapidly change in ways required by new organizations of work or content changes in the processes and performance of work. The strengthening of the skills of employment-bound youth is imperative as well because as the next chapter will discuss, as the global economy emerges, there is a concomitant globalization of the work force, an expanding pool of persons, educated and technically competent, with whom American employment-bound youth will increasingly compete. Only if American youth can compete effectively for available and emerging jobs and be equipped to change with change can their individual economic security and that of the nation be assured.

In essence, a central argument that guides the content of this book is not that employment-bound youth are inferior to other youth and, therefore, should receive a second-rate education or limited support. Rather, the view here is that employment-bound students constitute such an important proportion of the labor force, certainly of the technical, skilled, clerical, retailing and distribution system of the nation, that their needs must be given national, state, and local priority. As any administrator knows, it is the clerical support staff of an organization, most of whom are high school graduates, whose skills, insights, and loyalty literally make the organization function. Whether their jobs are in data entry, word processing, customer contact, financial record keeping, or other vital areas, these persons are the institutional memory and the maintainers of the organization's systems. So it is with the vast array of jobs in the construction trades, the trucking and railroad distribution industries, the wholesale and inventory systems, road, water and sewer systems, building and vehicle maintenance, and telecommunications installation and repair. These vital elements of the national and, indeed, international infrastructure rely on a constant infusion and availability of employment-bound youth and young adults, most of whom enter the labor force with a high school diploma, not a baccalaureate degree. This perspective can be further illustrated by examining Table 1 (Silvestri, 1993, p. 74) which reports on the U. S. Department of Labor projections about the occupations with the largest job growth, from 1992-2005. Conservatively, 19 out of 31 occupations represented will be filled by high school graduates or less, primarily employment-bound youth, not college graduates.

Table 1.				
Fastest Growing Occupations, 1992-2005, moderate alternative projection				
(Numbers in thousands)				
Occupation	Employment		Numerical Change	Percent Change
	1992	2005		
Home health aides	347	827	479	138
Human services workers	189	445	256	136
Personal and home care aides	127	293	166	130
Computer engineers and scientists	211	447	235	112
Systems analysts	455	956	501	110
Physical and corrective therapy assistants and aides	61	118	57	93
Physical therapists	90	170	79	88
Paralegals	95	176	81	86
Teachers, special education	358	625	257	74
Medical assistants	181	308	128	71
Detectives, except public	59	100	41	70
Correction officers	282	479	197	70
Child care workers	684	1,135	450	66
Travel agents	115	191	76	66
Radiologic technologists and technicians	162	264	102	63
Nursery workers	72	116	44	62
Medical records technicians	76	123	47	61
Operations research analysts	45	72	27	61
Occupational therapists	40	64	24	60
Legal secretaries	280	439	160	57
Teachers, preschool and kindergarten	434	669	236	54
Manicurists	35	55	19	54
Producres, directors, actors and entertainers	129	198	69	54
Speech-language pathologists and audiologists	73	110	37	51
Flight attendants	93	140	47	51
Guards	803	1,211	408	51
Insurance adjusters, examiners, and investigators	147	220	72	49
Respiratory therapists	74	109	36	48
Psychologists	143	212	69	48
Paving, surfacing, and tamping equipment operators	72	107	35	48

SOURCE: Table 3, page 74, George L. Silvestri, Occupational Employment: Wide Variations in Growth, *Monthly Labor Review, 116, 17,* 58-86.

Similarly, if one studies Table 2, (Silvestri, 1993, p. 75) which reports the Department of Labor's fastest projections of the growing occupations between 1992 and 2005, only 11 of the 30 occupations clearly require college graduates. While several other occupations would require some training beyond high school to enter, at least 15 of the 30 occupations portrayed could be entered by persons with a high school diploma or, in a few instances, less. What the data in Tables 1 and 2 also suggest is that there is a new emphasis rising in the American occupational structure for whom employment-bound youth are often prime candidates. This emphasis is the rise of technicians as a major part of the American work force, workers who have specialty technical skills that typically exceed those of traditional skilled workers but do not require a baccalaureate degree, although some technicians are college graduates or even possess a Master's degree. Called "a new worker elite who are transforming the American labor force and potentially every organization that employs them"..."the technician is becoming the core employee of the digital information age" (Richman, 1994). According to available statistics, the number of technicians has increased by nearly 300% since 1950—triple the growth rate for the work force as a whole. As reported by the Occupational Outlook Handbook (U. S. Department of Labor, Bureau of Labor Statistics, May 1994), "Workers in this group provide technical assistance to engineers, scientists, physicians, and other professional workers, as well as operate and program technical equipment. Employment in this cluster is expected to increase 32 percent, faster than average, from 4.3 to 5.7 million. Employment of paralegals is expected to increase much faster than average as use of these workers in the rapidly expanding legal services industry increases. Health technicians and technologists, such as licensed practical nurses and radiological technologists, will add large numbers of jobs" (p. 15).

As suggested above, technicians appear across industries. They include air traffic controllers, broadcast technicians, computer programmers, dental hygienists, medical technicians, drafters, engineering technicians, library technicians, nuclear medicine technologists, and science technicians. There are many other types of technicians but they have in common the ability to use increasingly powerful, versatile, and user-friendly technologies to accomplish complex and challenging tasks

Table 2.

Occupations with the largest job growth, 1992-2005, moderate alternative projection

(Numbers in thousands)

Occupation	Employment		Numerical Change	Percent Change
	1992	2005		
Salespersons,retail	3,660	4,446	786	21
Registered nurses	1,835	2,601	765	42
Cashiers..	2,747	3,414	670	24
General office clerks	2,688	3,342	654	24
Truck drivers light and heavy	2,391	3,039	648	27
Waiters and waitresses	1,756	2,394	637	38
Nursing aides,orderlies and attendants	1,308	1,903	594	45
Janitors and cleaners, including maids and housekeeping cleaners	2,862	3,410	548	19
Food preparation workers	1,223	1,748	524	43
Systems analysts....................................	455	956	501	110
Home health aids....................................	347	827	479	138
Teachers, secondary school	1,263	1,724	462	37
Child care workers	684	1,135	450	66
Guards	803	1,211	408	51
Marketing and sales worker supervisors	2,036	2,443	407	20
Teacher aides and educational assistants	885	1,266	381	43
General managers and top executives	2,871	3,251	380	13
Maintenance repairers, general utility	1,145	1,484	319	28
Gardeners and groundskeepers, except farm	884	1,195	311	35
Teachers, elementary	1,456	1,767	311	21
Food counter, fountain, and related workers	1.564	1,872	308	20
Receptionists and information clerks	904	1,210	305	34
Accountants and auditors	939	1,243	304	32
Clerical supervisors and managers	1,267	1,568	301	24
Cooks, restaurant	602	879	276	46
Teachers,special education	358	625	267	74
Licensed practical nurses	659	920	261	40
Cooks, short order and fast food	714	971	257	38
Human services workers	189	445	256	136
Computer engineers and scientists	211	447	236	112

SOURCE: Table 4, page 75, George L. Silvestri, Occupational Employment: Wide Variations in Growth, *Monthly Labor Review,116,17,* 58-86.

(e.g., trouble shoot robots, maintain and operate computer and telecommunications networks, perform and evaluate medical tests) that require judgment and skills and that arise from the increasing information- dependent technical work environment.

Persons enter the ranks of technicians with varying levels of formal education and credentials. Many enter technical fields with no more than a high school diploma and training acquired on the job. Others have received training as technicians in the Armed Forces which they translate into civilian occupations. Many technicians come to their careers from a trade school or a community college and an increasing number of them have a college or graduate degree (Richman, 1994). Such circumstances again reflect the importance and the potential of, as well as the opportunities for, well-trained high school graduates as major assets to the American occupational structure.

These observations are in no way intended to demean the importance of a college degree in a changing society, one which is information rich and where knowledge is increasingly important to perform jobs at many levels of the occupational structure. The issue here is the importance of employment-bound youth in the total economic structure of the nation and the need to educate them effectively and fully in the high school years so they will have the basic academic skills in reading, writing, computer literacy, communications, interpersonal and other general employability skills which many of the jobs which they will enter will demand. Some examples will illustrate the reality that qualifications for today's and tomorrow's" middle and low-wage jobs are rising even more rapidly than in the past. "In 1965, a car mechanic needed to understand 5,000 pages of service manuals to fix any automobile on the road; today he must be able to decipher 465,000 pages of text, the equivalent of 250 big-city telephone books... The secretary who once pecked away at a manual typewriter must now master a word processor, a computer and telecommunications equipment. Even the cashier at the 7-Eleven store has to know how to sell money orders and do minor maintenance jobs on the Slurpee and Big Gulp machines" (Whitman, 1989, p. 46). Many other examples could be identified which affirm the expanding roles played by employment-bound youth as they enter the labor force and the essential roles that basic academic skills play in a growing number of the jobs they perform.

Given the importance of such workers within the complex needs of the occupational structure, opportunities must be made available in the economy of the 21st century to ensure that employment-bound youth are provided access to "jobs with a future, that they do not experience unemployment rates that are substantially higher than other segments of the labor force, or that the real income available to these persons does not continue in deep decline" (W. T. Grant Foundation, 1988). To achieve such goals requires new perspectives on the education of employment-bound youth, on the school-to-work transition, and on the counseling and other support systems available in schools, communities, and in workplaces. These responses to employment-bound youth need to be sensitive to the diverse characteristics by which employment-bound youth can be described.

Employment-Bound Youth: Their Characteristics

The 20 million or so employment-bound youth in the United States are a diverse, not a homogeneous, group. They are typically high school graduates, mostly free of difficulty with drugs, crime, teenage pregnancy, or alienation from adults, and with aspirations for a job, a family, a place in the community of which they can be proud (W. T. Grant, 1988).

Employment-Bound Youth in Vocational Education

Employment-bound youth appear in all school curricula—academic, business, general, and vocational. A large proportion of the students described here as employment-bound are enrolled in a general curriculum or, more likely, in some form of vocational education for some part of their schooling. While stereotypes abound about general education and about vocational education and about the students who occupy such curricula, neither general or vocational education nor the students who participate in them are easy to label.

The general curriculum tends to be seen as one which is neither rigorous nor clearly related to either academic or vocational goals. It is one in which students are seen as academically inferior to students in other curricula, possessing neither the intellectual or psychomotor skills valued in the college preparation or vocational education curricula. It is one in which students are seen as tending to take easier, less rigorous courses, frequently at a survey level, which lead to no specific outcome except a high school diploma. During the height of the Career Education movement in the United States, U. S. Commissioner of Education Sidney Marland, in one of his speeches, called the general curriculum "a swampland of irrelevant pap" to illustrate his concern that students in that curriculum were not gaining the intensity of skills or the quality of academic preparation required by the occupational structure which most of them intended to enter as employment-bound youth. Subsequent to Marland's comment in the early 1970s, some school districts have abandoned the general curriculum and required students to enter either a clearly defined academic or vocational education track. How many students are now in a general curriculum is difficult to assess. It is also difficult to determine accurately the rigor of the basic academic skills acquired by employment-bound students in the general curriculum since many such students in that curriculum combine college preparatory courses and vocational courses into a blend of courses which allows them both to acquire the academic requisites to enter college and some vocational skills to enter the work force. Thus, they keep their options open without committing themselves precisely to one or the other academic or vocational paths. The latter use of the general curriculum by some students is particularly likely in a school district where curriculum boundaries are rigid, where the official policy is that if you matriculate in the college preparatory curriculum, you cannot take vocational education courses and vice versa. Where the general curriculum exists, one can usually take both college preparatory courses and vocational education courses in some combination, usually without much guidance or control by the school. It is possible that many students who do so are basically employment-bound.

Beyond the alleged problems with the general curriculum, while it is true that some vocational education programs in some comprehensive high schools may be "dumping" grounds for students of low achievement (Aring, 1993), there are vocational programs in regional or area vocational technical schools for which the requirements in science and mathematics are as stringent as they would be in any secondary school college preparatory program and, in such cases, there are students queuing up to obtain admission. Thus, vocational education programs in many facilities offer courses or curricula requiring intellectual ability on a continuum from below average to the very highest. As such, vocational education is not a narrow curriculum of courses only for those with low intellect and strong psychomotor skills but rather a continuum of opportunities, the requirements of which span the intellectual and psychomotor skill range. According to the National Center for Educational Statistics of the U. S. Department of Education (1992), "The vocational curriculum appeals to a diverse group of students. Individuals from all racial-ethnic backgrounds and all levels of academic ability and socioeconomic status take vocational education courses. The majority of secondary students preparing for college have taken at least one vocational course other than typing. Similarly, most postsecondary students enrolled in less-than-four-year institutions routinely participate in vocational education programs." (p. xix).

Using the 1987 high school senior class in the U. S. as an example, the National Center for Educational Statistics found that 98 percent of all public high school students completed at least one course in vocational education during their high school careers and almost 90 percent of all graduates completed at least one course in specific labor market preparation. Overall, public high school graduates in 1987 earned an average total of 22.8 carnage units in high school. Surprisingly, perhaps, on the average they earned 4.4 units in vocational education, or about 20 percent of their total units. White students tend to have heavier concentration in vocational education than minority students. Again, using the national high school class of 1987 as the sample, the National Center for Educational Statistics found that about 15 percent of White students earned 8.00 or more units in vocational education compared with 11 percent of Black students, 9 percent of Hispanic students, 4 percent of Asian students, and 12 percent of Native American students. Further, handicapped students were more likely than nonhandicapped students to be heavy concentrators in vocational education; 26 percent of the former earned 8.00 or more units of vocational education compared to 13 percent of nonhandicapped students (xx). Such partici-pation in vocational education in high school was positively related with full-time employment (xxii).

The national statistical data describing vocational education students indicates that participation in most vocational areas decreases as graduates' socioeconomic status, academic ability, and high school grades increases. Graduates in the highest socioeconomic status and academic ability quartiles are significantly less likely than graduates in the lowest quartiles to complete at least one course in agriculture, business, marketing and distribution, occupational home economics, and construction trades. In addition, graduates in the highest academic quartile are less likely than those in the lowest academic quartile to participate in trade and industry programs. Similarly, graduates who earn mostly A's in high school are significantly less likely than graduates with lower grades to participate in agriculture, marketing and distribution, occupational home economics, and trade and industry (xxii).

Interestingly, when one turns to postsecondary vocational education, the National Center on Educational Statistics (1992) reports that in the fall of 1990, about 6 percent of the U. S. population 18 through 34 years of age were taking vocational courses. About 43 percent of those students (3 percent of all 18 through 34 year-olds) were taking vocational courses in public 2-year colleges. Almost 19 percent were taking courses from a vocational, trade, or business school, while only 5 percent were taking courses provided directly by employers (p. 74).

The data about vocational education students in the United States reported by the National Center for Educational Statistics (1992) has been affirmed by the findings of the Congressionally-mandated National Assessment of Vocational Education, carried out from 1987 to 1989. In reports from the studies conducted under this national assessment, it was stated that, "A striking characteristic of secondary vocational education is that student participation is nearly universal. As expected, students who plan to complete their education at the end of high school [employment-bound students] are the largest consumers of vocational education. Surprisingly, college-bound students also take substantial amounts of vocational education, and not just general, introductory, or consumer and homemaking courses, but occupationally specific vocational education as well." (National Assessment of Vocational Education, July, 1989, p. x). In follow-up national studies of the high school class of 1982, it was found that students planning to attend postsecondary vocational institutions or colleges accounted for nearly three-quarters of all vocational credits taken by high school graduates (p. x). In contrast to such findings, the National Assessment of Vocational Education found as well that academically disadvantaged students and students with handicaps clearly take more vocational education than do academically advantaged and nonhandicapped students (p. xi).

The intent here is not to critique vocational education but to try to clarify the characteristics of employment-bound youth. As suggested above, these youth are not homogenous in their characteristics. But to the degree that student concentrators in vocational education comprise a significant group of employ-ment-bound youth, it is useful to consider some of their char-acteristics beyond those already noted. In data reported in 1982 (Berryman, 1982), the results indicated that vocational students differed substantially from academic students (basically college-bound youth) in such ways as the following:

- substantially lower school performance and measured ability than academic students
- they derive from families of much lower socio-economic status than those of academic students
- they show more self-esteem than academic students, but have less sense of control over events that affect them
- they value occupational security and family happiness more than academic students
- they value occupational contacts and steady progress in work more than the academic group
- they participated in extra curricular activities less than academic students
- their postsecondary plans differed substantially from academic students

Berryman summarized her findings in this way:
"When we look at this array of variables, we see a group that, relative to one or both of the other curricular groups, comes from the socioeconomically lower-status families in the com-munity; does not do well at what schools tend to define as their highest status mission—cognitive development; is not part of the high school's extracurricular structure except for that part

directly related to the vocational curriculum; rates the quality of the school positively; is not alienated from the high school; does not regard itself as having been channeled into its curriculum; wants money, steady work, and a happy family out of life; prefers to work after high school; selects practical (technical/ vocational) postsecondary education; has higher postsecondary employment rates and higher numbers of hours worked per week; and is more satisfied with jobs as a whole and with their specific dimensions" (Berryman, 1982, p. 184).

Such perspectives on characteristics of vocational education are undoubtedly descriptive of many vocational education students, but certainly not all. For example, the research of Dayton and Feldhusen (1989) among secondary schools in Indiana has made it clear that gifted students are not found only in academic or college-preparatory curricula. There are also vocationally talented high school students. These students tend to manifest academic talent or high ability, vocational talent or high ability, high levels of motivation/persistence, study skills, and leadership. Among the difficulties these talented students had as enrollees in vocational education were difficulties in scheduling both academic and vocational classes, boredom, and maintaining self-motivation, the lack of articulation between vocational and postsecondary programs, and dealing with parent, teacher, and counselor pressure to stay in the academic track even though as students they wanted to be in vocational education. Career guidance services for such students were seen as needing to deal with the unique pressures they face, to assist them in scheduling and in clarifying options, and to provide career education in more depth than usual.

The needs for greater attention to the career guidance needs of students in vocational education is not confined only to those who are gifted and talented. Various studies done over the past twenty-five years have shown that students in vocational education have received less access to career counseling or career guidance than other students (e. g., Campbell, 1968; Kauffman, et al, 1967; Palmo and DeVantier, 1976; Stern, 1977; the Business Advisory Committee, the Education Commission of the States, 1985; the Research Policy Committee, the Committee for Economic Development, 1985). Other longitudinal studies that have examined the student career maturity of students in different curricula have shown that largely because of the developmental experiences that differ for socioeconomic groups, students in academic curricula tend to be more career mature and to have experienced more comprehensive career-related exploratory behavior than have vocational students (Herr, Weitz, Good, & McCloskey, 1981). Basically, these findings suggest that the degree to which career development experiences are encouraged or provided by different curricula and by parents at different socioeconomic levels differ in major ways in parallel with the differing access of students to career guidance opportunities. The further extrapolation from these findings is that employment-bound youth, in whichever curriculum they are found, receive less career counseling and guidance or counseling of any kind than do college-bound students and this is not necessarily in relation to their needs or desires for such services.

It seems accurate to suggest that if career counseling for employment-bound youth is to be improved in the United States, more emphasis must be given to its availability for students in vocational education. At present, while there is a large literature on career counseling and career guidance in the secondary school, that literature tends not to be differentiated in terms of the needs and treatment of vocational education students. On the positive side, it could be argued that the meaning of an undifferentiated literature on career guidance is that all secondary students should have equal access to career counseling and career guidance. Since that does not appear to be the reality, the less positive side of an undifferentiated literature is that the unique needs of vocational education or, more broadly, employment-bound youth are not being responded to in a systematic manner.

Some Employment-Bound Youth at Risk

However important vocational education is as a major niche in which to find employment-bound youth and provide career counseling for them, there are other perspectives on employment-bound youth that also deserve mention. For example, it is also important to acknowledge that where they live and the racial, gender, or other characteristics by which they are identified has much to do with the likelihood that they will meet their aspirations or find the type of job or the level of economic outcome they seek. Because of stifled ambitions, limited developmental experiences or role models, some proportion of employment-bound youth are at risk of academic failure in school and at risk of being cast into a jagged or inadequate experience in entering and adjusting to the labor market. Many of these young people are employed, or underemployed, in part-time and low-paying jobs which limit their ability to anticipate having or adequately supporting their own family. As results of such phenomena unfold, single parent families, absentee fathers, and teenage pregnancies have grown dramatically in the last several decades. Much of the burden of the economic dislocations and job transitions so pervasive across the nation, has now fallen on the youth and young adult (ages 16 to 24) populations of the nation. For example, in the late 1980s, the unemployment rates for teenagers were about 16 percent for all teenagers, more than 32 percent for Black teens. For workers 20-24 years of age, the employment rates were slightly less than 7 percent for Whites, 11 percent for Hispanics, and 20 percent for Blacks. The real median income of families headed by a 20-24-year-old fell 27 percent from 1973 to 1986; the percentage of 20-24-year-old males able to support a family of three above the poverty level dropped by nearly a quarter from 88.3 percent in 1973 to 43.8 percent in 1986. The rate of that decline for Blacks in the same age group was twice as high (W. T. Grant Foundation, 1989).

As suggested above, the population of employment-bound youth, just as is true of the broader American labor force, can be dismantled into many different subpopulations. These groups can be classified by a range of demographic variables (e.g., gender, race, socioeconomic background, geographic location, school leaver or completer), as well as by other characteristics: those who are functionally literate and those who are not; those who have an adequate command of basic skills and those who do not. The number of employment-bound youth and adults in the work force who are not functionally literate or who do not have an adequate command of basic skills is troublesome, although it certainly does not indict or suggest that all employment-bound youth or adults have such problems. Examples of data which do address literacy or academic skill problems in some subpopulations of employment-bound youth or adults include fairly old data (Knowles, 1977) that suggest that approximately 40 percent of the American adult population is coping inadequately with typical life problems (e.g., getting work, holding a job, buying things, making change, managing one's economic life, and parenting). Whether or not a figure of 40 percent is an over or understatement of adult life problems is not known but it is certainly consistent with other available data. One estimate is that 23 million Americans, 10 percent of the population, are functionally illiterate; one out of every eight 17-year-olds is functionally illiterate and one million youth drop out of school every year—in some urban schools the rate is over 50 percent (Katzman, 1991). "Nationally, one of every four students does not stay in school until graduation; the figure is twice as bad in inner city high schools and for specific groups it is often worse" (NEA, 1988, p.1).

Other studies speak more directly to deficits in basic academic skills which reduce productivity among workers. One national study of employers found that 30 percent of those surveyed reported that secretaries have difficulty reading at the level required by the job; 50 percent reported managers and supervisors unable to write paragraphs free of grammatical error; 50 percent reported skilled and unskilled employees, including bookkeepers, unable to use decimals and fractions in math problems; 65 percent reported that basic skills deficiencies limit the job advancement of their high school graduate employees (Center for Public Resources, 1983). In another example, the New York Telephone Company, in a major recruitment effort, found that from January to July 1987, only 3,619 of 22,888 applicants passed the examination intended to test vocabulary, number of relationships, and problem solving skills for jobs ranging from telephone operator to service representative (U. S. Department of Education/U. S. Department of Labor, 1988). In a further example, a consortium of New York City banks made a commitment to hire 300 high school graduates from five inner-city schools, but found that only 100 students were able to meet entry requirements that included an eighth-grade comprehension and mathematics skills (Berlin & Sum, 1988, p. 25).

The interaction between poverty, poor basic skills and the nation's economic future has been addressed in several national reports that are of relevance to employment-bound youth. For example, the Panel on Adolescent Pregnancy and Childbearing of the National Research Council has noted that "Inadequate basic skills, poor employment prospects and the lack of successful role models...have stifled the motivation of many to...avoid pregnancy" (p. 1). In essence, a limited perception of future life options makes becoming a school drop-out or a teenage parent an acceptable choice. Therefore, the panel placed its highest priority on preventing adolescent parenting by enhancing young people's life options. In a different but related perspective, the Committee for Economic Development in its report entitled, *Strategy for U. S. Industrial Competitiveness*, has argued that the quality of education especially at the pre-college level, will determine the ability of the labor force to adapt to changes resulting from new productivity-enhancing technologies. Thus, counselors need, through programs of career education or other forms of career intervention, to link the importance of effective learning strategies and commitment to individual career development as ways of helping persons understand that chances exist and that help is available to make those chances realities.

The Importance of Basic Academic Skills for Employment-Bound Youth

These reports and many others suggest that to lift persons out of poverty, for them to develop self-esteem in a society of knowledge workers, or to provide the capability of a work force to master new technologies requires the same requisites—basic skills and the motivation to use them. The Ford Foundation Project on Social Welfare and the American Future (Berlin & Sum, 1988) has stated the matter in the following manner:

"Why are basic skills important? Because those with better basic skills—defined as the ability to read, write, communicate, and compute—do better in school, at work, and in other key areas of their lives. They are more likely to perform well in school, obtain a high school diploma, go on to and complete college, work more hours, earn higher wages, be more productive workers, and avoid bearing children out of wedlock. Conversely, those who are deficient in basic skills are more likely to be school dropouts, teenage parents, jobless, welfare dependent, and involved in crime. Moreover, in an interdependent world economy, the skills of the nation's work force are becoming an increasingly important determinant of American industry's competitive position, worker's real wages, and our overall standard of living. In short, basic skills bear a direct relation to the future well-being of workers, families, firms, and the country itself" (p. 2).

As large numbers of low-skilled or semi-skilled jobs are exported to other nations or eliminated by the rapid application of advanced technology, automated machine systems, and robotics in the work place, there is a redistribution of learning requirements in the United States, and in other nations that receive manufacturing and service jobs formerly done in the United States. This redistribution of learning requirements begins with an emphasis on the importance of basic academic skills as the foundation for being able to learn and to perform the tasks expected in the emerging occupations as well as in many of the traditional occupations. As forecast in many studies of how the occupational structure is changing through the 1990's and into the next century, the conclusion is that "very few new jobs will be created for those who cannot read, follow directions, and use mathematics" (Hudson Institute, 1987, p. 1). In one study that ranked new or emerging jobs according to the skills required, the rising educational requirements can be seen in fairly dramatic terms. When compared across six skill categories according to the math, language, and reasoning skills they require, only 27 percent of all new jobs fall into the lowest two skill categories, compared to 40 percent of current jobs that can be performed with these limited skills. By contrast, 41 percent of new jobs are in the three highest skill groups, compared to only 24 percent of current jobs (Hudson Institute, 1987, p. 1).

Drucker (1989; 1992) has continued to argue that knowledge has replaced experience as the primary requisite for employability and has become the economy's foundation and its true capital. To the degree that his suppositions are accurate, one can predict that a lack of basic academic skills will constitute a major problem for individuals trying to enter the occupational structure and progress in it, as well as for corporations who experience a mismatch between the skills that new employees bring and those that new work processes require. Such a reality now exists in many segments of the current work force. For example, a joint publication of the U. S. Department of Education and the U. S. Department of Labor (1988) has suggested that, "New technology has changed the nature of work—created new jobs and altered others—and, in many cases, has revealed basic skills problems where none were known to exist" (p. 3). Such findings suggest that new technology has intensified cries for educational reform and has stimulated the need for literacy audits among workers and the need to introduce basic skills training directly into the work place where such audits show that it is needed. Such findings also suggest that a functionally literate work force is a fundamental requirement to implement advanced technology. Indeed, to provide the flexibility, judgment, and skills necessitated by efforts to cope with international economic competition, competence in basic academic skills will be a fundamental necessity for employment-bound youth. The Bureau of Labor Statistics, U. S. Department of Labor (1994) summarizes these matters effectively when it stated that, "The trend toward higher educational attainment is expected to continue. Projected rates of employment growth are faster for occupations requiring higher levels of education and training than for those requiring less"..."opportunities for those who do not finish high school will be increasingly limited, and workers who are not literate may not even be considered for most jobs" (p. 12).

It would appear then, that as advanced technologies pervade the nation's work processes and workplaces in manufacturing and in services, basic academic skills may be the ultimate employability skills, the skills which are essential personal requisites to equity and opportunity in a society increasingly divided by education, employment, and wealth, a bi-level society polarized between haves and have-nots, a society of adolescent or young adult groups segregated into employment-bound or college-bound. Certainly, basic academic skills are related to the attainment of feelings of self-worth and self-esteem in a society where knowledge is power.

In the fullest sense, one cannot begin to attend to the high level intellectual skills required by advanced technology or many technology-intensive occupations until one first deals with the problem of inadequate basic academic skills among many segments of the youth or the adult population. Unless problems of learning or academic skill development are dealt with in the pre-college or early years of schooling, the proportions of persons likely to be able to go on to post-secondary education or to learn the skills required to participate in the new and emerging technologies will be inadequate to the demands of the nation. This problem is, of course, exacerbated by the decline in the absolute numbers of adolescents in education available to enter either the work force or post-secondary education. But there are other related concerns in addition to the need to tie learning and work together as they affect the lives of young people, particularly those who are employment-bound. Some examples follow as they appear in abridged or paraphrased form from the W. T. Grant Commission report, *The Forgotten Half* (1988).

The Effects of Inadequate Basic Skills in a Changing Occupational Structure

During the wage stagnation in this nation from roughly 1973 until the present, although nearly all groups of males in the population were adversely affected, within each age group males with the least education experienced the largest declines in mean earnings. For example, a comparison of the real mean earnings of twenty-to-24-year-old high school dropouts in 1973 with a similar cohort in 1984 shows that annual earnings declined by 41.6 percent from $11,210 to $6,552, while earnings of high school graduates, those with some college, and those with a B.S. or B.A. degree declined by a smaller amount: 30.1 percent, 26.1 percent, and 11.0 percent, respectively. Interestingly enough, although the real mean earnings of Black dropouts and high school graduates declined nearly twice as much as those of White or Hispanics, young Black male college graduates raised their earnings by 16.3 percent during this period.

As will be discussed more thoroughly in subsequent chapters, the median education requirement for the emerging occupational structure is more than a high school diploma, roughly 13.5 years of schooling. Thus, in increasing numbers of national reports, the argument is that to participate productively in today's economy, the minimum requirement is a well-rounded high school education. Indeed, more than ever, "the labor market is distinguishing between those with a high school diploma and those who left school before graduation." For 18-to-24-year-old-males, for example, the gap between the mean annual incomes of a high school drop-out and a high school graduate was 31 percent in the early 1960s, and in the late 1980s, it was 59 percent.

Since employers do not really have achievement test data on young workers, they tend to hire on the basis of attainment (e.g., high school graduation) as a proxy for achievement, for skills and knowledge as well as for "stick-to-it-iveness" which represents one piece of general employability skills as they are described elsewhere in this book. Again, employer valuing of skills and knowledge in young workers is related to the reality that workers who know more also learn more quickly and are more productive than workers who know less. The decline of the manufacturing sector as a major employer has had a particularly devastating effect on those young people with deficiencies in education and basic skills. Historically, there have been jobs in heavy industry—steel-making, durable goods-production, automotive manufacturing—in which one could earn enough to support a family even if one did not have a strong education. However, since 1974, the proportion of young male workers employed in manufacturing industries has declined by one-fourth, at the same time that employment in service industries has risen by more than 20 percent. Perhaps more important, in early 1974, blue-collar craft, operative, and foreman jobs accounted for nearly half (46 percent) of the jobs held by employed Black men, ages 20-24. These were jobs that were frequently unionized and paid above average wages with good fringe benefits. By 1984, these jobs accounted for about one-fourth (26.0 percent) of the jobs held by young Black males and their decrease has at least indirectly contributed to the expanding number of welfare and father-absent families in this nation.

As each new group of young male workers entering the labor market earned lower mean real wages and worked fewer hours annually during the past decade, the percentage of young men, 20-24 years old who are able to support a family of three above the poverty line has declined from 60 to 42 percent. By 1984, only 23 percent of young Black males had such earnings compared to 55 percent in 1973. A related result is that from 1974 to 1984, the percent of young Black men ages 20-24 who were married and living with their spouses dropped from 30 to 9 percent. Thus, as real earnings have decreased, there have been changes in family-formation patterns and increases in the number of single-parent families and children living in poverty. Other data indicate that two-thirds of the children who grow up entirely in single-parent households spend nearly their entire childhood in poverty as compared to only 2 percent of those who grow up in two-parent households.

The broad implications of these data suggest that the importance of employment-bound youth to the nation is not confined to their economic contributions, however important, but also to their roles in initiating and implementing families, as parents, as aspirants to the economic security and well-being of middle-class socioeconomic status and beyond, and as life-long learners who will serve as the major foundation labor force for many of the semi-skilled, skilled, technical, and entrepreneurial jobs in the occupational structure. Thus, the future success of employment-bound youth will likely be predictive of and parallel to the success of the larger American social, economic, and occupational structure.

Employment Conditions for Different Groups of Employment-Bound Youth

Obviously, not every employment-bound youth or young adult worker is affected in the same way by economic, educational or other factors. But, clearly employment conditions, opportunities, and concerns of and for young people vary with different social, economic, and political processes. For example, the number of young people available to enter the labor force has changed rapidly. By 1995, the population of 16-to-24 year-old persons is expected to be 20 percent less than its 1980 level. In numerical terms, it is anticipated that the number of young people ages 16 to 24 will be slightly below 29 million in 1995 compared to slightly over 36 million in 1980. These are reductions in the percentage of young men and women in the nation's civilian working age population from 21.5 to 15 percent (W. T. Grant Foundation, 1989). These figures affirm that the Baby Boom and its huge influx of young workers into the labor force is over for the foreseeable future. Therefore, one could be quite optimistic that this shrinking pool of young workers would be welcomed into the work place as replacements for large numbers of retiring workers. Not so!

The unemployment rates for this young population remain high for several reasons. One is that many of the entry-level jobs these young people might expect to obtain have been augmented or replaced by automation, reducing the number of such jobs available. Second, as firms are downsizing or merging, and made wary by the economic health of the nation and the world, they are reluctant to make permanent hires that increase their overhead, their commitment to health care and other fringe benefits; as a result, they would prefer to hire part-time workers, those available from temporary personnel firms, or those who can be secured on a time-limited contract basis, as part of contingency labor force, to do a particular task and then be terminated. Such hires frequently do not receive any form of health care or other fringe benefits that accrue to continuing, full-time employees (U. S. Bureau of Labor Statistics, 1988).

Thus, while employment opportunities and rewards are down across the 16-24 year age group, employment conditions also differ by youth groups. Rural youth have historically been seen as suffering from a lack of opportunities and information about jobs and they have fewer agencies, mental health or career counseling services to help them. In the inner cities, part of the problem is that there has been a relocation of jobs from the urban core to smaller cities and suburbs. By the nature of their environment, then, both rural and inner city young people experience job scarcity. Young people in these areas as well as in the suburbs or small towns are victims of discrimination: racism and sexism. Factors such as not achieving academically, having poor attendance, dropping out of school, and/or membership in a racial minority may combine to increase the significant difficulties associated with seeking, finding, and adjusting to work.

As different subgroups of employment-bound youth are studied, it becomes clear that both reality and stereotypes operate to differentiate the educational and occupational opportunities of these youth by geographical location and by other factors. Some examples follow as these have been abridged or paraphrased from a position paper on employment-bound youth prepared for the American Counseling Association (Herr and Associates, 1992).

Inner-City Youth.

For 40 or more years, classic movies and books (e.g., *The Blackboard Jungle, Westside Story, Up the Down Staircase*) have portrayed inner-city youth as gang members, violent, anti-school, anti-social and anti-establishment. Other movies (e.g., *Stand and Deliver*) have shown that with firm and caring leadership, inner city youth can be and are as academically capable and motivated to succeed as students in any other environment. Can both views of inner-city youth be accurate? They can and are! Inner-city youth are not monolithic in their backgrounds, neighborhoods, skills, family support systems or other characteristics.

The term "inner-city youth" is a phrase that is often used stereotypically and in a limited manner to mean youth who live in large core cities and who come from culturally diverse and low-income settings (Herr and Associates, 1992). Often the term "inner-city" is used as a negative or pejorative label when compared to labelling persons as suburban, small town, or rural youth. However, there are many inner-city youth, employment-bound or college-bound, who are among the nation's intellectually gifted, attend some of the nation's finest schools, have access to comprehensive career exploration programs, mentoring, and positive experiences with cultural diversity.

Various sections of cities tend to be microcosms of the larger society. While there are sections of any major city which contain populations that are economically depressed, have high crime rates and contain high ratios of ethnically diverse peoples and cultures, there are other sections of cities whose populations do not resemble any of these commonly expected stereotypes. Youth in either of these city sections may or may not be at risk or disadvantaged in comparison with their contemporaries in small towns or suburban communities or rural areas.

While hopelessness and despair may be more visible in cities as homeless persons, run-down housing, closed and abandoned plants are visible or more concentrated, cities also have other characteristics that can be highly positive. Among them may be the accelerated pace of life and the blurring of when work is done. When city businesses, entertainment centers, and other services remain open and function 18 to 24 hours a day as contrasted with 8 to 10 hours in other geographic locations, comprehensiveness in the form and content of work can be much greater than in geographic locations where work and the pace of life is much more restricted. Community and cultural resources available to augment formal educational settings in cities can be wide-ranging. The magnitude of information, experiences, role models, materials, businesses, and other work places offers significant opportunities to connect school and work in creative and meaningful ways. Some examples of programs designed to provide career counseling or career guidance in several of the great cities of the United States will be described in subsequent chapters.

Rural Youth

In contrast to the concentrations of resources, opportunities, role models, dramatic examples of achievement and of failure, possibilities and despair, ethnic diversity and structures of work in the cities, these factors, if present in rural areas, are diffused through a large geographical area. As a result, opportunities for career exploration and for many types of work are limited, if not non-existent. Population groups tend to be more homogeneous in ethnicity or cultural traditions, schools tend to be smaller as are tax bases, resulting in a more limited range of services to students. There tend to be fewer specialists in teaching fields, health care, or other work environments and fewer counselors per school than in urban areas.

Students in rural areas are less likely than are urban students to continue their education beyond high school, they tend to be more limited in their career aspirations and less exposed to a range of careers than are urban youth (Herr and Associates, 1992). A higher percentage of people live at poverty level in rural areas than in urban centers, and considerably fewer women work outside the home. The median educational level and median income are proportionally lower in rural areas. Teen depression and suicidal behavior are on the rise in certain rural communities, as are child abuse and neglect. Alcohol use and drug abuse are also serious problems in rural communities (Human & Wasem, 1991).

While some 70 percent of the school districts in the United States are in rural areas, only 25 percent of the population of the nation live in non-metropolitan communities. Consequently, schools in rural areas are smaller in enrollment and more isolated from industrial or service work places, although not agricultural careers, than are urban schools. However, given the constant decrease across the nation in the number and viability of family farms, in rural areas today, rural non-farm populations tend to outnumber rural farm populations by a factor of 7 to 1 or more. Manufacturing, mining, energy, and retirement populations together make up a larger portion of the total population than does farming. A proportionally higher number of under-17 and over-65 year olds live in rural settings, along with a disproportionate percentage of poor, elderly, and chronically ill persons.

Since desired educational and work opportunities require geographic relocations for many rural young people, the transition from adolescence to adulthood can be difficult, if not traumatic, for some. As Swift (1988), among others, has identified, the stress experienced during the transition from the secondary school to the work place to postsecondary education cause many rural youth to experience a time of fear and frustration. The stress and trauma associated with such transitions, tend to be exacerbated because in many rural areas, few mental and physical health services exist and often where the services do exist they are in remote locations making travel and the keeping of appointments difficult. Frequently, there is resistance to the use of such services because they are often perceived as outside intrusion (McIntire, Marion, & Quaglia, 1990; Murry & Keller, 1991).

Minority Youth

Whether they live in rural or urban areas, minority youth who are employment-bound frequently have to deal with the reality that their minority status is an additional stressor (Sue, & Morishima, 1982, p. 112) with which they need to deal. As such, it becomes a further factor of importance in the litany of problems of choice, preparation for, and adjustment to work. Minority youth, beyond any other barriers with which they must deal, "potentially face hostility, prejudice, and the lack of effective support during times of crisis (Sue, & Morishima, 1982, p. 162)… they may be treated as an outsider and discriminated against" (p. 164). Correlated with their minority status, African American, Hispanic and Native American students have higher drop-out rates, lower college completion rates, and are overly segregated into the lowest paying and least prestigious jobs in our society.

Although each minority youth group has unique difficulties, a core problem for most minority youth is poverty. Poverty creates an environment that frequently denies youth hope, comprehensive information about and assistance in planning for the future, and access to career opportunities that are secure, that provide sufficient income to support a family, and that encourage achievement. In the 1980s more than 50 percent of young urban Black men were unemployed, worked part-time jobs when they would have preferred to work full-time, worked in jobs without health benefits, or earned poverty-level wages (Lichter, 1988). Cheatham (1990), among others, has suggested that African Americans require some different career interventions. These include recognition of and response to structural or racial discrimination, culturally influenced perceptions of the meaning of work, differential availability of career information, and economic and labor market forces that uniquely affect African Americans. Hispanic youth also often tend to have a constricted knowledge of and exposure to occupations. In general, Hispanic workers are concentrated more in the lower paid, less skilled occupations than is the total work force and, thus, they frequently lack role models from which to learn the career planning skills necessary to aspire to professional and technical jobs. Native American youths have also experienced intense prejudice and limited access to viable work opportunities. They, too, suffer from formidable obstacles of stereotyping, lack of awareness of and access to a comprehensive range of work opportunities, and conflicts in values and expectations between majority normative structures regarding work behavior and those of their traditional communities.

Asian American youth, in contrast to other racial groups, are typically not seen as having major educational or occupational problems. They are seen as "having made it," as having succeeded in American society and not needing special assistance. As Leong (1985) suggests, Asian Americans suffer from the myth of being the "model minority," a myth that masks the fact that there is a bimodal distribution within the Asian American community: those who are highly successful and those living lives of poverty and destitution. It is from the latter group that many Asian-American employment-bound youth come. They, too, cope with poverty, with prejudice and hostility, with a restricted knowledge of and freedom to choose from a wide range of occupations.

Hotchkiss and Borow (1990) have summarized the experiences of minority employment-bound youth in the following manner:

> *"For minority youth, racial and ethnic bias in the job market exerts a two-way adverse influence. It restricts merit-based opportunity for employment and career advancement, and teenagers' awareness of it may also lead them to expect job failure. Although this is certainly not true of all minority youth, many do acquire a perception of the outside world that they will soon enter as essentially unmanageable. They are frequently burdened by negative self-images, feelings of inadequacy as workers-to-be, and disbelief in the efficacy of rational career planning. Unable to accommodate the notion that work may actually be pleasant and psychologically rewarding, they may make, at best, tenuous emotional commitments to their first jobs. Short-term monetary return is frequently the only aim they attach to work. Evidence is strong that the individual's and society's failure to deal early and effectively with such unrewarding school-to-work transition experiences may lead to protracted work-related difficulties. The early labor-market records of school-leaving teenagers and young adults are often prognostic of the dubious quality of their long-term career histories. For youths whose work entry is a negative and unsettling experience, episodes of chronic joblessness and underemployment are common consequences"* (pp. 301-302).

The reality for the United States, is that new and better ways to insure that persons of minority background receive training and other forms of work force education must be found and provided soon. Between now and the year 2000, some 57 percent of all labor force growth will be African-American, Hispanic, or other minorities (Whitman, 1989). In fact, that trend will not cease in the year 2000 but will continue far into the 21st century. Many of that number are now employment-bound youth who must have better education, access to excellent programs and opportunities and the support necessary to insure that they can realize their aspirations to be in the mainstream of jobs and mobility.

Youths with Disabilities

Perhaps the least known or visible of the employment-bound youth subpopulation are those with disabilities. Like minority status, a disability significantly adds to one's difficulties in making the transition from school to work regardless of socioeconomic level. Among the differences that youth with disabilities may experience in comparison to other employment-bound youth are:

1. Restrictions in awareness of work or career options that exist because of restricted early life experiences.
2. Lack of opportunity to develop work habits and skills that can be applied in a job.
3. For some youth with disabilities, possibly limited chances to develop communication and interpersonal skills with their non-disabled peers.
4. Less chance to compete for and obtain part-time or summer jobs during school years, further limiting opportunities to develop career exploration or job-seeking skills.
5. Often overt discrimination or lack of knowledge of disabilities by employers, by peers, or by adults in schools or in the community.
6. Inadequate physical facilities or accommodations in educational or social settings that tend to heighten awareness of the disability, promoting social dependency and stifling self-reliance.
7. Depending upon the disability at issue, the possibility of chronic pain, fatigue, attention deficits or other factors

than may cause chronic depression, or cause youth with
disabilities to limit the goals they set for themselves
(Hershenson, Personal Communication, 1992).

Campbell (1985) suggested that external influences affect the
employment opportunities for the disabled even when they are
qualified by knowledge, skill and motivation. These include
environmental access, job conditions, personnel management
practices, management attitudes and behaviors, employer relations practices, affirmative action efforts, law enforcement, and
protection of rights. Embedded in such environmental influences
are the effects of employment myths and stereotypes (for
example, persons with disabilities may be victims of social
stigma, as well as sexism, ageism, and racism), the degree to
which employers have attempted or will modify their work
places to accommodate the needs of disabled workers to function effectively or to comply with such legislative requirements
as those of the Americans with Disabilities Act, and apprehen-
sions about the productivity of disabled workers.

Persons with disabilities tend to have the highest unemployment rate and lowest mean earnings of any population in
the United States. But the problem of having a disability is not
only that of not working; it is also a function of self-percep-
tion. How does an employment-bound youth with disabilities
label himself or herself? What stereotypes from the able-bod-
ied population are internalized as valid about the inferiority,
incompetence, or worthlessness of persons with disabilities?
In a society where both political and economic realities suggest that it is inappropriate and wasteful of resources to
exclude any individual regardless of characteristics from the
work force, employment-bound youth with disabilities are a minority group who are at serious economic and psychological
risk and must be provided the support of counselors, transition
services, and employers that are sensitive and enlightened.

Gender Issues

Employment-bound youth are not only minority, poor, or
youth with disabilities. Obviously, in addition to all of the other
demographic characteristics cited there are both males and
females in this population. Gender-based and equity issues
affect both males and females although such discussions

typically tend to focus on females. There are concerns, for example, that females have not developed the self-efficacy or the self-esteem to choose and enter occupations that are non-traditional for women, particularly those that require prowess in science and mathematics. Such studies frequently argue that females are treated different than males in school classrooms and encouraged to use different talents or pursue different options than males. To the degree that such findings are true, they tend also to be true for males. That is, young males are not encouraged to enter occupations that are traditionally occupied by females. A young male interested in ballet, elementary education, child care, nursing, secretarial jobs frequently suffers a lack of encouragement, if not disdain, when pursuing non-traditional occupations for males.

To a large degree, employment-bound youth of either gender face major constraints in choosing, preparing, and entering positions that are not historically dominated by the sex of the chooser. For females, the equity issues are typically considered to be of greater moment because traditionally male occupations have been better paid, had more opportunities for advancement, and greater status than have had those of women. Therefore, if female workers are to move toward income parity for work done, it will be necessary for them to have increased access, information about, encouragement, mentoring and other types of support to enter what is for them nontraditional occupations. While the equity gap between males and females has been slowly narrowing since the 1970s, there are still many problems that remain.

One of the most pervasive of the issues associated with gender-based career development is that of the continued stereotyping and gender role socialization that occurs in families, in the media, and in educational institutions. There are numerous studies that suggest that many boys and girls from an early age have sex-stereotyped attitudes about how they should behave in school or workand what jobs are appropriate for them, as well as about other gender issues such as family roles, the division of labor within the family, and toward women with small children working outside the home even though more than 50 percent now do so (Hedin, Erickson, Simon & Walker, 1985; Herzog & Bachman, 1982; Hansen & Biernat, 1992). There are also other gender-related issues that are pervasive in the American society if workplaces and educational settings are to be congenial to gender equity. Among these are sexual harassment, gender-based violence and other similar phenomena. As long as such processes occur at current levels, females' ability to prepare for and choose occupations freely, to work with security and without sexual innuendo, to balance their homemaker and paid work roles more equally with those of males rather than, if married or similarly partnered, being required to do two full-time jobs simultaneously will continue to be compromised and unequal. This situation is true for employment-bound youth and for those aspiring to further education.

Constraints on the Entry to Work

In each of the categories of employment-bound youth discussed thus far in this chapter, there are potential implicit or explicit constraints on their anticipation of and transition into the labor force. For some, there are issues of racism and prejudice, for others sexual stereotype or discrimination against those with disabilities. For some, there is a changing opportunity to gain skills as a function of down-sizing in specific forms of employment (e.g., the Armed Forces). For still others, there may be legislative or other constraints which keep early adolescents from learning about or exploring work opportunities in an in-depth or systematic way. There are also issues of ageism and perceptions by employers of expected maturity to enter the primary work force—the sector where jobs are permanent, with more resources to devote to training and supervision, with career ladders, with health care and other fringe benefits—which limit employers' willingness to hire students immediately upon high school graduation. Instead, many young people, perhaps most, who are employment-bound, under current conditions in the United States, must enter the smallest firms or secondary labor market—the world of fast-food restaurants, temporary jobs in retailing and distribution—because employers are often not prepared to assume that these young persons will take responsibility, be punctual, remain with the firm for an extended period of time, or be prepared to perform ever more complex tasks. As a result, many young people are required to spend several years in minor and relatively unfulfilling jobs which generally do not do that much to enhance qualifications for future opportunities either until by the early or mid-20s they are seen as old enough to work with reliability and purpose.

It is important to acknowledge that small firms and the secondary labor market are not necessarily bad places to youth to make the transition to employment. Such firms allow young workers to establish credibility as a worker, to learn about work expectations and ways to cooperate with others, to apply skills and identify others they might need, and to acquire information about other jobs which may be available within a given industry or community.

While small firms are not necessarily the same as the secondary labor market, young workers, as compared to older workers, tend to work in the small or smallest firms (less than 99 workers or less than 19 workers respectively). One study suggests that 65 percent of young workers (age 25 or less) work in the small or smallest firms; 40 percent worked in the smallest firms. Similarly, high school graduates are more likely to work in the smallest firms, while college graduates are more likely to work in larger firms (Gray, 1994). While small firms are the major source of new jobs in the economy, unlike large firms, they are about one-half as likely to provide formal on-the-job training, they are also unlikely to have personnel officers and elaborate application processes; such firms are likely to look for new employees who already have relevant job skills from prior training in the military or a vocational school, compared to large firms that are more likely to look for new workers who are trainable to their precise needs. Small firms are less likely to reimburse employees for outside training costs. Again, because of their small size, they tend to have short career ladders compared to larger firms and a more limited variety of positions among which persons can advance or move. While the small firms want persons with vocational skills, they are also, because of size, very concerned about the person's fit with others in the firm. In a small firm, teamwork and cooperation can be as important as specific employee skills.

Within the small and smallest firms are not only those firms which are quite technological and innovative in a technical sense, but also others that are seen as primarily constituting the secondary labor market. Frequently stereotyped, but not confined to the fast food establishments, Hamilton (1990) defines the secondary labor market as jobs that pay little more than the minimum wage, offer no fringe benefits, demand few skills, are insecure, and lack advancement opportunities (p. 22). Thus, not all small firms meet these criteria to be considered part of the secondary labor market, but many do. In large measure, the forcing of youth into the secondary labor market or into small firms for their initial labor market experience tends to be largely a creation of employers in the primary labor market, the larger firms, who expect young workers to become seasoned in the secondary labor market until at age 25 or so, they are mature enough to enter the primary labor market.

Whether or not there are benefits to be gained by young workers in the secondary labor market, rather than in the primary labor market and in small firms, rather than large ones, is debatable. Nevertheless, such outcomes on constraints in the entry to work tends to be predicated on perceived limitations of young workers rather than on the assets they represent.

Borman (1991), in her study of young workers, has contended that the tendency to see the young as characterized by their weaknesses rather than by their strengths has been reflected in public policies and in attitudes of employers (and others) toward young people. "...Thus, although youths value work and wish to become economically successful in terms of a middle class standard, employers perspective toward this group remains negative... As a result of this bias, youths who seek employment rather than postsecondary education after leaving high school suffer 'an extended floundering period in the labor market before beginning a real career.' They do so as a result of employers' actions, adults' attitudes and expectations for their behavior, and the viability of local labor conditions, but not as a result of the inherent characteristics of youth" (p. 26).

Indeed, as the research of Veum and Weiss (1993), among others, has shown, "individuals demonstrate a great deal of job mobility during their early years in the labor market. Brief and transitory periods of employment are common among young workers. Previous research indicates that the first 10 years of a young worker's career account for about two-thirds of all lifetime job changes, and for nearly two-thirds of lifetime wage growth. During the first 10 years in the labor market, an individual works for an average of eight employers. Research also suggests that 1 of 20 male workers remains at his first job over a 10 year period. However, as workers age, employment patterns tend to stabilize and the probability of leaving or losing a job eventually declines.

Young workers change jobs and employment status for a variety of reasons. Information about how to find a job and the nature of employment are difficult to acquire, particularly for young workers. Some individuals get a job offer and remain in that job so long as the wage paid exceeds alternative wage offers.

Information about the quality of the match between a worker and a firm reveals itself over time. "Workers who are well matched remain on the job, and those who are poorly matched are most likely to leave... Individuals may also move into and out of the labor market because of decisions relating to schooling, marital status, childbearing or other factors. In particular, decisions relating to education affect labor market experiences for young workers" (Veum, & Weiss, 1993, pp. 11 and 12).

For these reasons and others, most employment-bound youth do not leave high school and immediately enter a stable job with a firm that provides security and upward mobility. Instead, "For many youths, the process of entry and adjustment to the labor market is lengthy and involves distinct periods. The behavior of the youths change over time, moving from a period of casual attachment to an increasing commitment to work and to stable behavior" (Osterman, 1989, p. 255). This view is focused on the characteristics of individual behavior, not on the interaction between individual and workplace or even on the skills, experiences, and attitudes that youth bring to the school to work transition or that employers reinforce or train young workers to incorporate and implement.

In the U. S. literature on the processes by which adolescents make the transition from school-to-work, it is almost an accepted truism that "typical high school graduates mill about in the labor market moving from one dead-end job to another until the age of 23 or 24" (Commission on the Skills of the American Workforce, 1990, p. 46). These young people are variously described as "floundering," "churning," in a period of "moratorium," from the point of high school graduation through the mid-20s, when they have only tentative commitment to work, they move into and out of the labor force, they hold numerous short-term and dead-end jobs, are frequently unemployed, and are, either in their perceptions or in those of observers, not moving toward some specific set of career goals. This period, then, particularly for employment-bound youth, is often seen as essentially unproductive, as not providing training or the elements of productivity which lead in the mid-20s and 30s to quality jobs in the labor market.

Such views of employment-bound youth as those advanced above are not shared by all researchers or theorists. For example, some longitudinal studies do not suggest severe employment problems for high school graduates, but rather, as a group, a smooth transition into the labor force (e.g., Meyer, & Wise, 1982). Other recent findings (Klerman, & Karoly, 1994) suggest that the adolescent school-to-work experience is not the same for all young males. "Based upon longitudinal analysis of the job patterns of the Class of 1972, the experiences of school drop-outs, high school graduates, persons with some college, and college graduates are different in the move to stable employment. While young men typically hold a large number of jobs after leaving high school, the largest number of jobs is held by school drop-outs, compared with other groups." The median male high school dropout had held 6 jobs by age 24 and 8 jobs by age 28" (p. 40). High school graduates held about one-half as many jobs by the same ages. It was further found that rather than stable employment being unavailable to young workers until the mid-20s, as commonly reported in the literature, many young workers are in stable employment (defined as holding one job for 3 years or more) by the early 20s. For example, 5 years after leaving high school, at approximate ages of 22 or 23 years of age, about one-third of high school graduates had already held a job that lasted 3 years. The median high school graduate had held a job for at least 2 years by the age of 23. Such data do not suggest that the average high school graduate who is employment-bound "mills" around unproductively until the middle 20s. While not all such persons settle into a long-term job immediately upon leaving high school (by 18 or 19), many do begin to settle into long-term job commitments by the early 20s. Implicit in such findings is the view that employment-bound youth are heterogeneous, not homogeneous, in the skills and attitudes they bring to the choice of and adjustment to work. In addition, they learn these skills and attitudes in many ways, formal and informal—in the home, the school, the workplace—with different results.

One informal mechanism through which youth learn about work is part-time work. Many employment-bound youth engage in part-time work because of economic necessity or for other reasons: as a way of filling free-time, as a method of providing some discretionary spending money, or as a way of being with friends or other family members. However, at its best, part-time employment has significant potential for providing bridges to full-time work by inducting youth into the adult or mature culture in which work occurs and by training them in the cognitive and psychomotor tasks that comprise work content. Such part-time employment or other formal work-related learning—career education, career guidance, vocational education, cooperative education, apprenticeship—can reinforce the insights inherent in the notion that work adjustment involves more than learning to cope with the technical demands of job-related tasks. Successful adjustment at work requires mastery of a range of social learning tasks such as when to take a work break, how and when to give advice to a co-worker, how to respond to and accommodate authority in the workplace, and, perhaps more important, how to understand and manipulate the culture of the workplace to one's personal benefit (Borman, Izzo, Penn & Reisman, 1984).

Research about the effects of part-time work on subsequent access to and adjustment in the workplace has frequently been equivocal but there are findings that indicate that high school graduates who had jobs during high school that give them the opportunity to exercise and improve their skills in dealing with people, things, or data are able to earn more pay per hour and spend less of their time looking for work. These findings further suggest that less unemployment and higher hourly earnings are obtained by new graduates who spend a larger number of hours per week in paid employment during their junior and senior years (for example, 16 compared to 10 hours per week) and who, in qualitative terms, had jobs during high school that give them more chances to develop and use skills (Stern & Nakata, 1989).

As will be discussed elsewhere in this book, not all employment-bound youth acquire part-time jobs or engage in formal work-based learning. The informal work-related mechanisms to which youth are exposed in the home, school or community are different and uneven, causing the learning about work content and processes, the availability of transferable skills, and the personal feelings of competence and self-efficacy to vary greatly among employment-bound youth from considerable career maturity to what might be considered impaired career development.

As suggested above, adolescent career development can be characterized as a "flow of experience" which incorporates personal career decisions and career decision points and the variety of social and economic factors and contexts which shape this flow. It has to do with developing an ability to cope with important career decision points, mastering effective decision-making processes as well as identifying satisfying content (Jepsen, 1991).

Messages Received by Employment-Bound Youth

Jepsen (1991) has addressed the effects of the adolescent's social environment, the principal agents of socialization, the primary reference groups, on the adolescents' perspectives and preparation to make choices at specific career decision points. These reference groups provide adolescents with different and intermittent messages about who they are, who they might be, and what actions they should take. Given the wide-range of potential groups of consequence to any given adolescent (e.g., family of origin, classes and activity groups, peers, teachers, co-worker group on a job, religious groups, neighborhood role models, community attitudes), it is obvious that not all adolescents get the same messages, with the same power, at the same time. Nevertheless, because they come from primary reference groups, groups of persons seen as authoritative and important in one's life, their messages are likely to be perceived as important, of great status with strong emotional overtones, and often contradictory.

As Jepsen (1991) has indicated, messages from different reference groups or from different types of exchanges with persons in these reference groups can take many different forms: direct inquiry about future plans, feedback on current roles and performances, information about opportunities, orientation, boundary description or boundary maintenance, facts, persuasion, role modeling.

While such intermittent social messages are undoubtedly present in every individual's life, they differ in their positive or negative connotations, in their support of actions or the reverse, in their characterizations of skills and abilities as strong, adequate, or inferior. It is within this context that the labels and messages to which employment-bound youth are exposed become critical. It is why terms like "non-college bound" or the "forgotten half" suggest that something is missing, not that something is present; that the status of adolescents so labeled are fixed and somewhat inferior, not fluid and that these are persons whose skills are of fundamental importance to the nation's economy. In order to provide employment-bound students with the messages as well as the knowledge, attitudes, and skills that affirm their impor- tance to the nation's economic development, it is necessary to provide such support in the schools, during the school-to-work transition, and upon entry to work. As the W. T. Grant Commis- sion (1988) has indicated "a college degree is not the only way to develop the talents of tomorrow's workers. For some, it is far from the best. There are many opportunities outside the college class- room to develop skills and talents and many ways to contribute to a stronger America and to a successful and personal life that do not require a college degree" (p.1). Subsequent chapters will address each of these periods and the types of programs that can be implemented by counselors and others to facilitate the employability, the career development of employment-bound youth. Before doing so, however, it is important to place into context, the trends that are shaping the economic environments, the organi- zations, the content, and the processes of work that are emerging as the twentieth century ends and the twenty-first century dawns.

Conclusion

Chapter One has suggested that employment-bound youths are not a homogeneous group. While empirical data is not available about the proportions of employment-bound youth by gender, by levels of career maturity, who are in vocational education or other curricula, who are at risk, who are minority or majority, who fall at different levels of academic ability, who have smooth or jagged early labor market experiences and so on, it seems clear that employment-bound youth can be located in each of these classifications. While primary assets to the nation's economic well-being, employment-bound youth frequently do not receive messages, information, and programs which would suggest that they are valued as much as those whose goals are to attend college and become professional workers of some type. In contrast, employment-bound youth constitute the technicians and the skilled labor force who construct, operate, and maintain the nation's manufacturing, transportation, retailing and distribution, construction infrastructures. Without the work ethic, the talents, the skills that are now present or can be nurtured in these segments of the populations, the nation's economic development would quickly deteriorate.

As suggested in the next chapter, the emerging work and economic environment for employment-bound youth is rapidly changing. As such, it will require new efforts to nurture and to ascribe full value to the importance of the contributions of employment-bound youth to the nation's economic progress and to its ability to compete in the global market place.

Chapter Two

The Emerging Economic Environment for Employment-Bound Youth

While it is possible to cite at length demographic and other statistical data describing and defining employment-bound youth, such information is only a part of the total set of dynamics related to counseling employment-bound youth. Indeed, such descriptive information can be abstract and sterile unless it is viewed within the context of major social and occupational changes affecting the lives of these youth and young adults. The importance of employment-bound youth to the nation, the labels used to describe them, and the opportunities made available to them do not occur in a vacuum. They occur in relation to external events, to policy, to paradigms that characterize employment-bound youth as assets or as problems to the nation, as a population to be provided special priority or not.

For the foreseeable future, based upon the growing body of policy, legislation, and interest by the mass media, employment-bound youth will be seen as a special population deserving particular attention and support in education, in business and industry, and in government funding or other schemes. In subsequent chapters, we will discuss some of the specific needs of employment-bound youth and responses to them at three important periods: prior to high school graduation, during the school-to-work transition, and during their induction to the workplace. Before turning to those perspectives, however, it is necessary to describe the emerging economic context for which employment-bound youth will need to be educated and counseled. To do so requires a brief snapshot of the national and international economic dynamics that are now unfolding and shaping the educational, skill, and psychological challenges that employment-bound youth will face in the near future.

The Emerging Global Economy

As the structure of the world's economy is undergoing rapid change, the political, social, and economic corollaries of such change are placing new demands upon human resources in nation after nation. One of the common themes in international and national reports is the direct linkage between human development and economic development. It is becoming increasingly clear in national development plans, in strategic industrial goal-setting, and in various international forums that the key factor in a nation's ability to compete in the growing global economy is the quality of its work force as defined by the literacy, numeracy, flexibility, and teachability which characterizes it. Many nations in Europe and in Asia have understood this challenge clearly for several decades. They have set new standards for the unparalleled development of human resources as national priorities and they have created technological and organizational systems necessary to support the maximization of the productivity of these human resources (Schlosstein, 1989, p. xiv). In particular, they have created methods of training and of induction into the labor force that emphasize the importance of employment-bound youth as national priorities and national assets (Echikson, 1992). These nations have worked systematically to create the "social ecologies" which imbue their students, citizens, and workers with the knowledge, attitudes, habits, and skills that are necessary in the societies they hope to create for the 21st century.

What has become particularly evident in the concerns about identifying, preparing, and supporting human resources as major national assets is the reality that it is insufficient to focus only on the intellectual or social elite of the society. Rather, creating a work force that has the skills, the flexibility, the teachability required to understand and implement the emerging technologies and the industrial and business processes that arise from such technologies requires a work force that has the capability to be productive and purposeful from the managerial and professional levels through the skilled and semi-skilled levels of the occupational structure. Without a work force that can function with quality and efficiency at the levels of creativity and invention as well as at the implementation and application levels, the occupational structure becomes fragmented, divided into the have's and have not's, and is encumbered by an underclass of persons who have neither the skills nor the motivation to be trained and retrained as the occupational structure requires new skills and ways of being productive. The issues involved are quite wide-ranging and diverse. Certainly of major importance is incorporating into schools and colleges career relevant knowledge, attitudes, and experiences that address somewhat differently the segments of the work force that schools and colleges and universities educate, respectively the clerical and skilled members of the work force or the managers, designers, and professionals.

It is useful to acknowledge that among the issues related to supporting human resources as national assets to be given priority and nurturance there is more involved than reforming education. Also at issue is the creation of policies and resource allocations that support such goals, the restructuring of work organizations and how they induct and orient young workers, and efforts at job creation, as well as the psychology of achievement and success in the society. These are not simple issues. In a global economy, nations approach such matters differently and from varied cultural perspectives. And they change as nations go through different phases in their own evolution, placing different demands on their human resources.

For example, Maccoby and Terzi (1981) studied work ethics in different periods of American history and argued that "each work ethic implies a different social character, different satisfaction and dissatisfactions at work, and a different critique of society" (p. 165). Divided into five historical periods in the evolution of the United States, Maccoby and Terzi suggested that each ethic—which they called protestant, craft, entrepreneurial, career, and self-fulfillment—suggests a dominant way of coping or achieving personal flexibility at a different historical period in the United States; the residual of each period tends to be combined in different balances in the American character that has been variously described as "competitive individualism." Such a view reflects different skills or attitudes that are valued in a worker in the United States at a particular point in American society. These are likely to be different from how such skills or values are perceived or reinforced in other nations. A good example of this phenomenon is Watts' (1981) analysis of perspectives on career development in America and in Great Britain. He suggested that: "The dominant focus in the USA has been on the actions of individuals, while in Britain, indigenous theoretical work has been more preoccupied with the constraints of social structures...the failure of the American social-structural evidence to have much influence on career development theory seems to be due basically to cultural and historical factors. From the beginning of its independent existence, the USA has been formally committed to the proposition that all men are created equally... As a result, there is belief that the individual controls his destiny [sic]; has appropriate abilities; and if these can be appropriately developed, his [sic] fate lies in his own hand (p. 3)." Thus, from this excerpt, one might suggest that the characteristics of how Americans and Britons are expected to act vis-à-vis individual power or adaptation to the social structure or the workplace are different and would yield different types of personal work behavior or work ethic. Such a circumstance is true in relation to Americans in comparison with persons from other nations. For example, Super (1984) in cross-national research has found that risk-taking as a work value is more highly valued in the United States than in Yugoslavia and more by English-speaking Canadians than by French-speaking Canadians. Peabody's study (1985) of the psychological characteristics of national groups also suggests that they are distinguishable and consistent and that their comparative differences are found in regard to (1) social relationships, (2) social rules, (3) control of hostility, (4) impulse control, and (5) authority and hierarchical relations. By extrapolation, different combinations of these dimensions would comprise what is considered to be acceptable work behavior within a particular culture.

Cultural constructions of achievement images and belief systems are likely to be shaped through the messages an individual receives from the mass media, the school, the family, peers, and the community and incorporated into the individual citizen's psyche as well as embodied in the economic and organizational systems that prevail in a given nation. If, for example, the expectation in a nation like the United States is that unfettered individual achievement, freedom, justice, liberty are the dominant social and economic values and that the burden of achievement lies with individual action, then work or other social organizations are likely to take particular forms.

They are likely to expect the individual to bring to the workplace appropriate skills and attitudes and to take responsibility for keeping them current. If, on the other hand as, for example, in Japan which is committed to such personal values as loyalty, conformity, hierarchy, duty, and obedience, it is likely that organizational forms will be created to respond to these individual values in a way that differs accordingly from those present in American organizational structures. To carry the analogy a bit further, institutions, policies, and social technologies in a given nation are likely to accommodate the values and the perspectives about human resources or individual behaviors that predominate in that society and the role of such institutions in using existing human resources to further the economy of that nation. Japan's economic and political system has been called a developmental model rather than a regulatory model as has been used to describe the U. S. and the United Kingdom (Wood, 1990). Developmental models applied to work organizations set clearly defined strategic economic goals, and attempt to insure that workers are constantly prepared to manage and implement the processes required to meet such goals, and to identify with the economic targets and their contributions to such outcomes.

The Japanese notion of a "developmentally" oriented work organization includes a major emphasis on harnessing the tacit skills and latent talents of workers from the factory floor to the management office. At all of these levels, workers are put to the task of diagnosing problems and organizing information that will improve productivity and corporate knowledge. In this sense, the management attitude is to make every worker an "industrial engineer" designed to help the organization collectively seek continuous improvement and to look beyond a narrowly focused view of immediate job completion. Within such a concept, training of workers is concerned with teamwork, multi-functional approaches, interpersonal skills, and problem-solving capabilities. Thus, the intent of the Japanese system of labor management is to create conditions under which workers will be encouraged to cooperate and develop their awareness and skills, including their collective and diagnostic ones (Wood, 1990). In this view, a developmental state or organizational model contrasts with that of a regulatory state which is more concerned with the processes and rules of competition, not the substance. Such perspectives also differ in the nation's or culture's stress on what economists describe as allocative or accounting efficiency versus X-efficiency. The former has to do with the efficiency that comes from getting all of the economy's resources put to use in ways by which they will yield most value, that will satisfy relatively short-term profit requirements in a shareholder dominated form of capitalism.

X-efficiency, on the other hand, is much more a matter of how people view their place in society and what the organization's responsibilities to its workers are. This kind of efficiency is less easy to calculate but it has to do with the efficiency which comes from paying attention to the work you are doing and not boring holes in the wrong place and having to scrap an expensive piece of work; it comes from making the right decisions because you have done your homework, got hold of all the market forecasts, collected as much information on your competitor's development plans as possible. It comes from caring about the quality of the work you produce and the service you give your customers, and from giving thought to how to improve them (Dore, 1987, p. 17). The latter form of efficiency is heavily colored by social arrangements—"the compromises made in favor of people who would lose out from the free working of market forces, the mobilizing of a sense of obligation and personal commitment in employment relations and 'customer market' relations—that generate a sense of fairness which enables people to work cooperatively, conscientiously and with a will" (Dore, 1987).

The intent here is not to set up a dichotomy of economic cultures that suggests that one is better than another. Indeed, it is likely that in a global economy the models identified will become more similar. Rather, the point is that, as a society, it is important, as part of the total effort in behalf of employment-bound youth, to monitor the achievement images and messages various social institutions send to this sub-population and how these may need to be altered. In addition, these perspectives suggest strongly that how work organizations are configured and how they induct young workers into their culture and create a work culture for them will have much to do with how young workers view themselves and express their loyalty to and identity with the work organization. Further, these perspectives suggest that the training of employment-bound youth needs to include attention to the norms, the expectations, the psychological environment which occurs in different work organizations in order to help employment-bound youth understand such expectations and develop skills and insights by which their adjustment to the workplace can be facilitated. Such needs will likely intensify as the demands and challenges of the global economy intensify.

Perspectives on Human Resource Needs in the Global Economy

In the past 25 years, national and global issues have radically altered. We are now in a historical period in which individual desires for higher standards of living have gripped the political world and in which the most recent quarter century has culminated in the explosive economic growth of the nations of the Pacific—not just Japan, but Taiwan, Hong Kong, Singapore, and South Korea as well—the economic expansion of the Western European nations, and the beginnings of the drive for economic revitalization in the nations of Eastern Europe, the Middle East, in South America, and in Africa.

As a function of such dynamics, societies throughout the world have entered major periods of transition or transformation. Some nations are leaping from underdeveloped to industrialized status in a generation. It is a rare nation, if it exists, that is not influenced by changing concerns about employment and unemployment, shifting characteristics and demographics of the work force, needs for training and retraining of a work force that is teachable and competent to implement new processes flowing from the adaptation of advanced technology to both the content of work and to the characteristics and organization of the workplace. These changes are interdependent; they each affect the other.

As various forms of advanced technology have become central to international competition and international trade, economic realignments and economic growth, the diffusion of scientific, engineering, and technological capabilities throughout the world has accelerated. The global spread of science, engineering and technological capabilities has brought with it an unprecedented integration of the global economy, exposing new dimensions of the interdependence of nations. It has become clear that as interim steps to a fully integrated global economy, *trading blocs* will be the economic way of life in the future and those nations outside of such economic alignments or without access to them will have their economic aspirations thwarted. National economies are rapidly eroding in favor of regional and global economies. Whether expressed in terms of the European Economic Community of 1992, the U.S.–Canada Free Trade Agreement of 1989, the North American Free Trade Agreement of 1993, the Association of South Eastern Asian Nations, or the Asian Pacific Economic Conference, it has become clear that the economic growth of nations is no longer sustainable within their political boundaries. Just as environmental sovereignty is a thing of the past, so is economic sovereignty. Just as pollutants flow from nation to nation, so capital and technological knowledge flow across national borders, altering economic sovereignty as they diffuse (White, 1990, . 10).

But the creation of a global economy is not simply an interesting structural artifact. It has implications for what nations must do to compete in the international economic arena, the skills their workers will need, and the forces driving such global economic dynamics.

Within any of the economic alliances where national boundaries are no longer operating as barriers to member states (e.g., European Economic Community, 1992), companies which had branch plants in other nations within the alliance in order to position themselves behind national tariff walls no longer need to do so. Similarly, firms of different nations are likely to more frequently merge to lock in their mutual competitive advantages or to take advantage of "economies of scale" to acquire the breadth and depth necessary to operate effectively under the new economic conditions. Many firms will continue to "downsize" or change the skill emphases in their work forces and purchase new technologies by which to increase their productivity and reduce labor costs. Other firms may reduce some parts of their organizations that have historically been required to manage the trade regulations, standards, or statutes that have affected commerce between specific countries. As such regulations or statutes are modified or eliminated, the need for certain types of workers may be reduced or eliminated. Beyond such points, the mergers, downsizing, joint ventures, or other

corporate transformations are likely to create worker dislocations of various kinds. Many of the workers displaced through
these processes will not have the skills to participate in the
emerging technologies implemented by the employment
requirements of the merged or changed corporate environments. In such situations, counselors likely will be heavily
involved in working with workers being terminated through
outplacement counseling, with brokering of training and
retraining opportunities, and with the psychological demands
associated with unemployment and underemployment.

As trade restrictions are eliminated across nations involved
with the European community or the North American Free
Trade Agreement or the emerging alliances among Pacific Rim
countries, the freer movement of workers will escalate across
nations. Mechanisms are being implemented now in Europe
and in North America to allow workers employed by specific
corporations in one nation to move easily with plants relocated
to other nations, to merged facilities, and within other economic
realignments. Potential problems are that some nations will
not gain enhanced employment opportunities in jobs requiring skilled, highly trained, better paid sectors because such
persons will be brought into the country by corporations coming to do business under the new economic agreements. From
a career counseling standpoint, free migration of workers from
one nation to another creates a much larger potential opportunity structure from which individuals may choose. But it also
challenges counselors to be sensitive to and help clients give
attention to cultural differences, languages, and traditions
which will mediate work adjustment in the country to which
they are considering migrating. Counselors will, in addition,
need to facilitate and broker worker preparation for cultural
transitions, including procedures by which to access the social
institutions of the host nation: e.g., financial services, religious
institutions, schools, health and legal care. Such perspectives
are likely to broaden the paradigms and content of career counseling from a current concern on cross-cultural counseling to
issues of cross-national migration.

Many of the factors inherent in worker migration within a
global economy are psychological issues, not simply economic
or placement issues. Thus, it is not unlikely that counselors
will, in the future, need to help workers and their families

anticipate and process decisions about whether they should immigrate or transfer to another nation on a temporary or on a permanent basis. Issues of economic and psychological trade-offs in such transfers; the need to modify or lose a cultural identity; the processes of cultural adaptation, accommodation, and assimilation; sources of specific information about policies and benefits; sources of social supports, ways to manage family disruption, separation, and the loss of family care-givers are each areas about which career counseling will increasingly be concerned as the full implications of the global economy ensues.

Career counselors must acknowledge in their conceptions and practices that to a large extent now and to a greater extent by the turn of the century, the career development of the citizens of every nation will be indirectly if not directly influenced by the content, status, and economic alliances undergirding a global economy. In such cases, workers who are bilingual or multilingual will be more prized and their careers will be enhanced by such skills. Knowledge of cultural differences, world history, political, legal, environmental and economic systems will be as important for many jobs as are accounting procedures, machine skills, and other technical competencies. Given the variety of physical and social ecologies in which a global economy must be played out, the need will increase for persons who have skills in the legal and regulatory systems of other nations and the abilities to examine and plan in accordance with the environmental impact of construction projects and industrial processes as they are integrated within differential national environmental laws and circumstances. So, too, will the need for managerial and entrepreneurial skills related to new and decentralized organizations of work.

A Global Labor Force

Perhaps of even more fundamental significance is the reality that with a global economy, there is emerging a truly global labor force, "talented and capable of accomplishing just about anything, anywhere. Thus, the average American doesn't realize that there is a truly competitive work force out there that is vying for their jobs. The rest of the world is catching up" (O'Reilly, December 14, 1992, p. 52). The meaning for

American workers, including employment-bound youth, is that American jobs or factories are not being sent to other nations simply in search of cheap labor or less expensive economic conditions, but in search of competent workers who can perform as well or better as American workers and do so at less cost. These distinctions may be subtle but they are highly important. Multinational corporations, even though owned by U.S. financiers, employ many foreign nationals in the countries where their offices, manufacturing plants, or hotels are located. They do so rather than taking American workers to these nations because foreign nationals know the language, the cultural issues, the networks on which the success of the multinational corporation rests *and* the foreign national is likely to perform without the overhead costs or the annual wage that would be required if an American work force were transported in mass to another nation to do the work of the multinational corporation.

But it is not only the large multinational corporations that are seeking and employing talented workers in other nations. A growing number of American corporations are parceling out increasingly sophisticated work to other nations where their work forces are exceedingly capable. Unlike 10 or 15 years ago when American, European, or Japanese companies located plants overseas and tried to produce and do everything they needed themselves, they are now much more likely to "outsource," to contract for parts and labor from independent local suppliers. This is essentially an extension of the domestic American companies' increasing propensity to subcontract work to suppliers of labor, temporary or contingent workers, or material. In outsourcing abroad or subcontracting in the United States, American companies are able to reduce their permanent investment in buildings and in people, thereby keeping to a minimum their overhead costs of maintenance, repair, health benefits, training, and other expenditures that accrue when companies have large physical plants and permanent work forces. They are essentially creating a contingent work force that can be called upon at times of specific need for particular skills to supplement those of the permanent work force (Fierman, 1994).

The parceling out of work generated in the United States to persons in other nations takes many other forms as the work forces of these nations become able to do sophisticated work that American companies need at lower cost and as made possible by technological advances. For example, in Jamaica, hundreds of persons now work at office parks connected to the U. S. by satellite dishes. As information flows to them through sophisticated telecommunication links, the Jamaican workers make airline reservations and process tickets, handle calls to toll-free 800 numbers, and do data entry. A similar set of events is occurring in Ireland as a result of the Irish government's investment in the island's telecommunications infrastructure. All over Ireland, from Dublin to Cork and in between, scores of offices handle complex service work originating in the U. S. Irish clerical workers handle medical insurance claims from the U. S., American employee pension claims, and a range of complex software development and implementation tasks as well as customer service questions about products and processes. Ireland's work force is not confined in its international work to responding to U. S. needs but also has well-trained, multilingual workers who do many of the same tasks for other European nations. There are many other examples of American companies finding national work forces that can do the work required with high technical capability, with a strong work ethic, and at lower costs: e.g., software programming in India, lighting manufacturing in Hungary, computer component design in Mexico, and a variety of data entry locations in the Caribbean, the Philippines and in China (O'Reilly, 1992). These skilled workers in other nations not only need the technical capabilities to perform the work to American standards but they also must know about American regulations, policies, and other information if they are going to process life insurance applications, medical claims, or pension information for American companies. These are different levels of work, requiring far more capability and understanding than is true, for example, of the exploitation of uneducated persons sewing garments manually in Haiti or in other cottage industries around the world.

It needs to be noted here that just as the globalization of the work force expands and affects the jobs and work expectations for Americans, there is also a growing global labor surplus. One of the corollaries of the globalization of the work force is that as foreign investments in and mergers occur among corporations in Western and Eastern Europe, or the U. S. and the newly industrializing nations, the facilities and processes created through the application of advanced technology and other innovative processes make the resulting factories or other workplaces much less labor intensive. Consequently, the number of blue-collar workers, staff, and managerial employees are reduced or kept limited with the use of outsourcing, subcontracting, part-time work and other processes used to keep the permanent employees at a minimum. As a result, there are many examples where major capital improvements, better technology, and reengineering of the way work is done, has reduced the work forces in acquired plants to one-third or one-tenth of the previous work force while maintaining higher productivity and competitiveness than before the plant was purchased. The workers unemployed through such processes become part of the global labor surplus. As several observers have noted, the surplus is not comprised simply of unskilled, uneducated workers; there is now a world-wide glut of surplus labor at all levels of education and technical ability (Martin, 1992; Wander, 1987).

The implications of such perspectives are that the emerging global economy has stimulated the emergence of an increasingly skilled global work force against which American employment-bound youth will increasingly have to compete. Such competition means that the education, the work ethic, the performance skills, the teachability, and the personal flexibility of employment-bound youth in America are increasingly being placed in direct confrontation with their counterparts around the world. But, there are other specific issues as well.

The Effects of Advanced Technology on the Content of Work

In contextual terms, there are many examples to be drawn about the interactive effects of shifting economic and social "ecologies" on individual behavior. One major factor, as suggested previously, is the effect of advanced technology upon the economic climate and the occupational structures of the nations of the world. The wide-spread application of advanced technology in workplaces and homes takes many forms, e.g.: microengineering; self replicating robots; genetic reconstruction and bioengineering; magnetic flight or levitation;

computer science; fiber optics, lasers, and semiconductors; synthetic materials or material sciences; synthetic energy sources; aquaculture and ocean mining. Simply put, there is not one advanced technology, there are many technologies that arise from different disciplines, applications, or categories of problems. There are industrial, medical, educational, social, computer, materials, agricultural, military, and many other forms of technology. There are hard and soft technologies. The former usually refers to physical technologies—machines, equipment, products—whereas the latter has to do with processes, problem-solving techniques, organizational structures.

Technology can also be identified as low or high technology. According to Dyrenfurth (1984), high technology typically refers to the most sophisticated, and often the most recently advancing technological knowledge, skills, and hardware applications. Minshall (1984) has extended such perspectives by applying the term "high technology" both to workplaces and processes as follows:

- High technology signifies high-growth occupational areas in which technological applications are rapidly changing job knowledge and skill requirements in terms of an arbitrary percentage of a worker's useful working life.
- High technology refers to (1) products, processes, and applications stemming from the latest scientific and technological developments, (2) utilization of high-level machine intelligence and information decision capability, and (3) the extension of human manual and intellectual capacities through the use of computer technology and the application of sophisticated physical principles (pp. 29-30).

Castells (1985) provided a somewhat different view of high or advanced technology. His perspectives probe the underlying characteristics of advanced technology:

*"Two features are characteristic of the stream of technological innovation under way. First, the object of technological discoveries, as well as of their applications, is **information**. What microelectronics does is to process and eventually generate information. What telecommunications do is to*

*transmit information, with a growing complexity of
interactive loops and feedback's, at increasingly greater
speed and at a lower cost. What the new media do is to
disseminate information in a way potentially more and
more decentralized and individualized. What automation
does is to introduce preinformed devices in other activities.
And what genetic engineering does is to decode the information system of the living matter and try to program it.
The second feature concerns the fact that the outcome is
process-oriented rather than product-oriented. High
technology is not a particular technique, but a form of
production and organization that can affect all spheres of
activity by transforming their operation in order to achieve
greater productivity or better performance through
increased knowledge of the process itself "* (pp. 11-12).

Of primary importance to the counseling of employment-
bound youth is the reality that advanced technologies, however defined, change the organization and the language of
work, its content, the role of workers, and the skill requirements to engage in work, particularly in those occupations
which involve either high technology or technology intensive
processes. As particular nations spin off their routine or stand-
ardized manufacturing and assembly operations to other
nations where wages are lower or resources are better, while
retaining control in their own nations of non-routine or innovative operations, the result is an elevation of formal qualifications or skill requirements in each nation (Nijkamp, Bouman,
& Verhoef, 1990). Studies in several nations have suggested
that the availability of technical and skilled workers largely
determine the location of production and the presence of
industries developing or using advanced technologies within
and across national boundaries. Thus, both in economic and
technical terms, advanced technology stimulates a major process of urban-regional restructuring of jobs availability and
population concentrations around the world. Regional differences across nations increase rather than decrease as high technology or technology-intensive occupations are introduced into
the manufacturing and distribution sectors of a society, with
persons in these regions experiencing major differences in
occupational opportunities, quality of life, education and training or, other such disparities. These conditions are among those

which stimulate migration within and across national boundaries, urban congestion and stress, potential widening of gaps between rich and poor, an erosion of family and community support systems, a dilution of feelings of personal responsibility for one's fate and a blurring of behavioral sanctions which tend to control individual behaviors, changing family structures, and other risk factors which create a seedbed for mental health problems and for the content of counseling.

From a global perspective, technology becomes critical at every step of international trade, production, and communication as raw materials, labor forces, and ideas are integrated into world systems of commercial interaction. Through global systems of telecommunications, satellites, fax, and computers, new technological developments and capital spread overnight around the world and become critical at every step of international politics, information dissemination, and world trade systems. As such, the pervasive implementation of advanced technology has altered the mix of jobs available and the content of work in a ripple effect across national economies. The playing out and success of life-long learning throughout its work force will be a major factor in giving individual nations the competitive edge in the future. It is unlikely that such goals can be achieved unless the work force of any nation is equipped with basic academic skills—literacy, numeracy, and communications. Without these skills, life-long learning, retraining, and teachability or adaptation to new management, production, and information-processing techniques are virtually impossible.

The Rise of Knowledge Workers

Alvin Toffler in the most recent of his classic books, *Powershift: Knowledge, Wealth and Violence at the Edge of the 21st Century* (1990), has offered the view that the world of the future will be divided, not into capitalist and communist societies or into the developed and the developing nations, but into the fast and slow nations, those that are technologically advanced and those that are not. In his view, knowledge has now become the world's prime commodity and its by-product is the use and acceleration of time—in terms of the speed of capital movements, transactions and investments, the speed with which ideas are converted into processes and products, the speed with which plans are translated into action. In his view, knowledge is rapidly replacing cheap labor and raw materials as the primary requisite to effective international competition and to improving the quality of life within communities and nations.

Toeffler's views have been accented by those of Peter Drucker (1989; 1993), the famous scholar of management, who has argued that the biggest shift—bigger by far than the changes in politics, government, or economics—is the shift to the knowledge society in all developed, non-communist societies. According to Drucker, all developed countries are becoming post-business, knowledge societies as the logical result of a long evolution in which the world has moved from working by the sweat of our brow and by muscle to industrial work and finally to knowledge work. Until quite recently, there were few jobs requiring knowledge. Knowledge was an ornament, or at least confined in importance to members of a few elite occupational classes, rather than a necessity for most workers. In the twentieth century, knowledge has rapidly become the economy's foundation and its true capital. Knowledge has replaced experience as the primary requisite for employability and cheap labor and raw materials as the primary national asset. In turn, work organizations are evolving into new forms; they are becoming knowledge, information and idea-based. They require employees in all settings who can work smarter and who can understand the various forms of knowledge exploding across disciplines, their central concerns and theories, the major new insights they can produce and their application to problem-solving. According to Drucker (1989), "Knowledge workers are fast becoming the pacesetters, the arbiters of value, in the societies of all developed countries... The essence of automated production is a system organized around information [working smarter]. But once the system has been designed, the need for manual work soon goes down dramatically. The center of gravity in production then shifts from manual workers to knowledge workers." Such a view clearly supports the rise of technicians, as described in Chapter One, as a new worker elite and, indeed, as a level of work to which many employment-bound youth should aspire.

Today, over 50 percent of the U. S. labor force are knowledge workers, white collar or information workers, ranging from executives, managers, analysts, and programmers to teachers, designers, illustrators and sales representatives, to copywriters, statistical clerks, and secretaries. Clerical workers constitute the largest single class of employees in the U. S labor force—about 20 percent of all employed people. Since 1950, industrial work has fallen from around 38 percent of the labor force to about 18 percent in 1984 and to closer to 15 percent in 1993. Just as the large decrease in agricultural employment over the last 25 years has been accompanied by a large rise in agricultural output so, too, has the decrease in industrial employment been accompanied by a continuing and accelerating rise in industrial output, signifying a long-term shift from labor-intensive to capital-intensive production. The latter reflects again the growing effect of the application of technology to production (e.g., numerical-controlled machine tools, computer-aided design and manufacture, robotics). Further, since 1960, service work has risen from about 18 percent of the labor force to nearly 30 percent and has led many to call the U. S. economy of the present future a distributive or service-based economy (Hudson Institute, 1987).

From another perspective, by 1982, only 3 percent of the labor force of the United States was engaged in agriculture (and an undetermined proportion of these workers are involved in agribusiness, which does not typically occur on farms or involve direct production of agricultural commodities), less than 30 percent was engaged in the production of non-agricultural goods (mostly manufacturing), and 70 percent was engaged in service occupations (defined in the broadest sense to include all enterprises not engaged in the production of goods—mining, manufacturing, and construction—or agriculture) (Ginzberg, 1982). Since 1978, the Fortune 500 companies and the large corporate models of the past 100 years have essentially created no new jobs in the United States. They have created new career ladders and job requirements, applied technology widely, and become increasingly international in work force and markets, but they have not added jobs. Since 1981, 19 out of 20 new jobs have been in the service sector. Up to two thirds of the new jobs since 1978 have been in three groups of occupations: business services, retail trade (including restaurants), and health care (*World Press Review*, May 1988).

The importance of knowledge as the foundation for economic development and international competitiveness in the United States and in other industrialized nations ripples through the society in implications for the necessary characteristics of the work force, in the stimulation of educational reform, and in the identification of sub-populations who are particularly vulnerable because of poor education and training or a jagged employment history.

With regard to the characteristics of the work force, American business and industry are increasingly worried about the quality of those potential employees from whom they will be able to choose. Such data come from many sources including major business news magazines. As an example, Simon and Button (1990) in *Forbes Magazine*, have indicated to business leaders that what has been learned from the late 1980's is that "a poorly educated labor force may cost the U. S. dearly. In a specific sense, the authors contend that as the "baby bust" generation moved into the job market in the late 1980's, companies got a taste of what lies ahead: a shortage of trained and trainable workers. They observe that "modern industry does not just require bodies; it requires trained minds." According to their data, the National Science Foundation projects a *shortage* of 540,000 scientists and engineers by the year 2000. (In 1988, the U. S. had 5.5 million scientists and engineers at work.) "Equally troubling is the lack of skilled workers for manufacturing, construction, and health care. Without extensive training, few of these slots can be filled by the unskilled who are out of work in inner cities or laid off from basic industries. If you can't read, you can't do much today, because most heavy lifting is done by machine." The authors indict American educational institutions at both the high school and college levels. They state that, "All too often our high schools are graduating functional illiterates, and even the colleges are graduating poorly educated people... Even without the educational deficiency, the prospects for the labor supply are not promising. There already have been spot shortages of entry-level workers in New England and parts of California. Blame a shrinking population of 18-to-24-year-olds. Fact is there will be nearly 40 percent fewer people entering the work force in the 1990s than there were in the 1970s" (pp. 103 and 104).

The perspective of Simon and Graham are in many ways echoed by Kuttner (1990) writing in *Business Week*: "Although it ultimately determines America's standing in the world, the U. S. work force skills aren't world class—particularly the lower half, which does not graduate from college, and the lowest quarter which can barely read, write, or add. The U. S., uniquely among industrial nations, has no systematic approach for continuously upgrading the quality of its workers and matching available capital to industry's changing needs. Demographics are predicting labor shortages in the 1990s. Good luck finding qualified workers" (p. 21).

The concerns expressed about the changing demands on the work force and its quality have also appeared increasingly in debates and in platforms of the Presidential elections of 1988 and 1992. In a Special Report, entitled "Needed: Human Capital," in *Business Week*, Nussbaum (September 19, 1988) and several other writers described the dimensions of an issue which was seen to be a necessary part of the political campaign. In sum, this special report and the subsequent essays addressed the view that after years of neglect, the problem of human capital had become a crisis. The United States had been seen as trying to solve its increasingly serious competitiveness problems by pouring billions of dollars into capital equipment and not into worker training, retraining, and other support systems. Several related dimensions are identified. One is the growing inability of a large percentage of the American work force to compete effectively in an integrated world economy. In this regard, Nussbaum quoted Professor Merry White, author of *The Japanese Educational Challenge,* that "Much of the success of Japan stems from the fact that its blue-collar workers can interpret advanced mathematics, read complex engineering blueprints, and perform sophisticated tasks on the factory floor far better than blue collars in the U. S" (p. 101). Thus, in such perspectives it becomes evident that building up human capital needs to be a national priority, that education and knowledge are critical to the American worker's productive capability, that skills of workers at all performance levels must be upgraded and, in particular, that if we do not increase the skills of the bottom ranks of the work force, we will have an even more divided society than we do now. These are direct challenges to viewing the importance of employment-bound youth more positively and providing a national agenda of actions to insure that these workers are equipped to compete at world class levels.

Fundamental to such views is the growing realization in American business and industry and in other economic and government sectors that while in any economic period there is some gap between the demands of jobs and worker skills, the mismatch that has been apparent since the mid-1980's or so is growing and very large. Obviously, the pervasive effects of the application of advanced technology across industrial processes, business procedures, and the organization of work is not benign. According to a joint publication of the U. S. Department of Education and the Department of Labor (1988), "New technology has changed the nature of work—created new jobs and altered others—and, in many cases, has revealed basic problems where none were known to exist" (p. 3). Such new technology, then, in part because of its important role within the capability of the United States to compete internationally and because many new jobs quite literally require levels of education and basic academic skills that many young people seem not to have acquired in school, has caused national outcries for educational reform to intensify at the same time that it has stimulated the need for reassessments of the skills of adult workers and where they are deficient to introduce remedial education and other training directly into the workplace.

As advanced technology has altered skill sets in jobs where such applications of technology have changed the job performance content, it has also caused other jobs to be transferred to other nations. In a general sense, then, as jobs are relocated from one nation to another as a function of the dynamics of a global economy or as the job opportunity structure changes in any specific nation, so does the spectrum of skill requirements that are required to maintain or advance that structure. As technological applications replace many of the least skilled jobs in the occupational structure and as such technologies become more complex and interactive and inexorably become applied to an ever widening cluster of jobs, they transform the training and learning requirements throughout the economy.

The above notion was captured in a major national study, entitled *Technology and the American Economic Transition: Choices for the Future*, conducted by the Office of Technology Assessment of the Congress of the United States (1988), in the following observations:

"Technology can replace many of the most tedious, danger-ous and dehumanizing tasks while creating jobs that

require more intellectual and social skills. Machines are likely to plant seeds, weave cloth, fabricate metal parts, handle routine paperwork, enter data, and perform a vast number of other repetitive tasks more efficiently and more productively than people. By default, the majority of jobs created in the economy could be those requiring human, and not machine-like skills: designing, tailoring products and services to unique customer needs; teaching; caring; entertaining; promoting; and persuading. Ironically, one result of sophisticated technology may be a work force whose primary task is dealing with people—as customers or as colleagues" (p. 3).

Shifting Emphases in Work

Such contextual factors denote a continuing shift of jobs in the United States from manufacturing to service. As projected in 1987 and in continuing estimates (e.g., Bernstein, 1988), "U. S. manufacturing will be a much smaller share of the economy in the year 2000 than it is today." According to the Executive Summary of the U. S. Department of Labor's *Workforce 2000: Work and Workers for the 21st Century* (Hudson Institute, 1987), "Service industries will create all of the new jobs, and most of the new wealth, over the next 13 years." But, whether or not that projection is totally accurate, these projections further assert that, "The new jobs in service industries will demand much higher skill levels than the jobs of today. Very few new jobs will be created for those who cannot read, follow directions, and use mathematics. Ironically, the demographic trends in the work force, coupled with the higher skill requirements of the economy, will lead to both higher and lower unemployment, more joblessness among the least-skilled and less among the most educationally advantaged," (Hudson Institute, 1987, p.1).

What is implied beyond the obvious in this quotation is that the content of service jobs is wide-ranging; it is not just the world of fast-food or personal services (e.g., laundry, child care, etc.) that is at issue here. Health care, financial services, entertainment, and many other complex jobs are also included. What is less obvious is that in many jobs, while the names remain the same, the content of the jobs is not the same, particularly as the number of technology intensive occupations grow. For example, the automotive assembly worker of the year

2000 will not be the automotive assembly worker of 1980. In 2000, while such a job may still be in the manufacturing sector, the person occupying such a job is much more likely to trouble-shoot robots and other computerized processes designed to fabricate and assemble cars than to actually manipulate and build car components manually. Thus, the distinctions between manufacturing and service become blurred; so do distinctions between working and learning. Indeed, increasingly work can be seen as learning activity. As such, what happens in schools and what happens in the workplace are not mutually exclusive phenomena. Life in the United States and in other industrialized nations is no longer separated into three independent stages: one goes to school, one goes to work, one retires. These stages are now interdependent. What one does and how one progresses in work and the quality of one's life in retirement are typically quite directly related to the quality and content of schooling and other training one receives in one's life.

Shifting Demands on the Education and Skills of Workers

The point is that whether or not a worker is directly involved in a high technology occupation, the pervasive application of advanced technology throughout the occupational structure is one of the major functions causing the educational skills required in the workplace to rise. Part of this phenomenon is related to the fact that the automation of work is easiest in the lower skilled jobs; by eliminating many unskilled and semi-skilled jobs through technology, the average education or training required in the remaining jobs or in the emerging occupations is increased. Similarly, through world-wide communication networks, it is possible to locate specific jobs anywhere in the world where the economic conditions and quality are satisfactory but manage them from a central location in the United States. This phenomenon also tends to reduce the number of low skilled and semi-skilled jobs in the United States, as these jobs are exported to other nations where workers receive lower pay than in the U. S. and the overhead for production is lower. Such circumstances again reduce the jobs where educational requirements are low and thereby increasingly elevate, on average, the educational requirements for American workers.

Looked at from an educational perspective, national projections suggest that "among the fastest-growing jobs, the trend toward higher educational requirements is striking. Of all the new jobs that will be created over the 1984-2000 period, more than half will require some education beyond high school, and almost a third will be filled by college graduates. Today, only 22 percent of all occupations require a college degree. The median years of education required by the new jobs created between 1984 and 2000 will be 13.5 compared to 12.8 for the current work force" (Hudson Institute, 1987, p. 98-99). If this trend to higher education in the emerging occupations continues, the figures cited for median education required for the fastest growing and the emerging occupations will likely be conservative.

Undoubtedly, there will continue to be a very large number of jobs which have medium to low-skilled requirements. As has been noted in a number of essays and by statistics of the U. S. Department of Labor, including those reported in Chapter One, in absolute terms the largest number of jobs from now until the end of the century will be cooks, nursing aides, waiters, janitors, clerks, and cashiers. But even for these jobs, there will be rising expectations that these workers will be able to read and understand directions , add and subtract, and be able to speak and think clearly in order to be increasingly adaptable to job changes. From this perspective, jobs that are currently in the middle of the skill distribution will be the least-skilled occupations of the future, and there will be few net new jobs for the unskilled (Hudson Institute, 1987).

As the educational requirements rise and gaps become increasingly wide between job demands and work skills, another issue of serious moment to many observers is the shifting demographics of the work force itself. Through 1985, White males dominated the U. S. job market. Starting in 1985, however, that long established demographic reality no longer prevails; White males will play a much smaller part in the work force of the future. Indeed, new entrants to the labor force from 1985 to the year 2000 will consist of more than half who will be minorities, nearly three times the figure prior to 1985. Included in this figure are more than 23 percent of the new entrants who will be immigrants. Another 42 percent of the new work force entrants will be U. S. born White females. Thus, at a time when jobs, particularly emerging occupations, require higher levels of math, science and literacy than ever before, the economy is becoming increasingly dependent on the groups that often receive the poorest education: for example, as population groups of Blacks and Hispanics have the highest school drop-out notes in the country and lag significantly behind the national average on test scores (Hudson Institute, 1987; Nussbaum, 1988). They do so not because of inferiority or inability to learn, but because they have, for the most part, been located in geographic locations where the education and the reinforcement to study and to seek occupational mobility have been far less positive and evenly distributed than has been true for their counterparts in the majority culture.

The realities of rising educational requirements, the need to be able to change with changes in the workplace, needs for competence in basic academic skills, puts those with minimal training or capability of learning at the risk of being permanently dislocated or unemployed or constantly on the move to find jobs which they can do. Such persons become increasingly and constantly vulnerable to being replaced in their current work, likely to suffer a diminishing quality of life, or they choose not to be involved in attempting to participate in a dynamically changing occupational structure at all.

The implementation of advanced technology has also altered the psychological environment for workers and, indeed, created a social revolution related to effectively integrating technology into the workplace and helping persons interrelate with these technologies. For example, machines can now give us more information more quickly than people can possibly absorb it. The flow of such information has changed the distribution of power and authority within many workplaces and created new stresses and demands which had not existed before, including potential health and safety hazards associated with the constant use of or exposure to computer display terminals and related equipment. As information must be transformed into knowledge and intelligence, which by its volume and rapid availability strains human factors of decision-making, information processing, and creativity, morale in the workplace can plummet not only because job procedures and content change under the implementation of technology but because the gap between humans and machines seem to be widening.

Technostress is becoming apparent in many situations, and the rapidity of change is pushing persons to the limit of their resources to respond and to anticipate. "The relentless advance of technological development puts even highly educated people at risk of becoming to some extent functionally illiterate" (Weiner & Brown, 1989, p. 11).

What has been implicit but not explicit in this chapter is that the rise of an interlocked global economy, the globalization of a labor force and what Robert Reich, Secretary of Labor under President Clinton, has termed a global enterprise net (1991), has created needs that go beyond the basic academic and the technical skills to other knowledge bases that become critical to international economic competitiveness. Secretary Reich describes in vivid detail the transformation of American corporations into organizations that are rapidly becoming internationalized, in which much of the value of what they sell comes from other places around the world, is produced by workers in other nations, and is a process of combining components, problem-solving, strategic brokering into products that may have a familiar American logo but little direct input by American workers. Such dynamics are characterized by Secretary Reich in his description of what goes into the making of a traditional "American" automobile.

> "When an American buys a Pontiac LeMans from General
> Motors, for example, he or she engages unwittingly in an
> international transaction. OF the $20,000 paid to GM,
> about $6,000 goes to South Korea for routine labor and
> assembly operations, $3,500 to Japan for advanced compo-
> nents (engines, transaxles, and electronics), $1,500 to
> West Germany for styling and design engineering, $800 to
> Taiwan, Singapore, and Japan for small components, $500
> to Britain for advertising and marketing services, and
> about $100 to Ireland and Barbados for data processing.
> The rest—less than $8,000—goes to strategists in Detroit,
> lawyers and bankers in New York, lobbyists in Washing-
> ton, insurance and health-care workers all over the coun-
> try, and General Motors shareholders—most of whom live
> in the United States, but an increasing number of whom
> are foreign nationals" (Reich, 1991, p. 113).

It is a mistake to assume that there are no longer American corporations that hire thousands of workers who design and create products, market, and distribute them. There are such corporations, of course. But even in these cases, such corporations typically have had to engage in export-import activities to become internationalized in their marketing and selling, rather than confining themselves to a domestic orientation. What the U. S. had conceived only a quarter of a century ago as its unchallenged dominant share of world markets has now been converted to an economic environment in which 75 percent or more of all goods produced in the United States are now being produced elsewhere in the world and thus open to price and quality competition both in the United States and in foreign markets in ways never before experienced in this nation. Thus, in many instances, if American workers are in internationalized companies, corporations, or industries, even if they never leave the United States, they are likely to work in an international communications environment, linked through satellites or other telecommunications systems to counterparts around the globe as they buy and sell products, design and test components, and do strategic brokering. As a result, the skilled worker and the technician, not only the professional, has had to learn more about the history, languages, religious beliefs, cultural traditions, financial and legal systems of the nations with whom they must do business. A global economy and the globalization of the labor force will require greater sensitivity of Americans to the history, ethos, political and economic aspirations of countries with whom we trade as well as of immigrant populations entering into our own work force. It will behoove us to increase our language facility as a nation, to acknowledge that national languages are not neutral, they convey cultural nuances, ethnic dignity, traditions, ethics to which we as a nation must extend greater respect in our interactions, internationally and domestically. In addition to these types of knowledge that many employment-bound youth will need to acquire and use, such young workers will need to learn that as economic resources remain limited in this nation and around the world, creativity, risk management, innovation, entrepreneurial skills and vision will be needed to create new paradigms of how to use resources more effectively, preserve the environment, and create a positive quality of life that is more inclusive of all persons.

These are extraordinarily challenging requirements to direct toward employment-bound youth, but they are certainly not impossible challenges. Millions of employment-bound youth in Europe and Asia acquire many of these skills and knowledge bases. They are not intellectually superior to American employment-bound youth, but, certainly, the comprehensiveness of content and purpose expected of employment-bound youth in the United States must be more clearly defined in education and in counseling in the future. Employment-bound youth must be helped to understand, prepare for, and implement the elements of personal flexibility, purposefulness, and productivity as they journey through their educational experiences, the transition from school to work, and their induction into the community of full-time workers.

Conclusion

Counselors of employment-bound youth must acknowledge in their life-long learning, in their conceptions and their practices that to a large extent now and to a larger extent by the turn of the century, the career development of the citizens of every nation will be indirectly or directly influenced by the content, status, and economic alliances undergirding a global economy and by the skills and capabilities of a global work force. Neither employment-bound youth nor other citizens exist in a social or economic vacuum. Nor do American industries exist in isolation from an interdependent and integrated world economy. Therefore, counselors and employment-bound youth must take the challenges of an occupational structure in flux in response to international economic competition seriously and use such dynamics as a stimulus to the planning, preparing for, and implementing of personal career development. The specifics of the content and the techniques by which counseling might be more effectively directed to such goals will be discussed in subsequent chapters.

Chapter Three

Career Development for Employment-Bound Youth in Schools

In the preceding two chapters, we discussed, first, some of the characteristics of employment-bound youth in the United States and, second, the emerging economic and work environments into which these youth will move as they complete or terminate their high school education. Together these two chapters provide a context which suggests that employment-bound youth are not a homogeneous population but rather one which is diverse in gender, ability, socioeconomic background, school curriculum pursued, racial and ethnic characteristics. Therefore, career guidance or other career relevant programs in the schools, in the school-to-work transition, or in their entry-level induction into the workplace must be tailored to such individual diversity as fully as is possible. As such programs are formulated, even though they may be implemented to meet some very specific purposes, they need to be constantly cognizant of an overarching question, How can we best prepare workers for international competition?

Programs developed in American schools for the career development of employment-bound youth need to be increasingly alert to what can be learned from other nations and they must also be concerned about what skills American students need in order to develop the competence, the personal flexibility, the numeracy, literacy, and teachability required of employment-bound youth in the 21st century. Such a view is consistent with what Secretary of Labor Robert Reich (1991) has suggested in his book, *The Work of Nations: Preparing Ourselves for 21st Century Capitalism*:

"The real economic challenge facing the United States in the years ahead...is to increase the potential value of what its citizens can add to the global economy, by enhancing their skills and capacities and by improving their means of linking those skills and capacities to the world markets" (p. 8).

Such value addedness from schooling suggests strongly that as Wirth (1993) suggests, "The indispensable condition for creating a world-class economy in a democratic society is the creation of world-class schools" (p. 365). A consistent theme in this book is that one of the major aspects a school can add to the education of employment-bound youth is career relevance and, more specifically, the provision of knowledge and skills to facilitate positive individual career development.

Schools as Facilitators of Career Development

With respect to the school's role in facilitating the skills and the career development of its citizens, the United States has been in conflict about the purposes of education, particularly in the common schools or grades K-12, since the beginning of the Republic. In an overly simplified way, there have been major tensions throughout the last two centuries between the perspectives related to Thomas Jefferson's view, that education should be directed to literacy and informed citizenship, and the implications of Benjamin Franklin's view, that education should be for economic development and, therefore, students should acquire that knowledge which is both "ornamental and practical" (Herr, 1987). Periodically, there has been a third view that says both sets of purposes should be integrated as educational outcomes.

In virtually every decade since these fundamental views were advanced, education and its purposes have been debated, criticized, and assigned blame for a range of national problems from illiteracy to weak national defense, to chemical dependency, poor parenting, losing the technological edge in international competition, to economic downturns. Indeed, for the past 25 years, the crescendo of voices has risen about the purposes of American education. During this period, the intensity of concern has increased about such persistent issues as: the relevance of education to the world outside of the classroom; the accountability of education for a variety of outcomes defined by political, social, and economic interests; the degree to which students in school should learn about themselves in affective as well as intellectual terms; whether students are acquiring the skills necessary to cope with the demands of a highly technological society;

whether the schools are developing a labor force capable of competing with that of other nations in international economic competition.

Each of these questions relates directly or indirectly to larger questions of the relationships between education and work and, perhaps, more specifically to education as preparation for work for all students and, in particular, for employment-bound students. Such questions elicit a variety of values, content, and intervention issues as one considers such matters. One such set of concerns has to do with the reality that policies and practices in the U. S. have tended to place possible educational purposes into dichotomies between preparing those bound for college and those going directly into the work force, the academically oriented or the technically oriented, the gifted or the educationally impaired, the advantaged or the disadvantaged, focusing on the intellect or the affect, etc. As a result, we have tended in this nation to keep separate, by curriculum and by prestige, education for the college-bound and that for the immediate employment-bound. In playing out our national desires for upward mobility, success, and individual achievement, we have tended to give greater value to intellectual pursuits and to college going rather than to technical skills and vocational training, particularly at the subbaccalaureate level. In the future, we will find it less easy to place persons into simple dichotomies since more people will go directly into the work force and also pursue post-secondary education or many other diverse patterns of work and education.

Career education was a major educational movement in the United States and some other nations in the 1970s and early 1980s. Among other goals, career education tried to address the structural dichotomies between academic and vocational knowledge by arguing that both are important and that no student, whatever their ultimate goal, should be locked into only a limited set of courses which do not allow for exploration, or for keeping one's options open. Career education approaches and models also advanced other relevant concepts. Since its formal origins at the beginning of the 1970s, career education's traditional focus has been upon the teaching/learning process. Its attempt to make all education more career relevant has been translated into systematic efforts to "infuse" into any form of subject matter examples from work or career development concepts which help students make the connection between what they are studying, however scientific or philosophical it may be, and the application of this content in the problem-solving or task performances which characterize various forms of work. In the elementary school years and beyond, such an infusion process is intended to help students anticipate the future, make connections between the present and the future, develop an internal rather than external locus of control, and help educate them to the processes of exploration and choice, the technology of career planning, self-assessment, and use of resources.

Whether emphasizing infusion or other approaches—e.g., separate courses on decision-making and-self management or stimulating delivery systems that are teacher-centered or counselor-centered—career education has made a major contribution to the preparation for work, in its emphasis on "Education for Choice." Not only can career education activities emphasize the learning of decision-making strategies which can be used in the process of choice, such an approach also serves to accent the power of choice to create one's realities. Many young people and adults do not know or acknowledge that choice-making is the process by which one converts possibilities into actualities and in so doing shape or limit one's present and future opportunities. Thus, they are not able to deal with the reality that choice-making is both a powerful tool in planning for achievement and mobility and a serious constraint if misused.

Through providing simulation and other exploratory modes, career education also can provide the context in which the occupational structure can be demystified and ways can be learned by which to classify its possibilities in personal terms of reference. Whether this is accomplished through the cooperation of teachers and school counselors, field trips to industry, computer-assisted guidance programs, or other means, such exploration is a major raison d'être for career education.

As suggested in the expectations of the career education Incentive Act (PL 95-207) when it was passed in 1977, there are other contributions which career education can make to education and work connections: (1) It can make education experiential or hands-on, so that students can have greater awareness of and involvement with work and workplaces;

(2) through the activities and the personnel it embraces, it can encourage communities, especially business and labor, to offer greater responsibility for the education of the young by cooperating and collaborating with the schools; and, (3) it can reduce the separation of content and curriculum boundaries by encouraging students to explore and test themselves in courses across curricula and by reinforcing the fact that, depending how it is viewed, every type of subject matter has its own career relevant aspects.

Career education offers a medium by which the inherent variation in developmental experiences which accompany socioeconomic, racial, or ethnic differences can be neutralized so that all students, regardless of their level of advantagement, can be encouraged to learn about and use information about work, develop planning skills, learn about self management and discipline within the workplace, set goals, and understand the educational steps which are available and necessary to goal attainment.

Career education can facilitate the development of the insights and skills necessary to counteract the "thwarting conditions" found to affect many youth in the transition to work. Among them are: a lack of career information, inadequate knowledge of personal abilities and aptitudes, restricted occupational socialization, inadequate job-seeking skills, and lack of understanding of the requirements of the work context (Haccoun & Campbell, 1972; Stern, 1977; Herr & Cramer, 1992). These positive outcomes, among others, of career education initiatives were well documented in the 1970s and 1980s (Herr, 1979; Hoyt, 1980) and there are many school districts still implementing career education principles following the demise of the career education Incentive Act in 1981.

Even though career education programs were documented successes, in one of the periodic shifts in education policy in the United States, the effect of the 1983 Commission on Excellence in Education and its report, *The Nation at Risk*, swung the balance in education toward greater emphases on requiring a larger number of academic courses for high school graduates and, because of its elective status, to an erosion of career, and especially vocational, education programs throughout the nation. Such shifts in educational offerings and emphases were potentially detrimental to many employment-bound youth who were interested in more hands-on, technical training, not abstract academic work which was unrelated to their interests. As antidotes to such trends, the Carl D. Perkins Vocational Education Act and more recently the Carl D. Perkins Vocational Education and Applied Technology Act have tried to influence national and state educational policies by a range of initiatives including funding curriculum development which integrates academic and vocational skills, that advances the articulation of vocational/technical programs from the high school into the community college and beyond, that advocates comprehensive career guidance programs for all students and that promotes equity and excellence for minority persons in relation to their opportunities in vocational education and in the occupational structure. Almost simultaneously, the U. S. Department of Labor initiated for the first time a set of policies that focus on the importance of work-based learning and new approaches to the utility of a much increased availability of youth apprenticeships. There are also related initiatives in place, or in process, that are designed in various ways to bring American students and, indeed, adult workers to higher levels of technical skill, purposefulness, and productivity. They include the Joint Training Partnership Act, the School for Work Opportunities Act, customized job training, and a variety of other emergent initiatives. Some of the goals promoted in these legislative actions will be discussed more fully later in this book.

Suffice it to say here that a cynic could argue that the initiatives just cited are the periodic flurry of legislative activity that happens whenever there is a national period of concern about the processes and outcomes of education. That is not the view taken in this book. Rather, it is assumed here that the realities that were described in the previous chapter—international economic competition, the erosion in many industries of what Americans traditionally believed was their uncontested major share of the world market, the emergence of trading blocs (North American Free Trade Agreement, the European Economic Community, and potentially a bloc comprised of the ASEAN or Pacific rim nations) as the interim phases of a global economy, as well as the pervasive influences of advanced technology on the content of work, the organization of work, and the required skills of workers—have created challenges that must transform American education and the preparation of workers for international competition into the 21st century. From a variety of vantage points, we are now in the throes of that transition across education systems.

International Emphases on Human Resources

As the precursors of the emerging global economy have become evident during the past decade, American education, industrialists, and policy-makers have increasingly become sensitive to how other nations with whom we are now competing have and are preparing their work forces. We have discovered that many of the nations of Europe and Asia do not see a dichotomy between academic and vocational skills, rather they see each reinforcing the other in societies which are increasingly technical in their international export-import contexts and transactions. While career education efforts and programs have ebbed and flowed in the U. S., other nations have not been so ambivalent.

Many of these nations have, for much of the past quarter century, been facing the reality that as the structure of the world's economy is transformed from a collection of separate national economies to an interdependent global economy, new demands will be placed upon human resources. It has become clear in national development plans, in industrial strategic goal setting, in international forums, and in the world's media that the key factor in a nation's ability to compete in the growing global economy is the quality of that nation's work force as defined by the literacy, numeracy, flexibility, teachability, and commitment to lifelong learning that characterize it. Many nations are learning that it is no longer adequate to concentrate educationally on the social or intellectual elite of a nation. Rather, the need for workers at all levels of industry or business to deal with technological processes, problem-solving and knowledge work requires that educational reform must be addressed to all levels of education and training, not only higher education or technical education.

These nations in Europe and the Far East have learned that "personal flexibility," or literacy and numeracy, or personal competence, or other technical or general employability skills do not appear spontaneously. Rather, educational and social institutions, work organizations, and systems of counseling must be provided with the resources and the policy directions to empower them to facilitate individual competence, purpose, and productivity or such individual characteristics will be far more uneven across populations in any nation than will be adequate to the demands of a global economy.

Basic to these notions is the reality that skills learned in school and skills learned on the job are complementary. Thus, together they are the major factors accounting for a nation's growth and productivity and their importance is likely to grow in the next century. The acquired skills and abilities of the population have become the pivotal resource in establishing a nation's competitive edge (Carneval & Gainer, 1989). In essence, any nation that wishes to remain in the forefront of economic competition in a world economy cannot compete on the basis of low-wage/low-skill production but must create the conditions and resources to provide a service and information-based economy in which highly skilled persons and the comprehensive application of technology are the critical factors. They must concentrate on developing innovations and reducing the time it takes to get such innovations through the competitive product cycle and into the marketplace. Learning is critical through every step of this cycle as are employees' creativity, problem solving and team skills, as well as the ability to function within a work environment heavily dependent on advanced technology.

Schools as Mediators of Student Career Skills

A national priority on human capital development rests upon viewing schools as mediums for "social engineering," in the most positive sense of that term, of all the attitudes and skills of significance to the work force. It has been said of Japan, for example, that "Americans have yet to recognize that we are competing not only with the Japanese factory, but with the Japanese school as well"... "The Japanese have not only invited us into competition at the market place, they are also inviting us into educational competition" (Duke, 1986). The Japanese have obviously recognized the interrelatedness of the factory and the school. In their view, "the industrial productivity of a nation is intimately related to, as it were, the productivity of its schools" (p. 20). While many American and European observers look at management style, quality circles, industrial processes, and factory output, to identify the elements of Japan's success, they miss the fact that the Japanese's workers' skills, high rates of literacy and numeracy, attitudes toward loyalty to the group and to their employer, diligence and cooperation are carefully nurtured from the first grade forward in the schools. The lesson from the Japanese is that "a nation's competitiveness cannot be measured merely in terms of factory output, rates of productivity, or day-to-day management practices. Rather, the overall competitiveness of a nation's factories derives from the effectiveness of the entire infrastructure of the society, basic to that is the school system." (Duke, 1986, p. 20).

While Japan may be a clear and successful example of embedding in schooling the training of students to be "personally flexible" and competent in terms important to that nation's economic structure and work organizations, the primary role of schooling as the major medium for advancing the preparation of workers for a global economy is equally important in Europe, in Scandinavia, and many other nations in Asia, (e.g., Singapore, South Korea, Taiwan). In each of these locations, what happens in schools and what happens in the workplace are not mutually exclusive phenomena; indeed education and economic development are seen as intimately linked.

Within the education reform movements and national development plans of many nations, there are attempts to make schooling more career relevant, more attentive to the various elements necessary to better equip students with self-understanding, understanding of technology and of life options available to them, to teach skills of conflict resolution and social skills, and skills to plan and prepare for work more systematically and purposefully. Industrialized and developing nations have variously created approaches to the infusion of academic subject matter with career development examples and concepts to give learning greater connection to its importance and its application in the adult workplace; created decision-making courses and experiences, including individual career development plans; introduced required courses on the principles of technology to help students envision the effects of advanced technology in workplaces and as job opportunities in the occupational structure; established career resource centers and computerized occupational and information systems in schools;

expanded contacts between schools and the larger community; instituted work study, work shadowing, work experience schemes; enlarged apprenticeship opportunity; provided placement offices and youth information centers directly in schools; and instituted other career related mechanisms in communities, schools, and work places (Herr & Cramer, 1992).

The degree to which various career development opportunities are present in a given nation depends in large measure upon the "country's vision about the value of employment to the lives of individuals, their development and the society as a whole. These overarching issues are critical to understanding and improving connections between education and employment"... "Clearly, there is a difference between U. S policymakers and practitioners and many of their counterparts in Europe, with the latter who clearly view the targeted goal of education as preparation for employment versus the more diverse and more general goals for education held by Americans" (The Council of Chief State School Officers, 1991, p. 6). Indeed, as observers have visited and examined the educational systems of Europe and contrasted them with those of the United States, they have noted that "Work as an integral part of life and well being is central to the education provided in these countries. The philosophy is reflected in the curriculum and the pedagogy of the school and of the workplace. Hence, career guidance is begun at an early age. Structured pathways to education and employment are multiple, both divergent and convergent. There is much adding to and subtracting from these approaches as needs and interests dictate" (p. 6).

One of the major differences between American approaches to the preparation for work of its young people and those of most European nations is the comprehensive and systematic attention of the latter to the collective responsibility of many sectors of the population and of the combined private and public sectors to prepare youth for employment because it is both in the national interest and a service to youth as they prepare to take over their economic and social responsibilities. In this context, "a great variety of resources from the public and private sectors is committed to preparing youth for responsible roles in the workplace and, more broadly, for adulthood. Youth are given not just one chance, but many opportunities to succeed. Standards for success are reflective of the standards of the workplace and co-determined by employers, employees, and educators. These standards, however, are never lowered; nor are shortcuts devised for students. As a result, few youth are left on the margins of society" (p. 6). In summarizing their analyses of the European systems of school and workplace collaboration in the preparation for work, the Council of Chief State School Officers identified four dimensions that seemed to be of particular significance. They included the following:

Inclusiveness—availability and access to a broad segment of the population. For example, two-thirds of German youth are educated in the dual or vocational training system; and 15 percent of college graduates hold an apprenticeship certificate. Publicly supported training is not limited to entry-level jobs or to special populations of the countries.

Flexibility—ability to change curricula relatively quickly in time with changing job requirements and the needs to initiate new training and career-path options for individuals. The relation-ship of government, business and unions provides the mechanisms required for rapid change in response to new labor and economic needs.

Competition among different types of institutions and the autonomy to provide the types and quality of programs required to improve their efficiency and attractiveness to students. There is also great competition among the best and the brightest of students for training positions in high-status industries, firms and occupations.

High Standards of quality, skills and expectations that apply to all students and result in high levels of knowledge in a broad spectrum of careers (e.g., mechanics that have knowledge of calculus). The apprenticeship certificate is the credential of a fully accomplished adult in society. It is the ticket to a wide range of middle-management positions in a variety of professions, crafts and careers in small and large companies (p. 7).

Aring (1993) has compared in some depth the German system of vocational education with that of the United States. As she indicates, all education is considered inherently vocational

in Germany and thus many of the stereotypes and dichotomies inherent in American education are not present in the
same way in Germany. Since some 70 percent of German youth
between 16 and 19 enter the dual system of youth apprenticeships, it is a formidable aspect of the preparation for technical
productivity in that nation. It is clearly one element of a career
ladder for persons who are employment-bound youth as we
define them in this book and who often progress to further
technical education after completing the dual apprenticeship
system. By one estimate (Marshall and Tucker, 1992), one-third
of the German university-trained engineers came through
Germany's apprenticeship system and then attended the university, a path that would be virtually impossible for most U. S.
engineers. Aring has identified what she defines as the most
salient features of the German vocational education system.
They include in a slightly abridged form:

1. The system is called *dual* because students learn
   in two interconnected settings—the workplace
   and the school—by means of an interrelated
   curriculum.
2. Students' education and training are provided in
   the context of a particular industrial sector.
3. Because students in the dual system have to meet
   very high standards of education and skills,
   educators and employers are willing to give them
   far more responsibility and at a much earlier age
   than their counterparts in the U. S.
4. Disadvantaged students are expected to meet
   the same requirements as everyone else.
   However, they are provided with substantially
   more resources in the process.
5. Education and training are not test-oriented.
   Students are seen as workers who are expected to
   acquire whatever competencies are necessary to
   do the job right.
6. The dual system of education requires that
   labor, business, education, and government
   collaborate closely.
7. There appears to be no evidence of a "forgotten
   half," and there appears to be virtually no
   secondary labor market (for example, dead-end

jobs in fast-food chains or mall stores) where young people spend significant amounts of time.

8. Education and training at the job site are not job-specific or entirely company-specific. Instead, the emphasis is on socialization and on broad, indus-try-wide training, so that the young person will have maximum job opportunities and mobility within the companies that make up the industry.

9. Education and training paths are structured so that virtually all young people can pursue further education, enter an occupation with a good future, or change industries and retrain.

10. Students going through the dual system must meet stringent requirements set by industry/state examination boards. They must not only spend a certain amount of time in an apprenticeship but must demonstrate their knowledge and skills during a two- or three-day examination period. Performance standards for the final exam are determined by a consortium that represents the particular industrial sector along with the labor union and the ministry of education" (p. 399).

It is always useful to acknowledge that the approaches taken by other nations to career guidance and counseling, career or vocational education, or other approaches to the preparation of youth for work are shaped by and responsive to such vari-ables as their national economic conditions, political ideology and cultural belief systems, and conceptions of the freedom of choice their citizens should have in preparing for and entering educational and occupational options of various kinds. There-fore, the models of preparation for work that these nations embody may not be possible to replicate in the United States. Even so, with due respect to that caveat, there appears to be much activity and much commitment among the European nations that can stimulate or, indeed, reinforce American approaches to the preparation of youth for work. The dual system of vocational education in Germany is one such example. Another example is what appears to be the growing importance attributed to the role of career(s) guidance and counseling in the European nations and the convergence in how such processes are con-ceived in the United States and in other industrialized nations.

For example, Watts, Dartois, and Plant (1988) conducted a major study of educational and vocational guidance services for youth in the 14 to 25 year age group in the nations of the European community. In summarizing the evolving key concepts that are descriptive of career guidance in the schools, Watts, et al, discuss perspectives that are very familiar to and compatible with American notions that have grown during the twentieth century. Such trends include:

"The first [trend] is that educational and vocational guidance is increasingly being seen **as a continuous process,** *which:*

- *Should start early in schools.*
- *Should continue through the now often extended period of transition to adult and working life.*
- *Should then be accessible throughout adult and working life.*

So far as schools are concerned:

- *Guidance is more and more being seen not as an adjunct to schools but as an integral part of the educational process.*
- *This is resulting in the growth of specialist guidance roles within the schools.*
- *It is also producing a recognition of the need to involve* **all** *teachers in guidance to some extent, and to develop ways of supporting them in their guidance roles.*
- *Guidance elements are increasingly being built into the curriculum, in the form of careers education programmes, work-experience programmes, etc.*
- *Where external agencies work into schools, their role is now more and more viewed as that of a partner or consultant to the guidance services within the school itself.*

    The second key trend is the move towards what we have termed a **more open professional model,** *in which the concept of an expert guidance specialist working with individual clients in what sometimes appears to be a psychological vacuum is replaced, or at least supplemented, by a more diffuse approach in which:*

- *A more varied range of interventions is used. These may include:*
  - *Guidance elements within the curriculum of education and training programmes.*
  - *Group-work alongside one-to-one work.*
  - *Use of computers and other media.*

- *More attention is given to working with and through networks of other individuals and agencies. This may involve:*
  - *Supporting 'first-in-line' teachers, supervisors, etc. in their guidance roles.*
  - *Involving parents and other members of the community as resources in the guidance process.*
  - *Working with 'opportunity providers' to improve the opportunities available to young people.*

Such a model offers the prospect of being a more cost-effective approach to guidance, as well as being based more closely on the ways in which choices actually tend to be made in practice.

*The third and final trend, closely linked to the other two, is towards a greater emphasis on the **individual as an active agent**, rather than as a passive recipient, within the guidance process. This can be seen in, for example:*

- *The growth of programmes of career education, work experiences, etc., designed to provide young people with a range of skills, attitudes, knowledge and experiences which will help them in making their own career decisions.*
- *The growth of interest in counseling as opposed to advice-giving.*
- *The reduced emphasis on psychometric testing, and the increased interest in encouraging self-assessment rather than 'expert' assessment.*
- *The development of self-help approaches in occupational information centers and in computer-aided guidance systems.*
- *The interest in 'education for enterprise' as a way of developing young people's self-reliance and initiative.*
- *The participation of young people in the preparation of information booklets and in running youth information centers.*

The individual young person is thus now increasingly seen as the active center of the guidance process, with the guidance specialist being available partly as a specialist referral point and partly as a means of activating other resources for young people to draw upon" (pp. 93-95).

More recent research by Watts (1992) and his colleagues (e.g., Watts, Guichard, Plant, and Rodriguez, 1993) have been designed to understand in considerable depth what functions vocational counselors actually perform in each of the 12 European Community nations, their primary locations (e.g., schools, ministries of labor), and their education and training qualifications. The intent is to both examine the comparability of vocational counseling in these nations and to facilitate stronger communication and collaboration between guidance services in different countries. Implicit in such activities is also a clear commitment to strengthening the role of career guidance and counseling across the European Community.

Finally, unlike the U. S., many of our competitors have put far more societal value on learning. In addition to their growing implementation of career guidance systems in schools, they have created national curricula standards, and they have used tests to assess who has learned and how much they have learned as credentialing methods. They have recognized as Peter Drucker (1993) has articulated that we are engaged in becoming knowledge societies and that the world's social center of gravity has shifted to the knowledge worker. Thus, they have conceived career guidance and career counseling as both a support to student learning and academic progress and a bridge between the school and the workplace.

Student Skills Required in a
World of Economic Competition

Beyond the perspectives on career relevant initiatives found in the schools of Europe and of Asia, there are also fundamental perspectives present in this nation that are relevant to shifts in educational emphases in schooling. Given the shifts in the occupational structure, the increase in the educational requirements to gain access to or to perform many of the jobs emerging as a result of the global economy, and the needs for career planning and other general employability competencies documented elsewhere in the book, there are clearly needs to revisit and reconceptualize the content and processes provided by the common schools for employment-bound youth as well as for students pursuing other options. As Wirth (1993) has so powerfully indicated, "When hammers and wrenches are displaced by numbers and buttons, a whole new kind of learning must begin" (p. 362). Recommendations for the contents and the processes that should be incorporated into educational reform directed to the preparation of youth for work take many forms, just as the abilities, needs, and interests of work-bound youth will likely differ in the types of learning they will require. For example, Hull and Pedrotti (1983) have identified six educational implications common to all high technology occupations that include the following:

1. They require a broad knowledge of math, computers, physics, chemistry, electricity, electronics, electromechanical devices, and fluid flow.
2. They involve heavy and frequent computer use [including knowledge of practical applications of programming].
3. They change rapidly and require lifelong learning.
4. They are systems-oriented [and involve working with systems that have electronic, electromechanical, electrical, thermal, optical, fluidic, and microcomputer components].
5. They require a fundamental understanding of a system's principles, as well as practical skills in designing, developing, testing, installing, troubleshooting, maintaining and repairing the system.
6. They require substantial employee flexibility and adaptability (pp. 28-31).

While something of an aside here, it is worth noting that in international terms, these bodies of knowledge and skill are those included in Germany's dual system of education. They also appear as outcomes in the abilities of some of our competitor nations' work forces. For example, as reported earlier in this book, Professor Merry White, author of the *Japanese Educational Challenges*, states that "much of the success of Japan stems from the fact that its blue-collar workers can interpret advanced mathematics, read complex engineering blueprints, and perform sophisticated tasks on the factory floor far better than blue collars in the U. S." (Nussbaum, 1988, p. 101). Thus, Japan and Germany have seen the building of human capital as a national priority and they have built into their education and training systems, knowledge and technical skills that are seen as essential in relation to their industrial and economic goals.

Within such contexts, it is clear that if the prime requisite of economic competitiveness and a strong trading position is the skill level and preparation of the work force, a first necessity for any nation is to know what the work force needs to know and be able to do and, second, to determine what processes will facilitate the development of such skills. But once such insight is achieved and implemented in the common schools, in American parlance from kindergarten to grade 12, it must be maintained and enhanced by continuous upgrading of skills over each worker's lifetime (Kuttner, 1990).

As nations attempt to develop their particular model of how schooling should be related to work force development, they, in fact, engage in a search for the types of career relevant knowledge, attitudes, and skills that enable young people to emerge from the secondary school with the elements of personal flexibility by which they can compete in a rapidly changing occupational structure. They figuratively ask, "What is the hidden or emerging curriculum in international economic competition that lays a claim on the educational preparation of adolescents, and, perhaps more particularly, employment-bound youth?" But in this complex process of preparing young persons and, indeed, older adults for work and for change in work, Simon, Sippo and Schenke (1991) remind us that we must constantly keep before us in our planning questions such as, "What do we mean when we say that someone is a competent participant in a workplace? What does it mean to say that someone has a good working knowledge of how things are done?" As they further suggest: "Working knowledge includes more than just the notion of a technical ability to perform certain tasks such as typing invoices, back-stitching upholstery, using micrometers, supervising outdoor play, washing hair, making cheesecake, and developing photographs. These are, of course, included in the meaning of the concept, but there is much more. Each and every task in a workplace is embedded in a particular set of social relations within which people define the facts, skills, procedures, values, and beliefs relevant to particular jobs in their own organizations. For this reason, job competency often means understanding how the particularities of one's workplace defines what one needs to know to get a job done. Perhaps more to the point, there is no work in the abstract; there is only work in context. 'Learning work' thus often entails not only the development of technical and social skills but also an ability to understand how and why such skills are used, modified, and supplemented in different situations" (pp. 27-28).

These Canadian authors employ the term "working knowledge" as a useful concept for the study of how people in different workplaces define what is important to know in order to be competent workers and to do competent work. They suggest the following as a partial list of different workplace features that suggest some things it might be important to know in order to be an effective worker in any given workplace:

Workplace materials—material objects that are basic to a workplace. These include, for example: tools, equipment, decor, supplies, raw materials, and finished products, clothing.

The language of work—the specialized words and phrases, technical jargon, abbreviations, codes and forms as well as names, nicknames, slang, clichés, tones of voice, gestures and modes of conversation.

Workplace facts—the information and beliefs taken as objectively true, incontrovertible, and accurate by at least some group of people in a workplace. These 'facts' include not only task-related information but also reputations, workplace customs, rituals, and traditions.

Skills and techniques—the set of capacities and competencies necessary to perform certain procedures and complete certain tasks required by the organization of work in a particular workplace.

The frames of reference for evaluating workplace events—the principles used by workers to determine the good or bad qualities of things, people, events, and/or ideas; for example, the criteria used by others to determine a 'fair day's work,' 'a job well done,' 'a good supervisor' or a 'harebrained scheme!'

Rules and meanings—the implicit and explicit rules, understandings and expectations that regulate interactions among people in various situations. Implicated in these are power structures, lines and areas of authority, questions of responsibility, status, prestige, and influence" (p.28).

Such perspectives on the content and processes of career relevant schooling are very useful complements to those found in the United States. They often overlap but there are also orientations and priorities which differentiate European, Asian, or U. S. views of the content and processes of work force education.

In the United States, in addition to such concepts about necessary educational content as those of Hull and Pedrotti, or, indeed, those of Simon, Dippo, and Schenke, there are many national reports that could be cited that speak to the needs for extended and comprehensive services, including career counseling and guidance, as students approach high school graduation and move into post-secondary education or the world of work, and to how the education experiences of all children should be made more career relevant, not only in the content they learn, but in the incentives they receive for doing well, for learning good work habits, and for being helped to make connections between what they study and its relationship to future educational and occupational options. There are a number of observers who would argue, that without greater attention to the career relevance of schooling, students experience a delayed transition to adulthood and an often mindless moratorium on responsibility for some years after high school. Others would argue that what we need is a coherent system with a sequence of steps through which young people can move, a veritable career ladder through which employment-bound youth would move on their passage through schooling, the school-to-work transition, and entry into and adjustment to work.

Such views, among other concerns, are searches for and often presumptions about the types of career relevant knowledge, attitudes, and skills that enable young people to emerge from the high school with the knowledge, skills, and attitudes by which they can compete in an occupational structure which is in constant flux. As suggested in the observations of Simon, Dippo and Schenke (1991), these issues are described in somewhat different ways but they also exhibit considerable commonality. One such model has been described by The Secretary of Labor's Commission on Achieving Necessary Skills (June 1991) in its report, *What Work Requires of Schools*. This report contends that schools should provide five categories of competencies or workplace know-how and a three-part foundation of skills and personal qualities that are needed for solid performance.

The five competencies include the ability to:
1. identify, organize, plan, and allocate resources such as time, money, materials, and facilities;
2. work with others;
3. acquire and use information;

4. understand complex interrelationships; and
5. work with a variety of technologies.

These five competencies were described in the U. S. Department of Labor's SCANS report (1991) as spanning the chasm between the worlds of the school and of the workplace. Equally important is the declaration in the SCANS report that these five competencies involve a complex interplay with the three elements of the foundation on which they rest, that is, what schools must teach: the basic skills, higher order skills, and the application of selected personal qualities. As defined in the report, demonstrating basic skills means that the student "reads, writes, performs arithmetic and mathematical operations, listens and speaks"; demonstrating thinking skills shows that the student "thinks creatively, makes decisions, solves problems, visualizes, knows how to learn, and reason"; by effectively applying personal qualities the student displays responsibility, self-esteem, sociability, self-management, and integrity and honesty" (pp. 4-5).

The recommendations of the SCANS report bear some overlap with what Reich (1991) has argued is required in the current transformation of work and the need for new qualities of learning in the emerging workplace. In his view, the current global system as it is evolving and being refined is made possible by technology, but also by four key human skills that underlie symbolic-analytic services (problem-solving, problem-identifying, and strategic brokering) using symbols, data, words, oral and visual representations as work media that are now important in so many jobs. While it is not likely that most employment-bound youth will become symbolic analysts in their early career, the skills that Reich identifies as important in such roles are similar to those that others suggest are important in greater proportion in emerging occupations and even in increasing degree for employment-bound youth. Such skills include:

Abstraction—the ability to work with, bring order to, and make meaning out of large amounts of information; to shape raw data into patterns that can be dealt with.

Systems Thinking—being able to see the whole, to see how parts are linked, to determine how problems arise and their connection to other

Experimentation—having the capacity and perspective to set up procedures to test and evaluate alternative ideas, ability to systematically explore a range of possibilities and outcomes.

Collaboration—ability to work in teams, to collaborate, to engage in the communication of abstract concepts, to dialogue, to share perspectives and to create consensus as necessary.

From a somewhat different perspective, Lynch (1991) has synthesized various reports on the skills needed in the future work force and presented the following as important for both high school and post secondary graduates. Under the rubric "skills workers will need," he has identified the following broad-based categories:

Computers and technology—programming simple jobs, using software extensively, maintaining equipment.

Problem-solving, critical thinking, decision-making—knowing how to learn, find answers and solve problems.

Resource management—scheduling time and personnel, budgeting, using human and capital resources appropriately.

Economics of work and the workplace—understanding organization, profit, work relationships, work ethics, national and international systems.

Applied math, science, social science and communications—using numbers, theories and fundamental math and science principles and effective language skills in the workplace.

Career and personal planning—setting priorities, taking advantage of continuing education and training opportunities, managing parenting and family life, maintaining personal health.

Interpersonal relationships—having appropriate values and attitudes toward teamwork and working effectively with customers.

Information and data manipulation—finding and managing information, using data, understanding systems and symbols, keeping records.

Technical skills—to the level required to sustain career employment (p. 29).

While there are many additional examples that could be cited, those used as illustrations here suggest that a work force that possesses the characteristics required by a global economy must be equipped with the knowledge, skills, and attitudes necessary to cope with both the economic and the personal challenges of the future. Such traits do not normally arise from short-term and intermittent job-related training. Rather long-term commitments of schools, families, labor unions, business and industry, and other social institutions must be involved in collaboratively accomplishing such outcomes, certifying their attainment, providing reinforcement of their importance and the provision of incentives when they are achieved.

At the risk of being redundant, there are also other conceptions of knowledge and skills that need to be fostered in schools as requisites to the choice of, preparation for, and effective transition to work following high school or to some form of post-secondary education They include the following:

Basic Academic Skills. Given the characteristics of the emerging technologies that are increasingly critical to international competition, and the emergence of knowledge workers, basic academic skills—literacy, numeracy, communications—are perhaps the ultimate employability skills for employment-bound youth. Within the industrialized nations, very few new jobs will be created for those who cannot read, follow directions, and use mathematics. In an information era, knowledge has replaced experience as the requisite for a growing proportion of the jobs being relocated or created around the world. Without basic academic skills, it is difficult to comprehend how individuals can possess personal flexibility, teachability, or be capable of engaging in life-long learning, a condition that increasingly will be required to maintain career competency. The future of the occupational structures in the industrialized world is to eliminate more and more unskilled jobs and to put an increasing premium on higher levels of reading, computation, communication, and problem-solving or reasoning skills. In essence, the skills learned in school and the skills learned on the jobs will be increasingly seen as complementary and interactive.

Adaptive Skills. As the SCANS report and other national reports have indicated, personal career competence and flexibility will not be confined to intellectual skills. As technological adaptation of a variety of forms continues to be implemented in the occupational structures and workplaces of the world, the economic development of individual firms and other enterprises will suffer if its employees are not able or willing to learn new production systems or new management strategies. While academic skills in reading, mathematics, and science are important to such processes, there are other qualitative skills likely to be critical in such employment environments as well. One set of such overarching skills has been defined by the U. S. Congress's Office of Technology Assessment (1988) as including:

Skills of Problem Recognition and Definition
- Recognizing a problem that is not clearly presented
- Defining the problem in a way that permits clear analysis and action
- Tolerating ambiguity

Handling Evidence
- Collecting and evaluating evidence
- Working with insufficient information
- Working with excessive information

Analytical Skills
- Brainstorming
- Hypothesizing counter arguments
- Using analogies

Skills of Implementation
- Recognizing the limitation of available resources
- Recognizing the feedback of a proposed solution to the system
- The ability to recover from mistakes

Human Relations
- Negotiation and conflict resolution
- Collaboration in problem solving

Learning Skills
- The ability to identify the limits of your own knowledge

- The ability to ask pertinent questions
- The ability to penetrate poor documentation
- The ability to identify sources of information
  (documents and people)

These skills are important not only to manufacturing but to service industries. They represent the survival skills necessary in an environment of rapid change and one which is information rich.

In addition to the skills cited above, an increasing number of employers are extending their conception of basic skills to include self-discipline, reliability, perseverance, accepting responsibility and respect for the rights of others (U. S. Department of Education/U. S. Department of Labor, 1988). Other observers are discussing the needs for adaptive skills and for transferable skills. *Adaptive skills* are also referred to as coping skills, occupational employability skills, work survival skills, or, sometimes, career development skills. They frequently involve skills necessary for positive worker-to-worker interaction or worker-work organization interaction. *Transfer skills* "enable a person to draw upon prior learning and previous experience for application to these and different situations" (Pratzner & Ashley, 1985, p. 19). Such skills include those involving learning to learn, dealing with change, being a self-initiator, coping, and self-assessment skills. *Mobility skills* are those related to making a career or job change and include job-seeking and job getting, interviewing skills, resume preparation, and carrying out alternative job search strategies. Each of these skill sets are increasingly defined as general employability skills as contrasted with technical or work performance, occupation-specific, or firm-specific skills which tend to emphasize the technical content rather than the affective dimensions of choosing, preparing for, and adjusting to work. These general employability skills do not substitute for the basic academic skills nor the job performance skills noted above, but they are clearly mediators of how such academic or job performance skills will be practiced and they are important dimensions of personal flexibility.

Another set of skills is becoming increasingly important and reinforced by shifts in the settings where new jobs are being created in the society. In addition to the shift from manufacturing to service, in the United States we have also had a shift from the large Fortune 500 companies to companies which employ less than 100 workers as the sources of new jobs in this economy. In addition, the United States is experiencing a major rise in self-employment, in part-time and contract work, and in small businesses which require sets of skills embodied in such terms as entrepreneurial behavior and innovation. It has also been contended that as the larger corporations require down-scaling in size and "deinstitutionalizing," there are needs for entrepreneurs within such organizations. As the work place, the organization of work, or the content of work undergoes transformation, there are needs for persons who have the skills and desires to manage innovation and change. The skills associated with entrepreneurial behavior involve acquiring understanding of systems, risks, change. These skills are essential to systematic innovation whether in creating a new, small business or modifying an existing one to take advantage of new market forces and potentiality (Drucker, 1986, p. 35).

Part of the problem related to designing programs in schools for employment-bound youth is that there are many and diverse basic skills expected by employers for entry-level workers. These skills include those identified in government reports (e.g., the SCANS report) and those from many other sources. Depending upon what survey of employers one reads, he or she is likely to identify such skills as reading, writing, computation, communication, the ability to learn, creative thinking, problem solving, negotiation, teamwork, and leadership (Keeley, 1990). All of these skills can and should be taught to employment-bound students in academic and in vocational programs. Frequently, they are not. If they are, their meaning or application in the workplace often has not been identified and made clear to the students. Thus, the issue is not simply what academic skills are important in the workplace but how are they applied in different jobs or occupations in the workplace? Are they done alone or with other workers? How are they applied and for what purposes? Is there a specialized vocabulary necessary? The relationships between critical tasks on a job, the scientific principles or academic skills involved, and, indeed, how reading, writing, and other literacy skills are combined become elements essential to helping students increase their "workplace literacy" both in specific and more general terms.

Vocational education, as one partner in the national move to integrate academic and vocational skills, is increasingly being seen as the possessor of both content and methodology of importance to helping all students, not only employment-bound students, to acquire the career development and the technical skills necessary to be an effective worker. Methodologies such as job task analyses as the basis for curriculum development, outcome-based education, the application of academic skills to occupational problem solving on a hands-on or experiential basis, and the use of cooperative learning to develop teamwork skills in completing tasks are each common in vocational education but typically not in academic classrooms. There are also other perspectives that have evolved in vocational education related to content and process issues in learning that are worthy of consideration; these are discussed at other places in the book.

Other Learning Processes Necessary for Career Relevant Schooling

While many of the rudiments of the skills, attitudes and knowledge bases identified in the previous section need to start being introduced in the elementary school and be infused throughout curricula at all educational levels, there is a large inventory of ideas available by which schooling can be made more career relevant. These learning processes provide exploratory opportunities, occupation or industry-based skill development, the foundations for advanced technical training and, depending upon the configuration or school-industry partnership at issue, transitional skills directly to the labor force. Examples of these include:

- Making college and career options known to children beginning in the middle schools if not before. Helping them link what they are studying in academic areas to the occupational problems where that subject matter is relevant or, indeed, critical. Helping them to understand that they have options and the skills to address and master them.
- A career guidance system, K-12, that focuses, among other goals, on helping students develop individual career development plans,

the acquisition of self-knowledge and of educational and occupational opportunities, and the ways to explore and choose among these.

- The infusion of career development concepts into academic subjects to help students understand how course work fits together and forms a body of knowledge and skills related to performance in work and other aspects of life.

- The promotion of schools-within-schools, career academies, and alternative preparatory academies. The scale of these can vary dramatically in urban, suburban, or rural areas. These are typically not seen as academic tracks per se but rather as opportunities to provide special programs available to students that promote student pride and participation as well as family and community involvement in schools. For example, career academies, in which students get work experience as well as coursework that draws upon a particular vocation, such as communications, computers, or teaching, help provide the kind of "real-world" experiences students need to better appreciate the education they are receiving. These schools-within-schools that occur in a number of states, including California and Pennsylvania, are part of a larger continuum of special programs that give students learning experiences outside, and in addition to, the traditional classroom structure (Massachusetts Institute of Technology, 1990).

- The development of clear expectations for student learning, including the use of competency-based or OBE approaches. In a study by the U. S. General Accounting Office of the strategies used to prepare employment-bound youth for employment in the United States and four competitor nations—England, Germany, Japan, and Sweden—several findings were particularly telling (Warnat, 1991).
  1. The four competitor nations expect all students to do well in schools, especially in the early years. U. S. schools expect that many will lag behind.

2. The competitor nations have established competency-based national training standards that are used to certify skill competency. U. S. practice is to certify program completion.
3. All four foreign nations invest heavily in the education and training or employment-bound youth. The U. S. invests less than half as much for each employment-bound youth as it does for each college-bound youth.
4. To a much greater extent than in the United States, the schools and employment communities in the competitor countries guide students transition from school to work, helping students learn about job requirements and assisting them in finding employment.

• Requiring participation in community service programs for high school graduation. The Clinton Administration's 1993 National Service Initiative for high school and for college students will undoubtedly advance this trend and increase the awareness that community or national service can be a major career exploration mechanism as well as one in which career relevant skills can be acquired.
• Providing educational opportunities that acknowledge that not only technical skills but multilinguality, leadership and social studies skills, and knowledge of cultural differences, national histories, political and economic systems of nations with whom we trade will become increasingly important in international trade.
• Focusing on life skills. Secondary schools, including middle schools, should provide training in "life skills" such as formulating good work habits, interaction with public agencies, job hunting, appropriate areas and behavior for the workplace, how to work in a team, how to complete applications and follow instructions, and how to look for meaningful employment. Many of these skills can arise from helping young people understand that school is their work and that attitudes dealing with punctuality, accepting constructive supervision,

honesty, and self-discipline are those valued as well by the workplace. Many of these skills and others can be gained through a variety of cooperative education and work based learning opportunities. In this regard, it would be possible to provide and use summer and academic year internships, apprenticeships, and cooperative work site training (Massachusetts Institute of Technology, 1990).

• Enlarging the availability of cooperative education (which now enrolls about 5 to 10 percent of all students in high school and college) that structures students' experience in paid jobs to promote learning to extend what is taught in the classroom. The "co-op" method gives students direct practice in learning at the workplace. Many vocational-technical education programs also operate their own school-based enterprises, which likewise provide opportunities for students to learn through the process of producing real goods and services for community agencies. These options make deliberate use of work as part of the learning experience and bridge school and work directly.

• Providing certificates that recognize the demonstrated skills of students meeting articulated requirements for such skills in technical training or other program offerings in high school. Such demonstrations of skills will undoubtedly increase the use of portfolios describing examples of students skills, more precise discussion of their skill development experiences, as well as greater clarity about their achievement of competency-based career development experiences and associated attitudes.

• Increasing Tech-Prep or 2+2 programs. As defined by the U. S. Congress in 1990, a tech-prep program means a combined secondary/postsecondary program which (a) leads to an associate degree or a two-year certificate; (b) provides technical preparation in at least one field of engineering technology, applied science, mechanical, industrial, or practical art or trade, or agriculture, health, or business; (c) builds student competence in mathematics, science, and communications (including through applied academics) through a sequential course of study; and (d) leads to placement in employment (Congressional Record. 101st Congress, 2nd Session, August 2, 1990). These programs increase the availability of more rigorous course work tied to occupational skills and at the same time give more students the option to go on to post-secondary education. They help students see more clearly the connection between school and work, the importance of continual or life-long learning, the integration of academics and vocational skills, and the need to bridge both work-oriented courses and those oriented toward further schooling. In their articulated structures they expedite student movement from high school programs to related community college programs and beyond with emphases on efficiency and equity.

- Modifying the school curriculum to combine academic and vocational courses. Such an approach to an integrated curriculum, which like tech-prep and several other of the recommendations here are strong emphases in the Carl D. Perkins Vocational and Applied Technology Education Act, gives students the benefit of occupational preparation and college preparation at the same time. It also potentially infuses academic courses with the task-oriented, problem-solving, and cooperative learning approach to learning that have been successful in vocational-technical education. These approaches incorporate the findings of research in the cognitive sciences which suggest that abstract information is often best learned through authentic application in task or problem solving learning (U. S. Department of Education, 1991).
- Apprenticeship schemes also need to be expanded in availability after high school in new ways that begin in the high schools and provide skill development opportunities during that period in similar ways to what is available in several of our competitor nations. Currently, apprenticeships in this

country enroll hardly any students in high school and fewer than 2 percent of high school graduates although in Europe, 30-60 percent of employment-bound students are likely to be in apprenticeships following high school (U. S. Department of Education, 1991). National and state youth apprenticeship legislation which is now in place or to be implemented in the near future is an excellent vehicle for this effort.

Implications for Counseling in the School

As one of the possible initiatives cited above noted, "there is a need for a career guidance system, K to 12, that focuses among other things on helping students develop individual career development plans, the acquisition of self-knowledge and educational and occupational opportunities, and the ways to explore and choose among these." It is clear that such a goal has not yet been achieved in all school districts in America. While, at one level, the United States may offer its citizens the widest range of career guidance and counseling opportunities of any nation in the world, research, national reports, legislative initiatives, and other evidence suggest the need for more such services, better planning, and new paradigms about how these services should link the school and the workplace, maximize the cooperation among community resources of all types, and provide for the career planning of employment-bound and other students.

Representative examples of the concepts advanced by national reports to strengthen career counseling and career guidance in schools, particularly for employment-bound students, include the following perspectives. The National Commission on Secondary Vocational Education (1985) stated:

Inadequate student knowledge subtly but formidably constrains student access to vocational education. Students and parents need to be accurately informed about what vocational education is, how it relates to their personal and career goals, and how it can be used to help them achieve their goals. One does not choose what one knows little about or is constrained from choosing by

unexamined social attitudes... We need comprehensive career guidance programs that will provide
this information and remove some of the subtle
status distinctions involving vocational education.
Comprehensive guidance means counseling that is
available to all students, covering all subjects,
leading to all occupations (p. 10).

The National Alliance of Business and the National Advisory
Council on Vocational Education (1984), in a major analysis of
the nation at work and particularly of relationships between
education and the private sector, has argued for more school-
to-work transition programs including job placement assistance, career counseling, cooperative career education activities
with business, and counseling about vocational-technical
program alternatives to college degree programs.

These perspectives and those that are reported at the
beginning of Chapter Four from various national business and
educational forums make clear that the problems experienced
by different sub-groups of employment-bound youth cannot
be solved by schools alone. They need to be seen in larger community and policy terms and addressed in comprehensive
ways. Even so, however, there are attempts to define the roles
of school counselors that would complement the needs to make
schooling more career relevant and to support such current
efforts in work-based learning as tech-prep initiatives. Some
examples of perspectives about counselor roles within such
contexts are exemplified by the following perspectives.

Aubrey (1985) in advocating greater participation by
counselors in the learning environment of students, employment-bound or other, has suggested seven tasks that include
in paraphrased form:

1. Monitoring and assessing the student's
   educational progress;
2. Helping students plan for and complete a
   semester of service in either a community agency
   or other setting;
3. Providing instructional units that focus on
   guidance activities, such as human relationships,
   communications, values development, ethics;
4. Constructing coursework in technology, future
   thinking, cultural awareness;

5. Helping students acquire critical thinking and decision-making skills through problem-solving challenges related to the real world;
6. Guiding students in the acquisition and use of information related to their first tentative career decisions;
7. Assisting teachers in the recognition and accomplishment of specific developmental tasks that each student needs to master.

Both explicitly and implicitly, counselors engaging in such tasks would be dealing with helping students personalize, apply, and plan based upon much of the career relevant content and experience suggested as important earlier in this chapter. If counselors in schools were concerned with more resources in order to facilitate the knowledge and skills of employment-bound youth, it could be more readily expected that high school graduates would obtain the outcomes associated with effective school counseling programs that a variety of research studies and observers have suggested are both possible and desirable (Sears, 1991; Perry, 1993):

- develop effective relationships with others
- apply their interests, skills, and aptitudes in the world of work
- use a decision-making process when making important decisions
- control and direct their feelings/emotions
- resolve conflicts, peaceably at home, school, or work
- resist using alcohol and other drugs and engaging in other harmful forms of behavior
- manage stress
- utilize resources to set and reach educational goals
- achieve realistic career goals
- value life-long learning
- value traits/characteristics of people who are different

Implicit in these counselor roles and student outcomes are assumptions that school counselors will help employment-bound youth learn about changing work force and job trends, encourage them to consider the potential meaning to them of various educational pathways, and to learn the life skills that will provide them the personal flexibility, the problem-solving skills and the ability to anticipate and prepare for change in systematic and deliberate ways.

Beyond perspectives on counselor roles that relate to general career and change skills, some authors recommend more specialized counselor roles associated with new educational initiatives in work-based learning. As suggested earlier in this chapter, tech-prep is one of the major curriculum reforms now under way that has significant potential to improve the school-to-work transition for many employment-bound students. Among the specific roles of counselors that have been suggested by Chew (1993) as particularly relevant to tech-prep initiatives are the following in abridged form:

1. Counselors and school districts should implement a comprehensive developmental guidance model for K-12 students emphasizing technical career opportunities within the career component.
2. Counselors should provide all students with interest and aptitude assessments (beginning no later than the eighth grade) to help them plan meaningful four-year educational goals.
3. Counselors can provide school-wide activities that promote the awareness of technical career opportunities.
4. Counselors can provide students with information about community or technical college summer camp opportunities.
5. Counselors should give attention to women and minorities by providing them with information regarding technical careers.
6. Counselors should assist special needs students (e.g., learning disabled, physically disabled, teen parents, economically disadvantaged, etc.) in making transitions from secondary to post-secondary education.
7. Counselors must have access to appropriate materials and resources that explain the options of tech-prep and technical careers.
8. Counselors should help students develop a portfolio that summarizes their credentials, both educational and experiential.
9. Counselors should utilize career planners with students (Chew, 1993, 32-35).

Similar to the counselor's role in support of tech-prep is that of the counselor in support of vocational education. The counselor can implement several different emphases that relate to the choice of vocational education or success in completing such courses by employment-bound youth. Thus, one such role that the counselor can play is informing appropriately talented and motivated students about options within vocational education and the likely outcomes that could ensue from such instruction. A second role is that of assisting in the selection of students for admission to various vocational education programs. Such a role involves the assessment of individual aptitudes and preference and helping students match these to what research indicates are the characteristics of these successful in different vocational education options (e.g., business, electronics, construction trades, applied health occupations, etc.). A third role that the counselor can play is in direct relation to instruction itself. For example, the counselor may work with vocational educators as consultants or collaborators as career development concepts and general employability skills are infused into and taught in vocational education curricula. A fourth role is the contribution of the counselor to the placement of vocational education students as part of the school-to-work transition (Herr, & Cramer, 1992).

Conclusion

The emphases suggested here—integrated curriculum, structured work experience, infusion of career development concepts in academic subject matter, systematic attention to the transition of employment-bound students from school to work, exploration of and acquisition of vocational skills by college-bound students, new paradigms of career counseling and career guidance, particularly in combination with community resources—can positively reinforce each other. They offer the opportunity for all students to have the benefit of rigorous academic instruction and practical vocational education at the same time. If academic reform were to take such possibilities seriously, then in comprehensive terms every "high school student would be able to choose among several possible curricular specialties, some of which would organize the core academic curriculum around a particular occupational theme, and would provide related part-time employment during the school year and summer" (U. S. Department of Education, 1991, p. 3). Some students might enter related full-time employment after completing the program, hopefully with increased opportunities for apprenticeships or other transitional industry-education programs. Others might go on to college or other forms of post-secondary education, equipped with the skills that will enable them to support themselves and to possess a clearer sense of purpose and productivity along the way, to have a better sense of why they are in higher education and the goals they hope to achieve.

The connections between school and work identified here are not abstract or esoteric; they are in place and effective in other nations and in some communities in the United States. But they need to be expanded and made more comprehensive. They need to be seen as affirmations that the workplaces of the nation are changing in ways that require knowledge workers, persons who use information to solve occupational problems and manage technology in the new information-based work organizations that are being created. They need to be embedded in programs that emulate the learning-intensive and continual learning work environments emerging in this decade and that are likely to accelerate in the 21st century.

While the emphasis in Chapter Three has been on what can and should be done in schools to enhance the skills of students preparing to enter the workplace, it is clear that the ultimate success of such efforts depends to a large degree on the effectiveness of governmental and business efforts to expand job creation that provides creative and challenging career ladders for the work force, that shares information meaningfully between government, industry, and schools to improve program planning and student choice, that is based on industrial and employment policies that take a long-term view of education and training related to the creation and maintenance of a work force that is flexible, teachable, and equipped with basic academic and vocational skills that allow them to engage successfully in learning-intensive workplaces. Such policies need to provide job training and retraining for anyone who wants it—the unemployed, those who are dissatisfied with their current job, those who want to learn new competencies as a hedge against job changes. These policies must reflect societal convictions that education and training are both indispensable and that to provide them successfully requires comprehensive and sustained interactions between education-business and industry-labor unions-government (Education Writers Association, 1990).

Perhaps the major void yet to be filled in addressing the needs of employment-bound youth is that related to seeing the school-to-work transition as a bona fide and distinctive life stage for which counseling and other support services must be tailored and provided. To do so will require a concerted effort at the community level to orchestrate the contributions to the school-to-work transition of the schools, business and industry, labor, the Job Service, the Joint Partnership Training Act and other government resources.

Chapter Four

The School-to-Work Transition for Employment-Bound Youth

Perspectives on the School-to-Work Transition

If there has been a major void in the provision of counseling and other support services for employment-bound youth, that void has occurred at the point of the school-to-work transition and at the point of entry into a specific job. Indeed, the Commission on Skills of the American Workforce (1991) stated the issue directly in the following manner: "The lack of any clear, direct connection between education and employment opportunities for most young people is one of the most devastating aspects of the existing system" (p. 72). While it is thought that we have the finest higher education system in the world, children completing our K to 12 system of education are being outdistanced by children from other countries in their acquisition of mathematics and science skills in the pre-college grades. More important, for the purpose of this chapter, "we have the least well-articulated system of school-to-work transition in the industrialized world. Japanese students move directly into extensive company-based training programs, and European students often participate in closely interconnected schooling and apprenticeship training programs...In Austria, Sweden, the former West Germany, and Switzerland, it is virtually impossible to leave school without moving into some form of apprenticeship or other vocational training..." (Berlin & Sum, 1988).

As stated in *From School to Work* (Educational Testing Service, 1990), there are two difficult life-time transition points—into the work force for young people and out of the work force for older people. Given the rapid shifts in the American economy, currently the more difficult transitions are into the U. S. work force. "And the U. S. record in assisting these transitions is among the worst in the entire industrial world" (p. 3)..."school counselors are overburdened, and helping with job placement is low on their agendas. The U. S. Employment

Service has virtually eliminated its school-based programs. Our society spends practically nothing to assist job success among those who do not go directly to college. On the whole, the answer to the question, who links school and work? is "the young themselves, largely left to their own devices" (p. 3)... "in the United States the institutions of school and those of work are separate and most always far apart. There are quite limited arrangements to facilitate this transition [to work]" (p. 4)..."most developed countries have highly structured institutional arrangements to help young people make this transition; it is not a matter left to chance, West Germany does it through the apprenticeship system, combining classroom work and on the job instruction. In Japan the schools themselves select students for referrals to employers, under agreements with employers. In other countries, there is either a strong employment counseling and job placement function within the school system or this function is carried out for the student by a labor market authority of some type, working cooperatively with the schools"... To be sure, there are some school systems that have good linkages to the work world, often found in the guidance offices of vocation education schools or as the natural operation of cooperative education programs. But the general pattern has been one of doing a whole lot more to link high school students to college than to work" (p. 22).

Also with major emphasis on the transition from school to work is a report written by Mangum (1988) for the W. T. Grant Foundation Commission on Work, Family, Citizenship. Many of the conclusions of Mangum are similar to or extensions of those just cited in the report, *School to Work*: The Executive Summary of Mangum's report includes the following selected conclusions:

1. The transition from adolescence into the adult world of work is inherently difficult in a society which persistently separates home and workplace and extends adolescence. Nevertheless, most American youth make the transition with a minimum of pain and reasonable success. Yet there is a substantial minority, primarily from culturally and economically deprived backgrounds, who are permanently scarred by their unsuccessful experiences. The transition process can be improved for all but the latter deserves the priority.

2. There are cultural norms, labor market realities, and human development processes which compose the transition environment. No program to improve a transition can expect success which does not take into account these constraints. Employers control and dispense jobs and any successful program must ultimately help youth to meet employer expectations.

3. Job security is declining in the United States. Employers increasingly seek to carefully select and invest in a core group of employees who they seek to retain while avoiding commitment to a peripheral group who they prefer to employ only temporarily. Youth are typically in the peripheral category.

4. The family is the single most important contributor or deterrent to the career success of youth. It is possible to increase parent effectiveness in aiding their children's careers. But it is less likely to happen in those families doing the greatest harm.

5. The discipline of successful school performance is helpful in preparing for labor market participation. A career education concept which could have made a major contribution to career success has been rejected. Still, there are less draconic measures which could be taken to enhance the schools' contributions. Among the desirable curriculum additions would be values clarification, assertiveness training, decision-making skills, and familiarization with labor market dynamics.

6. Vocational education has suffered bad press because it has misconstrued its own best role. At the secondary level that is career exploration with career preparation pushed primarily to the post-secondary level.

7. Apprenticeship's potential for contributing to the transition is very limited in the United States. It and on-the-job training serve primarily employer needs and, in essence, the transition out of adolescence must be made before training access is attained.

111

8. Second chance programs of employment and training have made a modest contribution which can be strengthened with some recommended reforms. Some major advances are being made in alternative high schools with employer involvement. Local initiative is among their irreplaceable strengths.

9. What is needed more than research to develop additional knowledge of the youth transition process is application of the knowledge we already have. The essence of that knowledge is to work within the bounds of reality set by labor market dynamics and career development theory. The critical question to be asked is whether it is possible to synthesize for the unsuccessful minority the practices and conditions of the successful majority.

10. It is possible to dream of an effort concentrated in the central cities on the now least successful, beginning with world of work oriented parent effectiveness training, carrying on through career education supplemented by experience-based alternative schools and second chance programs, buttressed with a world of work curriculum emphasizing job-getting and job-keeping as well as job-doing skills, supported by employers offering part-time and summer work experience and guaranteed placement of successful completers who are consistent performers. It is only a dream, but not an impossible one (Mangum, 1988, pp. i-iii).

In essence, a major issue in the United States is that the school-to-work transition has not been viewed as a process that begins in the early years of schooling and proceeds systematically or jaggedly through the secondary school years, into the period and processes of transition from school to employment and, ultimately, into the choice of and induction into a job. This process of transition, then, has three phases, the in-school phase, the transitionphase, and the job-induction phase. Historically, the school-to-work transition process has not been characterized in this way in policy or legislation nor have resources, support systems, or information been systematically tailored to such phases. In the future, however, it seems that successful transition from school to work as a national goal can only be assured if the responsibilities and the unique contributions of the school, transition services, and employers can be identified, integrated, and implemented.

Responsibilities for School-to-Work Transition Not Defined or Consistent

In particular, the school-to-work transition phase, the bridging period between school and employment, has not been treated as a period when youth experiencing the job search, the move from part-time to full-time work, the dynamics of interviewing and negotiating for a job have special needs that require the availability of sensitive, competent support services. However, as Barton has noted there are major obstacles that interfere with meeting such needs. Barton (1991) has suggested several factors, paraphrased here, that contribute to the lack of assistance employment-bound youth experience in crossing the bridge from school to work and, specifically, obtaining counseling and guidance about the process. His perspectives include the view that school counselors spend disproportionate amounts of time in counseling the college bound; only 6 percent of high school counselors spend more than 30 percent of their time helping students find jobs, so job placement assistance for employment-bound youth is almost non-existent; academic skills as taught in the school are often insufficient or not applicable to the workplace; high school graduates usually have no tangible credential or other way to demonstrate their employment potential; and large firms, those that offer career paths to well paid jobs, are reluctant to or do not hire new high school graduates.

Unfortunately, in the United States, the responsibility for assisting a youth to get a first job has been poorly defined. The schools have been vague about their responsibility in this process after the former student graduates or leaves the school as a drop-out. Community agencies have not had clearly specified assignments to assume major responsibilities for youth in the school-to-work transition although the Employment Service and personnel from Private Industry Councils or Joint Training Partnership Act programs all do get involved with some youth as they engage in the school-to-work transition.

Through the past several decades, the State Employment Services have been periodically provided resources to focus special support on the job placement of youth. When such resources have been provided, Youth Opportunity Centers, Human Resource or Vocational Planning Centers have been put in place to provide continuing help to young people pursuing job placement and the transition to work. Employment Service counselors have sometimes been seen as a supplement to the school counseling staff, sometimes directly located in the school or assigned on a rotating basis to serve several regional school districts, to provide employment registration, assessment, counseling, job referral, job development, and job placement for employment-bound youth. Employment Service staff are sometimes used as consultants to school counselors or vocational educators on employment issues and the job market. As specific youth-oriented national initiatives have been developed and included in various pieces of legislation, Employment Service Counselors have been expected to be directly involved with these initiatives: e.g., Neighborhood Youth Corps, CETA Summer Job Program, JTPA Summer Youth Employment Program, National Alliance of Business Summer Job Program, various local Chamber of Commerce Career Prep Clubs, Job Corps Centers (Jones, 1987). Unfortunately, the resources to provide such support have been jagged in their availability, or they have been available only for selected groups of employment-bound youth, e.g., economically disadvantaged, not all.

From a somewhat different perspective, the Joint Training Partnership Act (JTPA) uses economic indicators as the criteria for who is eligible to be served by JTPA Services. In this legislation, and largely also in the Carl D. Perkins Vocational Applied Technology Education Act, economic disadvantagement serves as the defining measure of being at risk and, therefore, of eligibility to receive services. Such a measure may overlap with but not fully encompass other factors that inhibit the successful transaction of youth from school to work: dropping out of school, teenage pregnancy, lack of basic academic skills, history of substance abuse, or a criminal record. These risk factors can, in turn, be the context that leads to poor work habits, attitudes, and interpersonal skills that further complicate the transition to productive, steady employment (Employment and Training Administration, U. S. Department of Labor, 1993). But, it must be noted here as well that there are many American youth who do not suffer economic disadvantagement or other risk factors who also need information, support, and career guidance during the transition to work for whom such services are unavailable.

Federal Initiatives Increasing

As America intensifies its involvement in international economic competition and studies what other nations are doing in providing mechanisms and support services to insure a successful passage through the school-to-work transition, it is becoming evident that the transition from school to work is a complex combination of experiences and events that often are not related to each other or to what the student learned in school. Rather than an event that occurs on the day the student graduates or leaves the high school, the school-to-work transition is beginning to be perceived as a process, a series of activities, job search, interviews, selection, training and retraining, that requires a variety of types of support and follow up over an extended period of time. While the school must help the student learn the basic knowledge, attitudes, and skills required to engage in career planning, job search, and job holding, the school's responsibility must become a collaborative process with local agencies and employers to see the young person through the process of job placement and into the work force.

There are hopeful signs that the federal government is currently prepared to revisit the issues involved and provide leadership to strengthen the nation's school-to-work transition system as a national priority. For example, in 1993, President Clinton proposed the School-to-Work Opportunities Act to spur the development of local partnerships between schools and industries to develop school-to-work programs and make them available to all students. On May 4, 1994, the U. S. Congress made the School-to-Work Opportunities Act of 1994 (PL 103-239) a law of the land. Programs funded by the School-to-Work Opportunities Act combine classroom learning with real-world work experience. They fund the training of students in general job-readiness skills as well as in industrial-specific occupational skills. The School-to-Work Opportunities Act provides help to high schools and community colleges to create programs in cooperation with business, to develop the academic skills and attitudes toward work that too many adolescents lack today and that both educational and community agencies have neglected.

The School-to-Work Opportunities Act provides for a school-based learning component, a work-based learning component, and a connecting activities component. It introduces the term "career major" to mean "a coherent sequence of courses" or field of study that prepares a student for a first job and that (A) integrates academic and occupational learning, integrates school-based and work-based learning, establishes linkages between secondary schools and post-secondary educational institutions; (B) prepares the student for employment in a broad occupational cluster or industry sector; ...(D) provides the students to the extent practicable, with strong experience in and understanding of all aspects of the industry the students are planning to enter;...(F) may lead to further education and training, such as entry into a registered apprenticeship program, or may lead to admission to a 2- or 4-year college or university" (Section 4, Definitions). The Act also defines Career Guidance and Counseling to mean programs: (A) that pertain to the body of subject matter and related techniques and methods organized for the development in individuals of career awareness, career planning, career decision making, placement skills, and knowledge and understanding of local, state, and national occupational, educational, and labor market needs, trends, and opportunities; (B) that assist individuals in making and implementing informed educational and occupational choices; and (C) that aid students to develop career options with attention to surmounting gender, race, ethnic, disability, language, or socioeconomic impediments to career options and encouraging careers in nontraditional employment" (Section 4, Definitions).

While the School-To-Work Opportunities Act specifies the elements of the school-based learning component and the work-based learning component of a school-to-work opportunities program, for the purposes of this chapter, it could be argued that the connecting activities, component is most directly relevant. That component (Section 104) indicates that the connecting activities shall include:

1. matching students with the work-based learning opportunities of employers;
2. providing, with respect to each student, a school site mentor to act as a liaison among the student and the employer, school, teacher, school administrator, and parent of the student, and, if appropriate, other community partners;
3. providing technical assistance and services to employers, including small- and medium-sized businesses, and other parties in—
   (A) designing school-based learning components described in Section 102, work-based learning components described in Section 103, and counseling and case management services; and
   (B) training teachers, workplace mentors, school site mentors, and counselors;
4. providing assistance to schools and employers to integrate school-based and work-based learning and integrate academic and occupational learning into the program;
5. encouraging the active participation of employers, in cooperation with local education officials, in the implementation of local activities described in Section 102, Section 103, or this section;
6. (A) providing assistance to participants who have completed the program in finding an appropriate job, continuing their education, or entering into an additional training program; and,
   (B) linking the participants with other community services that may be necessary to assure a successful transition from school to work;
7. collecting and analyzing information regarding post-program outcomes of participants in the School-to-Work Opportunities program, to the extent practicable, on the basis of socioeconomic status, race, gender, ethnicity, culture, and disability, and on the basis of whether the participants are students with limited-English proficiency, school dropouts, disadvantaged students, or academically talented students; and

8. linking youth development activities under this Act with employer and industry, strategies for upgrading the skills of their workers.

The implementation of the School-to-work Opportunities Act will undoubtedly rest on many concepts and recommendations that have been available for some time but not fully implemented. Among these possibilities are many that are identified in this book. For example, Chapter Three identified a number of initiatives, activities and emphases that are being encouraged or being implemented to make schools more career-relevant. Many of these programs carry forth models of career education that took shape in the early 1970s and have provided, in refined ways, possible methods by which the content and experiences of schools can be connected to the expectations and content of the adult work world. Particular techniques suggested embody the infusion of career development concepts and examples into academic subject matter, the use of adult resource persons to describe what they do in their occupation and how to prepare for it, computer assisted career guidance systems, job search strategies, career resource centers, field trips to and shadowing of workers in industry or other techniques by which to increase student understanding of their own characteristics and interests and how these might be more effectively matched with job opportunities and requirements. Chapter Three also identified other recent initiatives such as Tech Prep, which are designed to articulate the vocational and technical training of students from the secondary school into the community college or other post-secondary education experiences. Such initiatives reflect a changing national policy that supports increased attention to work-based learning such as youth apprenticeships, increased cooperative education, and related opportunities to help youth prepare for and span the school to work transition and to more fully involve planned collaboration between schools, government policies and legislation, and the resources of labor and industry in making such transitions effective and productive. Several of these initiatives will be more fully described later in this chapter. But the current initiatives reflected in the School-to-Work Opportunities Act is to make more explicit elements of the three phases of the school-to-work transition—in school, transition services, employers.

Selected National Perspectives on Counselor Roles

Inherent in background information that led to the School-to-Work Opportunities Act and throughout the discussions of the last decade about the problems in the United States with the school-to-work transition, issues of the form and substance of career counseling have been raised. Among the input to such debates has been a number of national reports focused on new models of how career counseling might be designed to facilitate the journey of employment-bound youth through the school-to-work transition.

There are many examples of such perspectives. One, The Commission on Workforce Quality and Labor Market Efficiency, supported by the U.S. Department of Labor (1989), strongly recommends that attention be paid to the dynamics of the school-to-work transition, with state employment security agencies and private industry councils establishing school-based employment services with direct connections to employers. The report further encourages employers, whether small or large, to provide information on job openings and to consider filling vacancies with recent high school graduates. The intent of these recommendations is to harness the possibilities of cooperation between government agencies in the community that are directly involved with job placement and job training with the school's efforts in career guidance so that concrete information on local job vacancies are provided to students in a timely and accurate fashion; to show that the system works for those who have the necessary skills (e.g., high school completion); and to argue that career guidance and counseling in schools must not only be active in educating students for choice but be directly involved in concrete steps to help place students in community jobs as an important aspect of their effective transitions from school to work.

The William T. Grant Foundation report by its Commission on Work, Family and Citizenship entitled *The Forgotten Half* (1988) has been cited elsewhere in this book. Among its many other emphases, this report has indicated that career guidance and other services for students not bound for college are unevenly distributed and available across the nation. Specifically, this report has advocated school, parent, and community cooperation in providing programs necessary for the effective transition of these students to work. Of particular relevance to the school-to-work transition for employment-bound youth is the advocacy of significantly expanded career information and counseling, career information centers, programs to train parents as career educators, and the involvement of community mentors and community-based organizations in supporting efforts to improve counseling and career orientation.

These important recommendations by the Grant Foundation are embedded in a context which articulates, in both realistic and poignant terms, the characteristics of the school-to-work transition:

> *"In the United States, the almost exclusive responsibility for youth's transition-to-work is lodged with parents and schools. Many parents have networks and associations that allow them to give their teenagers a hand in finding jobs. But particularly in poverty families, these informal but important connections are too often absent, leaving teenagers dependent on their own initiatives or on the schools. Yet our schools are largely isolated from the community and from the workplace. A host of blue ribbon panel recommendations calling for an end to the school's isolation from the larger community have been largely ignored"* (p. 39).

> *"Obviously, this is not a problem that can be solved by the schools alone. The Commission urges school authorities, business leaders, and community officials to join together in greatly expanded efforts to aid youth. The image of these foundering young people should not be seen as evidence that young people have failed, but rather that adults of the community have failed to give them a fair chance to get started"* (p. 40).

> *"The Commission urges new consideration by state policy makers, school and community leaders of a variety of out-of-school learning possibilities which use the schools as the nexus of community-based programs and resources"* (p. 41).

The particular examples suggested by the W. T. Grant Foundation of programs in which the community and parents can play major roles would include such examples as:

Monitored Work Experience
- Cooperative education
- InternshipsApprenticeship

- Pre-employment training
- Youth-operated enterprises

Community Neighborhood Services

- Youth-guided services

Redirected Vocational Education Incentives

- Guaranteed postsecondary and continuing education
- Guaranteed jobs

Career Information and Counseling

- Career information centers
- Parents as career educators
- Improved Counseling and Career orientation
- Community mentors and community-based organizations

School Volunteers

Organizations directly representing the business and industrial communities have also stressed the importance of career counseling and guidance to be seen as vital processes for various populations of employment-bound youth if they are to successfully negotiate the school-to-work transition. For example, the Business Advisory Committee of the Education Commission of the States (1985), in a report which focused on the growing problems of alienated, disadvantaged, disconnected, and other at-risk youth, recommends "new structures and procedures for effecting the transition from school-to-work or other productive pursuits" (p. 26). In particular, the report cites needs for consolidated programs including career counseling, financial assistance, summer jobs, cooperative education options, and role models to facilitate the reconnection of at-risk youth to schooling and to work. In 1985, in a major report dealing with business and public schools, the Research and Policy Committee of the Committee for Economic Development (1985), strongly urged that schools provide, among other emphases, exploratory programs to assist in career choice, the development of job search, and general employability skills. For example, (how to behave in an interview and get to work on time) and the provision of employment counseling" (p. 31). In 1984, the National Alliance of Business contended that education and the private sector need to collaborate more fully in providing more school-to-work transition programs including job placement assistance, career counseling, cooperative career information activities with business, and counseling about vocational-technical program alternatives to college degree programs (p. 8).

On balance, then, in these perspectives and others to be cited later, it is clear that the school-to-work transition is seen as a major national problem in the United States that is not shared by other nations that have instituted mechanisms to insure that the transition to work is smooth and purposeful. In addition, the reports cited view career guidance and counseling as vital components in successfully addressing the school-to-work transition. As they are implemented, however, the reports recommend that career counseling or career guidance not stand alone but that they need to be part of a larger program of financial incentives, appropriate information, training, and community action provided in a focused, goal-directed manner rather than one that is more abstract. Further, these perspectives suggest that neither an increase in career counseling nor in career guidance can address alone all of the issues combined in the school to work transition. Rather, there needs to be collaborative action between the school, government agencies, and business and industry. The latter is still emerging although there are a variety of initiatives beginning to appear that are addressed to various facets of the school-to-work transition.

Policy and Program Responses to the School-to-Work Transition

As policy-makers and educators in the United States compare what other nations do in preparing or supporting students as they make the transition to work, many possibilities for action have been found to exist. A number of possibilities were inventoried in Chapter Three but several of the most important will be examined more fully here.

The Integration of Academic and Vocational Skills

As many of our competitor nations have long known, academic and vocational skills are not independent. They complement each other. As advanced technologies, high technology, and technology-intensive occupations become increasingly significant in the nation's attempt to retain a competitive edge in the international economy, such work will require people who have proficiency in basic academic skills and in the technical skills that rest upon literacy, numeracy, computer literacy, and communications skills. Vocational educators have long known that applying basic academic skills to the solution and clarification of applied problems is a very effective way to learn both academic and technical skills. Indeed, in broader terms, both vocational education and the movement toward career education that was prominent in the 1970s and early 1980s, but began in the late 1960s, strongly contended that a major goal was the permeability for students of the often rigid curriculum boundaries between college preparatory and vocational education courses, the integration of academic and vocational skills and, therefore, the blurring of academic and vocational education.

In an era when the long-standing classifications of jobs as manufacturing or service are being blurred and the two components are being integrated, it makes particular sense that a similar phenomenon would occur within education and in the characterization of the skills, both academic and vocational, prerequisite to performing the emerging occupational procedures of the 21st century. In the school of the immediate future, as academic educators and vocational educators pursue curriculum development, the integration of academic and vocational skills for employment-bound youth, as well as for youth whose immediate goals are intensive post-secondary or baccalaureate education, will need to be seen not as a dichotomy but as mutually complementary ways of knowing. Such integration of skills will, among other purposes, be directed to current literacy problems, where literacy audits in workplaces show that 40 percent to 50 percent of workers need remedial training before they can learn new roles or perform new industrial processes, a situation that will have no place in the emerging occupations and work organizations of the future. Every available current indicator suggests that if students of the present are to keep open their occupational and educational options, to be able to change with change, to equip themselves with the skills necessary to be competent in and master the complexities of the future, possessing capabilities in basic academic skills *and* technical skills will be fundamental to employability and to flexibility.

A corollary goal of integrating academic and vocational education must be to make the experience of applied vocational education more accessible to academic students at the same time that advanced academic courses are made more accessible to employment-bound students concentrating in vocational education. A greater cross-enrollment or intermingling of academic and vocational education students would help to end both the stigma associated with vocational education and the social isolation of vocational students. Such an integration would also increase the opportunities for academic students interested in engineering and other technical areas to have the opportunity to work in vocational laboratories where they explore relevant content, project or task oriented problems and workplace literacy skills which they are unlikely to get in other academic contexts. In this sense, the integration of academic and vocational skills as supported by the Carl D. Perkins Vocational and Applied Technology Education Act, among other national initiatives, must be seen as a movement not only to reform vocational education but the entire secondary education curriculum as well as the preparation of students for postsecondary technical education and the school-to-work transition.

Another interesting corollary concern within school reform is the provision of educational opportunities to equip students with levels of proficiency in academic subject matters that they have not been successfully acquiring under many current models of schooling. Certainly within such contexts, the need to strengthen the instructional processes pioneered by vocational education have become more apparent in providing certain skills for employment-bound students. For example, the National Assessment of Vocational Education (NAVE) has affirmed the importance of vocational education in reinforcing the basic academic skills, particularly in mathematics. In particular, the research conducted by NAVE (Wirt, 1989) has shown that "an examination of math scores during the 11th and 12th grades for a nationally representative sample of students from the high school class of 1982 revealed that vocational courses in applied mathematics (e.g., business math, vocational math) and vocational courses that included substantial math content (e.g., electronics, drafting, accounting, agricultural science) were associated with significant gains in math learning. Math-related science courses such as chemistry and physics also made a large contribution to gains in math proficiency. These results support the general notion that significant gains can occur in applied settings while courses are heavily enriched with math content. This research estimated that taking five credits of a vocational education subject to which math makes a significant contribution *doubles* the average gain in math proficiency of non-college bound youths.

These results are particularly important for youth who are employment-bound. Such youth can experience significant math gains in a variety of applied course settings in vocational education and science. Moreover, youth not bound for college tend to take very little traditional math, particularly during their last two years of high school. They take a large amount of vocational education, however: about two and a half times more courses in vocational education than in math. Although math-enriched vocational courses result in math gains, most vocational education courses provide no math growth. Since most vocational education (about 80 percent) was not math-related as of 1982, if vocational education is to play a larger role in boosting the math proficiency of students, much of the current vocational curriculum will need to be substantially revised and upgraded. This is likely to be true as well in other areas of basic academic skills.

In the reform of vocational and academic education that needs to be accelerated in the United States, one of the major challenges to the integration of academic and vocational education skills has to do with creating instruction that responds to how basic academic skills are actually applied in the workplace. For example, the kinds of reading, writing and analytical tasks performed routinely in jobs are different from those which students are taught in schools or in general literacy programs. Typically, students read to learn information to be remembered for later use. While important for many tasks in the workplace, it is also important to recognize that worker's literacy tasks are oriented to satisfying more immediate and specific goals: "reading to do" and "reading to assess." It is within functional contexts such as those occupied by adult workers and used in the laboratories of vocational education that the application of basic academic skills can be embedded in real job tasks. But the fundamental skills of literacy, numeracy, and communications must be taught before students enter vocational education and elementary and junior high school teachers must be helped to understand how basic skills are applied in the workplace and encouraged to reinforce such functions as well as to cooperate with vocational educators in creating relevant learning tasks to facilitate such learning.

Basic academic skills must be seen in terms of the growing requirements of more and more occupations for these skills as part of the knowledge economy and as ways by which to process information. Research has found that the most successful workers are those who can process and organize information, monitor their own understanding, and who can explain the purpose of reading and writing for the accomplishment of a task (U. S. Department of Labor/U. S. Department of Education, 1988). In this sense, the integration of academic and vocational skills is both functional and conceptual. They allow one to perform and also to know why performance occurs and to what end. But it is also true that the teaching of reading and writing and computational or oral communication skills separately as is true in "traditional instruction does not facilitate the direct transfer to the requirements of job-specific tasks as necessary" (Wirt, 1989). Ways must be found to insure that students can integrate and apply basic academic skills to accomplish tasks, solve problems, and make decisions about which materials they need for these tasks, particularly within problem solving contexts where such skills are used frequently and comprehensively. Within vocational education, or combined academic-vocational education, integration of workplace literacy is facilitated when curricula are organized by job tasks, not by discrete basic skills, that include problems and simulated decision situations that call for the integrated use of basic skills as they will be used on the job. It is important to help students realize that the blurring of who is in manufacturing and who is in service occupations, as, for example, the person who previously fabricated automobile assembly by hand but is now trouble-shooting and servicing computers that are doing the fabricating, is really a function of how information processing now pervades the manufacturing and distribution systems of the nation. More and more jobs involve data gathering, monitoring, processing, editing, copying, storing, and distributing as routine elements of job tasks and such information cycles are no longer confined to white collar jobs.

The integration of basic academic and technical skills are inherent in processes throughout the business and industrial spectrum.

Tech Prep

One of the major and emerging initiatives that is related to, but not limited to, the integration of academic and vocational skills is that of restructuring vocational and technical education in the United States. One major approach to that goal is tech-prep or "2 + 2" education programs. Such programs have been embraced by the U. S. Congress, by many State Departments of Education, and by such legislative initiatives as the Carl D. Perkins Vocational and Applied Technology Education Act.

Tech-prep education programs mean a combined secondary/postsecondary program which (a) leads to an associate degree or a two-year certificate; (b) provides technical preparation in at least one field of engineering technology, applied science, mechanical, industrial or applied art or trade or agriculture, health, or business; (c) builds student competence in mathematics, science and communications (including through applied academics) through a sequential course of study; and (d) leads to placement in employment" (Congressional Record, 101st Congress, 2nd Session, August 2, 1990.) (Quoted in Hoerner, James L., 1991).

Tech-prep programs are carried out following the design included in a formal articulation agreement between the secondary school and the community college or other agency involved. They must include two years of secondary school preceding graduation and two years of higher education or an apprenticeship of at least two years following the secondary school that leads to a certificate and specific career field. In some instances, it is expected that articulation agreements will encompass the transfer of students to a four-year baccalaureate program following completion of the first two years of postsecondary education.

Tech-prep programs rest on improved or strengthened emphases on academic and vocational skills that will prepare students for immediate employment and for post-secondary education. Tech-prep programs have received their rationale from doing something constructive to "save the Forgotten Half" and other employment-bound students but, perhaps, without the emotion associated with such a quest. Nevertheless, it is clear that at the heart of tech-prep is an effort to provide increased pathways that connect the secondary school and employment that are clear, relevant, and likely to be successful. The Congressional commitment to tech-prep initiatives that has been discussed in the *Congressional Record* and implemented in the Perkins Act, also speak directly to the need for counselors to be enabled to do such things as: recruit students for tech-prep; ensure that such students successfully complete such programs; and ensure that such students are placed in appropriate employment. Again, such views portray counselors as being central actors in a program of initiatives designed to facilitate the school-to-work transition for employment-bound students. What is unspoken in many of the discussions about tech-prep is the potential tension between opening and limiting student freedom of choice and the availability of student options. As noted by Hoyt (1994), most career development theorists and researchers would contend that "Most youth are not ready to make reasoned long-term occupational decisions before age 20 or later." Traditional forms of vocational education in the secondary school and now most models of tech-prep tend to assume that high school students can choose effectively and commit themselves to a technical field and to a curriculum that may limit their career exploration and their ability to keep their options open once they enter such a tech-prep experience in, for example, the eleventh grade and remain in it through the community college. In a worst case scenario, such students can be swept into such new initiatives as tech-prep with a halo effect but little systematic exploration of the implications of such a choice or systematic knowledge of other alternatives they might pursue.

While as Hoyt also notes, adolescents can do career planning and make career choices prior to age 20, the likely validity of such choices rests upon having had the opportunity to participate in a comprehensive and effective career education or career guidance program. To be useful in this context, such a program should have provided students considering tech-prep or other alternatives the ability to engage in relevant self-assessment and exploration of work opportunities which results in a much higher level of accurate understanding of themselves, their occupational alternatives, and their skills of career planning than seems to be typical of employment-bound students in most American school districts. Thus, the success of tech-prep programs in opening rather than closing career options for adolescents and in expanding their career development rather than stifling it is a function of both the content and the flexibility built into the tech-prep initiative, as well as the effectiveness of school counselors and other educators in insuring that students are prepared with the knowledge and skills to consider the implications of tech-prep programs as one of several alternatives among which they might choose and to be able to assess the likely outcomes of each alternative for themselves. As the school counselor roles in behalf of tech-prep suggested by Chew (1993), and reported in the previous chapter, advocate, counselors, in implementing a comprehensive K-12 development guidance program, should emphasize technical careers, provide information and experiences that promote such awareness and how technical careers are facilitated by tech-prep participation, expose women and minorities to the opportunities available to them in technical careers, and help all students develop individual plans and portfolios that summarize their educational and performance credentials.

Work-Based or Field-Based Learning

Many of the initiatives that are now evolving in American policy and legislation have in one way or another a reference to work-based or field-based learning. However defined as on-the-job training, cooperative education, apprenticeship or in some other perspective which blends study and doing, learning and application, related directly to job performance or occupational skills, such approaches are being promoted as parts of the school program, vocational education, collaborative school-industry programs, or government schemes.

Work-based or field-based learning has been advocated in many national reports as a method of providing a better education-work connection, and for achieving more integration between institutions preparing people for employment and the workplace itself. For example, the Research and Policy Committee of the Committee for Economic Development in its

1990 book, *An America That Works: The Life-Cycle Approach to a Competitive Work Force*, contends that such integration requires four ingredients:

- Stronger business support for effective education
- Clearer identification of employability skills to guide educators
- A smoother transition for students from school to work at multiple points
- Improved entry-level training within business.

These perspectives echo other concerns for field-based learning that would occur in work sites provided by industry. For example, many national reports have contended that field-based learning is grossly underutilized and that supervised field-based learning experiences should be made available to all secondary vocational education students and employment-bound students, as we use the term here. Clearly, if this happens, it will also require considerably more cooperation among schools and business, labor, government, and community organizations. Optimism about the extension and comprehensiveness of field-based learning in the United States rests on several pieces of evidence. One is that the United States is finally looking at how our international competitors are managing their education programs, both vocational and academic, and the transition of youth in those nations from school to work. Nations in Europe and Japan are using apprenticeships, work-related learning, and direct placement from school into industrial training schemes in far greater magnitude than the United States (Berlin & Sum, 1988; Herr & Watts, 1988). In Austria, Sweden, West Germany, and Switzerland, it is virtually impossible to leave school without moving into some form of apprenticeship or other vocational training. In this country, *High School and Beyond* follow-up interviews with a representative sample of high school seniors from the class of 1980 revealed that only 5 percent of graduates were participating in an apprenticeship training program within the first year following graduation from high school, and only one percent of graduates reported being enrolled in an apprenticeship program three years after high school. In sharp contrast, between 33 and 55 percent of all those who left school at ages 16 to 18 in such European nations as Austria, Germany, and Switzerland had entered apprenticeship in the late 1970s (Berlin & Sum, 1988, p. 23).

In a recent report to Congress (Hilton, 1991), the U. S. Office of Technology Assessment concluded that only a few U. S. firms use training as part of a successful competitive strategy, in contrast to competitor firms in Germany and Japan. German workers receive two major types of training: apprenticeship and further training. About 65 percent of each class of middle school graduates in Germany enter apprenticeship training in fields ranging from skilled manufacturing to office work. Over three years, these would-be apprentices spend four days per week in on-the-job training and at least one day per week at a state-supported vocational school.

To respond to growing international competition, German firms and governments are stepping up the pace of further training. Traditionally, further training has taken the form of off-hours classes at state-supported schools, with employees and government paying tuition for workers who wish to be certified as master craftworkers and thereby qualify for promotion to supervisory positions. Such training is now being supplemented with on-hours and off-hours courses in the use of new technology and other subjects.

According to Hilton, unlike training in Germany, training by U. S. firms does not fall neatly into two broad categories. Although apprenticeship training does exist, it is quite small, accounting for only 0.16 percent of the U. S. work force, in comparison with 6.5 percent in Germany. The average U. S. apprentice is at least 23 years old, has previous employment or education, and works in unionized construction or manufacturing. Because of its limited scope, apprenticeship training is not the major mode of initial training for high school graduates in the United States. Instead, 57 percent of these graduates enroll in postsecondary education and the majority of these subsequently drop out, leaving to employers the task of completing their training.

But many U. S. firms fail to pick up where schools leave off: younger workers ages 16 to 24 receive a disproportionately small share of employer-provided training. Nevertheless, employers do invest in training and the amounts are increasing as international competition intensifies. Although the Office of Technology Assessment found that most calculations of U. S.

firms' training investments are unreliable, the most reasonable estimate is that U. S. employers spend about $30 billion annually on formal classroom training. Averaged across an employed work force of 114 million, American employers invest about $263 per worker per year in training.

These rough estimates suggest that German firms invest more than twice as much each year in worker training as their U. S. counterparts. The contrast with German apprenticeship training is especially stark: each year, West German employers invest nearly 17 times as much in training per apprentice as U. S. employers invest in training per average worker.

Part of the difference in training investment in the U. S. and in Germany has to do with the degree to which German firms and industry associations pool the costs and the benefits of worker training. In Germany, such pooling is commonplace as a matter of federal policy and as a matter of negotiation between German firms and labor unions. This is true both in large firms and in small firms. Typically, the latter are not involved in such training in the United States.

In Germany, industry associations are also involved in delivering training. As technology advances, apprenticeship has evolved away from "learning by doing" to a more theoretical training. Large firms have apprenticeship training centers where apprentices spend much of their time with instructors, especially during the first two years. Smaller firms, which rely more heavily on apprentices for daily production, send their trainees for a few weeks at a time to area training centers, administered and partially financed by their local Chamber of Commerce in conjunction with industry or Chamber of Artisans. The German Federal Government encourages such centers by contributing about half of their costs. Training advisors housed in the area centers and in the Chambers of Commerce and Chambers of Artisans not only oversee apprenticeship but also advise firms on strategies for further training.

As international research about vocational education in West Germany and other European nations, now required and supported by the Carl D. Perkins Vocational and Applied Technology Education Act, comes to fruition, federal policies and state practices will likely include far more field-based learning and school-community-business-labor cooperation. A significant, contemporary predictor of movement to such outcomes over the next decade is the recent policy document of the Employment and Training Administration of the U. S. Department of Labor, entitled *Work-Based Learning: Training America's Workers* (1989). The thrust of this document and the policies and models it recommends includes a major emphasis on support and expansion of structured work-based training programs, including apprenticeship, developing flexible approaches for accrediting work-based training programs, formally recognizing specialized training programs, and assisting small and midsize firms in sponsoring training programs. The reports from the National Commissions cited at the beginning of this chapter further suggest that if work-based learning is to be successful, career guidance and career counseling approaches tailored to the needs of employment-bound youth that provide linkages between schools and employers and that follow up students and provide support through the school-to-work transition are essential elements.

Apprenticeships

Perhaps the major form of work-based learning now undergoing considerable attention in the United States is the revitalization and extension of the availability and use of apprenticeships. Although apprenticeships have typically begun after one completes high school and fully enters the adult work world, demonstration programs are appearing in many states to begin youth apprenticeship programs while students are still in high school. Such programs obviously provide students with incentives to stay in school and begin the time earlier when a student will move through the apprenticeship process toward becoming a full-time, certified, journey person. Hamilton (1990) has proposed a comprehensive apprenticeship system that is integrated into the K-12 educational system. Unlike most other existing apprenticeship proposals, Hamilton argues for a "school-based apprenticeship," primarily for career exploration, and a "work-based" apprenticeship for students with clear goals and who have clear occupational choices. The latter would start at grade 11 and essentially merge with tech prep or 2+2 models.

In most youth apprenticeship programs now proposed, high school students in these programs go to school part-time and serve as apprentices part-time. Upon high school graduation, they are expected to continue with their sponsor as full-time apprentices. Sometimes students entering apprenticeships from vocational schools or the military receive advanced standing but these are less systematic than youth apprenticeships are likely to be.

In describing the characteristics of the Pennsylvania Youth Apprenticeship Program (PYAP), Wolfe (1993) indicated that this model is a school-to-work program that links the classroom to the worksite experience based on the premise that all students can learn. It stresses skills learned on a one-to-one basis, using mechanisms and processes that make academics relevant. PYAP grew out of a study done by the Pennsylvania Department of Commerce and the National Tooling and Machining Association which showed that the most serious obstacle to competitiveness in the industry was a lack of skilled workers. At the local level, the model is guided by local consortia of education, business, labor, and other community organizations. Model programs currently operate in six sites and include 79 firms sponsoring 100 students. Of the firms, 76 are manufacturers using metal working skills and three are hospitals which provide training and education in health care occupations.

While there are some differences in the models used in each site, the basic elements include a program designed around a four-year curriculum—approximately two years of high school and two years of post-secondary education. The assumption is that to be successful in a technical environment, students must have some post-secondary skills. At the end of two years in the program, the students receive a high school diploma and can choose to seek employment or continue the program for two more years and receive an associate degree at the completion of four years, or receive an associate degree and go directly to a skilled job, a registered adult apprenticeship program, or continue in a four-year program.

Other program components include: paying a wage for time spent in on-the-job training ($4.25 to $6.00 in 1993), which is negotiated at the local level; an integrated curriculum based on the needs of industries and one which provides academics that relate to the worksite; broad based skills that include critical thinking and problem solving; coordination between the teachers in the school and the mentors at the job site; and outcome, performance based assessments or portfolios for the students that serve as credentials that can be used to apply for jobs or to enter college.

Whether one talks about youth apprenticeships or the traditional apprenticeship, an apprenticeship is a formal, contractual relationship between an employer and an employee (apprentice) during which the worker (apprentice) learns a trade. The training lasts a specified length of time and one that varies in time required, depending upon the skills/learning expected by a particular occupation or trade. Apprenticeships usually last about four years but they range from one to six years in length. An apprenticeship covers all aspects of the trade and includes both on-the-job training and related instruction, which generally takes place in a classroom. The teaching by experienced craftworkers and other skilled persons requires the study of trade manuals and educational materials.

During the period of an apprenticeship, apprentices work under experienced workers known as journey workers, a status obtained after successful completion of an apprenticeship. Apprentices are employees, whose pay usually starts at about one-half that of an experienced worker in the trade being pursued. The apprentice's wage increases periodically through the apprenticeship to correspond with the increasing learning and skill level attained and the increasing ability to work with less supervision as the apprenticeship ensues. The sponsor of an apprenticeship program plans, administers, and pays for the program. Sponsors can be employers, employer associations, and typically unions are involved.

The national apprenticeship act of 1937 (The Fitzgerald Act) is the principal federal legislation identifying the criteria by which apprenticeship programs will be developed and evaluated and how the Secretary of Labor will work with appropriate state labor agencies and with State Departments of Education. Apprenticeship programs are commonly registered with the federal government or a federally approved state apprenticeship agency. These programs must meet federally approved standards related to job duties, wages, related instruction, and health and safety regulations. Currently, apprenticeships are offered in some 830 occupations. About 100,000 new apprentices are registered each year, with about 350,000 persons participating in approximately 43,000 apprenticeship programs. As of 1992, over 22 percent of the apprentices were minority and over 7 percent were women. In most states or local level apprenticeship programs, outreach counselors are available to provide information about admissions to programs, the prerequisites and tasks involved, and related topics, and they counsel participants about preparing for interviews, how to get technical task training and other issues (U. S. Department of Labor, 1992). Earlier in this chapter, some comparisons were drawn between the use of apprenticeships in the U. S. A. and other nations. Other comparisons can also be cited. One of note is that the United States ranks 14th out of 16 developed Western nations in the share of the work force enrolled in such programs (Glover, 1986), that less than three-tenths of one percent of the work force are currently enrolled in apprenticeship training programs (Elbaum, 1989), and that in comparison to such other nations, including Great Britain, in the U. S. A., beginning apprentices will be at least 20 years of age rather than 16 or so (Glover, 1986), giving increased credence to the current rise in availability of youth apprenticeship in the U. S. A., and that the number of high school trade courses taken by students has a highly significant impact on obtaining apprenticeship training (Gittner, 1994).

While much more could be said about work-based or field-based learning, the basic point is that, however defined, these processes help potential workers understand not only the specific skills or job tasks with which they are concerned but the broader picture of "working in context," understanding the characteristics of the organization, its norms, its expectations, its mission and the tasks at hand. These broader skills and understanding have the potential to clarify the young worker's contribution to the whole, to understand how his or her input relates to the productivity of the firm, and to give substance to such notions as the importance of life-long learning.

For employment-bound youth, particularly those for whom traditional classrooms and abstract skills have no appeal and make them increasingly vulnerable to leaving school before graduating from high school, formal work-based training programs—cooperative education, apprenticeships, tech-prep programs, curricula offering integrated academic and vocational skills—offer reasons for staying in schools and opportunities to bridge the gap between school and work.

Counselor Roles in the School-to-Work Transition

It would be accurate to suggest that most school-to-work transition programs have identified the role of the counselor as a vital element of such programs. However, as suggested at the beginning of this chapter, a number of national reports, largely from various business policy groups, have advocated more and different counseling availability in preparing students to anticipate and in support of the school-to-work transition. These roles take many forms. They include:

1. Help students obtain and learn from part-time employment in high school, in particular, to consider how such part-time employment has the potential to provide bridges to full-time work by inducting youth into the adult normative culture in which work occurs and by training them in the cognitive and psychomotor tasks that comprise workcontent. In these contexts, as well as those of formal work-based learning, the counselor can help employment-bound students to understand that work adjustment involves more than learning the skills inherent in the technical content of a job. As mentioned in a prior chapter, successful adjustment to work requires mastery of a range of social learning tasks such as when to take a work break, how to respond to accommodate authority in the workplace, and, perhaps more important, how to understand and manipulate the culture of the workplace to one's personal benefit (Borman, Izzo, Penn & Reisman, 1984).

2. Counselors in schools and in school-to-work transition programs can coordinate programs of assessment to facilitate choice of occupation, and of what work-based learning program or school-industry program might be best suited to prepare for that chore. They can also coordinate other types of programs that support the school-to-work transition: career counseling; summer jobs; financial assistance; involvement in in-school apprenticeship programs; choice of cooperative education options; employability counseling and exploratory programs to assist in career choice, job search, and general employability; job placement assistance; counseling about vocational-technical program alternatives to college degree programs; working with community resources —

e.g., personnel officers in industry, role models, minority groups of professional persons (e.g., engineers, accountants), and with parents to create a hospitable and supportive environment for the school-to-work transition.

3. Less explicit than it should be in most conceptions of counselor roles related to employment-bound youth is helping such youth take steps to keep their options open as fully as possible and to anticipate the needs for contingency planning. This was suggested earlier in discussing tech-prep, but the point also extends to vocational education and other forms of work-based learning, however good such initiatives are in providing alternative pathways to preparation for employment, depending upon how these are structured, they can also serve to restrict student choice by locking them into a rigidly prescribed set of courses with little opportunity for exploration of alternative opportunities or of emerging changes in work or the occupational structure that may require new patterns of preparation in a different career trajectory. Thus, a major function of counselors in the schools or in transition services is to protect the youth's right to choose and to provide such youth the career planning skills necessary to facilitate informed free choice.

4. Counseling services in support of the transition from school to employment cannot be confined to what school counselors do alone or even in collaboration with counselors in community agencies or personnel specialists in work places. Rather, new mechanisms must be instituted in this nation that learn from and adopt, as appropriate, from other nations, mechanisms that are directly related to employment counseling and to the transition from school to work. There are many possibilities. For example, in Australia, as fewer employment counselors are available to assist a larger number of persons seeking work, advocacy has grown to provide clients self-help resources

that may achieve many of the outcomes usually done in individual counseling. The intent is to use audio, video, and computer technologies more extensively for "the development of user-friendly, self-contained, client self-help packages focusing on specifically defined areas of employment counseling need." In addition, there are efforts to use the telephone more effectively as a medium for providing employment information to clients. For example, a nationwide telephone information service for career decision making has been established called "Career Line." It provides 15 three- to five-minute information messages on aspects of career planning, implementation and adjustment. Other telephone services are being planned or established covering job information, employment trends, job variances, and other relevant information (Pryor, Hammond, & Hawkins, 1990).

In Britain, government policy now requires each secondary student and, therefore, school-leaver to have records of achievement (ROAs) and individual action plans (IAPs). These documents are drawn up by students and their teachers or counselors listing achievements as a basis for future planning and to facilitate self-awareness and awareness of potential career outcomes to be sought. In addition, these activities are now incorporated into the government's Technical and Vocational Education Initiative and Extension policy that provides cash-value instruments to school-leavers to "buy" vocational training contingent upon individual action planning using a National Record of Achievement which includes a personal record, an action plan, an assessment record, and certificates of National Vocational Qualifications, acknowledgments of skill at four performance levels (Law, 1993).

There are many other important national approaches to the school-to-work transition or to employment counseling that should be cited. Among these is the development and use of group employment counseling in Canada (Amundson, Borgen & Westwood, 1990), as well as the delivery of career counseling through distance learning, psychosocial counseling for the unemployed with the collaboration of trade unions in the State of Bremen in Germany (Kieselbach & Lunser, 1990), the nation-wide network of Public Employment Security Officers (PESO) in Japan, their three-tier system of interventions for job applicants, and the national computer assisted information system by which labor supply and demand information can be made available.

This three-tier system of classifications for job applicants in Japan begins with a self-service section, the first tier, that deals with job applicants who are assessed as able to find a job matching their needs or conditions relatively easily with little assistance. These applicants have a clear understanding, adequate experiences, and appropriate knowledge of the labor market and job openings. The main role of employment counselors in this section is to conduct an appraisal interview to confirm whether jobs that the applicant has selected from "job-open files" fits his or her job-seeking conditions. It is also the employment counselor's task to prepare a letter of introduction to the job offerer (employer) when a job applicant decides to make an application. In this section, counselors intervene little in the decision-making process of job applicants.

The second employment counseling section deals with those job applicants who have difficulties in choosing and are assessed to need counseling and vocational training to equip them with job skills before being referred to job openings. Employment counselors in this section are involved with the decision-making process through individual counseling, interviews and assessment of aptitudes and interests, and so forth.

The third section, called the special service section, is set up for physically or mentally disabled persons and elderly people who generally have considerable difficulty in finding jobs and in preparing themselves for employment as well as with adjustment after placement. The functions of counselors in this section are individual centers to receive professional care. In this section, counselor stays with the client throughout the job-hiring process" (pp. 173-174).

This system is supported by, among other resources, a national computer assisted information network system by which labor supply and demand information can be made available to every PESO office (Watanabe, Masaki, & Kamiichi,1990).

Within the United States, there are a variety of important initiatives underway that represent different combinations of state and local actions in behalf of facilitating the school-to-employment transition. Barton (1990) has described several of these. They include:

- The Arizona Employment Service provides two programs of career development and job placement services for in-school and out-of-school 16 to 21 year olds. These programs are co-sponsored through the State Education Department and the Job Training Partnership Act.
- The commitment by the Missouri Employment Service to assign a full-time career counselor to each vocational-technical high school. This counselor provides instruction in pre-employment skills, and job search help.
- The Rhode Island Job Service operates a program for high school seniors on a statewide basis. It is a career exploration and job skill and search instruction program.
- The Youth Opportunity Centers in New York State and the New York City Partnership provide high school students with computerized occupational information, job search workshops, and a resource center to develop career plans. The counselors facilitate placement of current students and graduates into full- and part-time work.

While there are many other approaches to facilitating the school-to-employment transition youth and to supporting them through this transition, it is increasingly apparent that this process requires new and innovative approaches to counseling and career services as a central mechanism.

The Induction to Employment

Ultimately, students leave the familiar world of the school and make the passage into the world of employment. In an idealized sense, the successful transition from school to work requires young people to be responsive and mature, to be prepared to relinquish some roles and take on new roles, to hold positive attributes, habits, and values. In short, they are expected to be ready to perform as competent workers, understand the firm for which they will work, be able to manage interpersonal affairs on the job, accept responsibility and function responsibility. Some employment-bound youth can fit such a model; some cannot. In either case, employment-bound youth take multiple pathways to get from school to work. They may do so with a jagged process of floundering and trial commitments to work, they may do it as part of a process of apprenticeship or other school-business-industry cooperative scheme, they may enter the military or a program of national service, or they may go directly from school into the work force and into a specific job. As suggested in other parts of the book, many will enter the secondary labor market for some period of time to gain credibility as a worker and often because they have been discriminated against by employers in the primary labor market through ageism, sexism, or racism. Whichever way a particular employment-bound youth engages in full-time work, they will undoubtedly go through a process of transition where their expectations and those of the workplace and their supervisor may come into conflict. This process was described in a very useful manner by Tiedeman (1961) as a decision-making model. However, this paradigm can also be seen as encompassing the period up to and during the high school experience (the period of anticipation) and the period from the end of high school through the school-to-work transition and into the process of work adjustment itself (the period of implementation and adjustment). In sequence, the stages proposed by Tiedeman included:

I. The period of anticipation.
    a. Exploration (random and acquisitive activity)
    b. Crystallization (emerging of patterns in the form of alternatives and their consequences leading to clarification and comment).
    c. Choice (organizing in preparation for implementation)
    d. Specification (clarification)

II. The period of implementation and adjustment
    a. Induction (person largely responsive)
    b. Reformation (person largely assertive)
    c. Integration (satisfaction)

This model, unlike many other decision-making models, is concerned not only with the formulation of a choice, the process of moving from a very diffuse and general choice to a specific job, but also with the process that occurs when one tries to implement the choice that is made: the processes of induction, reformation, and integration. This model suggests that the process of anticipation is involved with creating and specifying alternatives that will allow one to meet preferences, expectations, self-concept notions related to work. When one engages in work-based learning or, more specifically, actually takes a job, all of the elements of anticipation—preferences, expectations, self-concepts—are tested and challenged by the performance and organizational characteristics which are inherent in the specific choice. During this period, there is a process of reciprocity, give and take, between the person's characteristics and expectations and those of the environment. If the individual's ability to take on role expectations as defined by the job context and work norms associated with the job chosen is not stretched beyond the person's level of tolerance for adaptation, the young worker will likely stay in the position and incorporate the job expectations into his or her self-concept and process of identification with the job. However, if, for whatever reason, the person cannot adjust to the job expectations, it is likely that he or she will leave that job, either voluntarily or involuntarily, and reinstitute the processes of exploration, anticipation, and choice.

In many ways, the period of anticipation and of implementation and adjustment just discussed are processes which require reconciliation between what the individual hopes to acquire from work and what work organizations expect of their workers. These are complex in their content and in their interaction. Morgan (1980, p. 65) has identified these two sets of dimensions:

Dimensions that individuals have expectations of receiving and organizations have expectations of giving:

1. A sense of meaning or purpose in the job
2. Personal development opportunities
3. The amount of interesting work that stimulates curiosity and induces excitement
4. The challenge in the work
5. The power and responsibility in the job
6. Recognition and approval for good work
7. The status and prestige in the job
8. The friendliness of the people, the congeniality of the work group

9. Salary
10. The amount of structure in the environment (general practices, disciplines, regimentation)
11. The amount of security in the job
12. Advancement opportunities
13. The amount and frequency of feedback and evaluation

Dimensions which organizations have expectations of receiving and individuals of giving:

1. Performing nonsocial job-related tasks requiring some degree of technical knowledge and skill
2. Learning the various aspects of a position while on the job
3. Discovering new methods of performing tasks; solving novel problems
4. Presenting a point of view effectively and convincingly
5. Working productively with groups of people
6. Making well-organized, clear presentations both orally and in writing
7. Supervising and directing the work of others
8. Making responsible decisions well and without assistance from others
9. Planning and organizing work efforts for oneself or others
10. Utilizing time and energy for the benefit of the company
11. Accepting company demands that conflict with personal prerogatives
12. Maintaining social relationships with other members of the company outside of work
13. Conforming to the pathways of the organization or work group on the job in areas not directly related to job performance
14. Pursuing further education on personal time
15. Maintaining a good public image of the company
16. Taking on company values and goals as one's own
17. Seeing what should or must be done and initiating appropriate activity

One of the tasks in career counseling in the school, during the school-to-work transition, or at the point of entry into a job is to help employment-bound youth recognize both their own reasons for working and the reasons why employers would hire them and the expectations they have for the worker's contribution to the productivity and climate of the workplace. That such reconciliation of worker and workplace needs does not always occur is seen in the shifts in jobs that ensue.

Patterns of Labor Market Entry and Work Adjustment

The shifts in jobs that young workers frequently experience have been described and analyzed in many ways. Super's paradigms of career development from the early 1950s through the late 1980s have tended to label the period overlapping the school-to-work transition as that of Trial-Little Commitment. It is seen as a point where a first job is located and is tried out as a potential life work. However, commitment is seen as still provisional, and if the job is not appropriate (if the implementation and adjustment process discussed above is not successful) or if such employer discrimination as ageism, sexism, or racism makes the situation intolerable or stifles learning and advancement, the person may reinstitute the process of crystallizing, specifying, and implementing a preference.

Within such perspectives, there are many patterns of dealing with the school-to-work transition. Some people flounder from one opportunity to another; some persons convert a previously part-time job into a full-time one; some persons approach jobs quite cautiously and hold back their commitment while they test their fit with the job tasks, co-workers, and organizations; some persons may choose or be obliged to take work in which they are essentially underemployed, their talents and abilities are only partially challenged by the job; some young persons are unable to find work and are unemployed.

The explanations for these patterns are wide-ranging. Some young people have not acquired the self-understanding, knowledge of educational or occupational opportunities or planning skills advocated elsewhere in this book. In essence, they have not acquired the planfulness, undergone the exploration, acquired the information, developed the reality orientation, or accepted the responsibility for choice that would characterize them as career mature in late adolescence (Super, 1985). Some young persons enter the school to work transition with little knowledge of their personal values, preferences, and skills and stereotypes of jobs and work contexts. They have not developed good work habits (e.g., punctuality, dependability, honesty, social skills) that elicit patience and training from their work supervisor. Many students experience difficulties in the school to work transition because of barriers imposed on their job search as a function of racism or sexism or, indeed, reverse ageism (employers assuming they are too young to handle a job independently and effectively).

A major problem which tends to linger into adulthood and, indeed, potentially throughout one's work life is early underemployment and/or unemployment. While throughout this section, we talk of the experimentation, the floundering, the trial and error behavior which characterizes much of the transition from school to work, the importance of such processes are of little consequence compared to the "hangover effect" created by extended joblessness among out-of-school teenage youth. In one of the first studies of this phenomenon, Adams and Mangum (1978) argued that...

> *"those who have unfavorable early labor market experiences are less likely than others to have favorable experiences later...Thus, early labor market experiences are related to subsequent measures of labor market success. They cannot be treated as benign phenomena which 'age out' nor as simple individual problems which have no implications for social policy or government intervention"* (p. 3).

Mangum (1988) has more recently stated, "There is a substantial minority, primarily from culturally and economically deprived backgrounds, who are permanently scarred by their unsuccessful experiences [in attempting to secure and be successful in work]" (p. 1).

Youth whose adolescence and young adulthood is characterized by unsuccessful labor market experiences are likely to be cast into marginal roles in adolescence and to have these reflected in their later life in economic marginality in adulthood. There are many reasons for these early labor market problems—families with low economic resources, a lack of significant role models, a lack of relevant information about jobs, disintegrating family support systems, poor educational preparation or early school leaving, teenage pregnancy, crime, substance abuse, discrimination. Such factors explain but do not justify why Hispanic and Black adolescent populations are characterized by unemployment rates two to three times that of White adolescent populations, frequently exceeding 50 percent in the inner cities.

Poor early labor market experiences have other problems associated with them. For example, they represent loss of work experience, information, and skills, as well as credibility as a worker which likely injures attitudes toward work and employer perceptions of the young worker's assets, stability, and probable contributions to jobs available. A related phenomenon is that negative early labor market experiences are frequently interpreted by adolescents or young adults as rejection, as indications of their worthlessness that reinforces both negative self-images and anxieties about the future. According to Borow (1989) such anxieties often result in "avoidance behavior, a reluctance to plan and to explore, and a resultant slowing of the process of career development" (p. 9). Borow goes on to contend that, "a disproportionate number of youths among socio-economically disadvantaged populations appears to exhibit depressed levels of achievement motivation, self-efficacy expectations, and other important indicators of competitive coping behavior" (p. 9). These are groups of young people, of employment-bound youth, whose need for the help of career-relevant schooling and of counselors who can bring to them information and caring exceeds what they have likely received in school or in the community.

For the above reasons and others, most youth do not leave high school and immediately enter into a stable job with a firm that provides security and mobility. As a group, most research studies show that young people typically enter the labor market gradually rather than abruptly on the completion of school (Stevenson, 1978) and that their attitudes about work, jobs, and careers are largely formed prior to the first job itself (Raelin, 1980). Such findings certainly validate the importance of career counseling, career education, and career guidance programs in the high school and earlier. At any rate, following the first job, a trial and error period typically precedes complete incorporation into the labor force. A large number of adolescents and young adults combine school and work before completing the transition to work. As Osterman (1989) has suggested: "For many youths, the process of entry and adjustment to the labor market is lengthy and involves distinct periods. The behavior of the youths changes over time, moving from a period of casual attachment to an increasing commitment to work and to stable behavior" (p. 255). Ostermann also describes the several year period following high school as a moratorium period, a period in which adventure seeking, sex, and peer group activities are all more important than work. He contends that: "This moratorium stage tends to be reflected in the reality that most youth spend their initial years after school in the secondary labor market (e.g., the fast food industry). Firms in such categories do not invest resources in training youth nor are there career ladders available to provide incentives to youth to settle into the firm and identify with it as an occupational commitment for an extended period of time. Such firms, with little investment in training, benefits, or long-term commitments to these workers, can accept the unstable behavior of youths in ways that primary firms cannot or will not" (P. 244).

Whether the behavior of youth moving through the school-to-work transition is stable or unstable undoubtedly varies from individual to individual. What seems not to vary in gross terms are the complexities that comprise the transition environment through which adolescents and other employment-bound youth pass. Mangum (1988) has stated, "There are cultural norms, labor market realities, and human development processes which compose the transition environment. No program to improve a transition can expect success which does not take into account these constraints. Employers control and dispense jobs and any successful program must ultimately help youth to meet employer expectations" (p. i). However, in Mangum's view "irresponsibility is a far more serious barrier to successful youth access to the labor market than inexperience and lack of skills. No more than one-third of U. S. jobs require pre-entry training and most job skills are learned on the job. Thus, job-getting and job-keeping skills are more critical to youth attractiveness as employees than are job-doing skills" (p. 1).

While Mangum's perspectives are generally accurate, other available data suggests that the transition to work is a multi-faceted process. Hulsart (1983) in an in-depth study of owners, managers, supervisors, and entry-level employees, identified 12 skill groups seen by these groups as needed by entry-level workers. They included:

1. Job seeking/career development
2. Mathematics
3. Computer
4. Reading
5. Writing
6. Communications
7. Interpersonal
8. Business Economics
9. Personal Economics
10. Manual Perspective
11. Work Activity
12. Problem Solving/Reasoning

In a related study of the transition and adjustment to work, Ashley, et al, (1980) studied the adaptation to work of 38 males and 30 females from 17 to 30 years of age. The findings of this study indicate that for those who adapt to work successfully, adjustments must be made sequentially in five areas: performance, organization, interpersonal, responsibility and affective aspects. Thus, adjustment to work has to do with attitudes, task-specific skills, knowledge and feelings. New workers must learn what is expected of them and how to do new job tasks; they need to learn the informal rules that operate in the workplace, the procedures required, the hierarchies of policies and persons and how and where they fit into the total organization of the company; the ways to adapt to co-workers and to their supervisor's styles; how to prove oneself and use training opportunities; how to maintain a good work attitude and willingness to work hard. When such adjustments are not made, particularly those which are affective or emotional in content, high school graduates or school leavers lose their jobs. Such perspectives are reflected in the research reported by Oinonen (1984) which indicates that the major reasons high school graduates or dropouts lose their jobs include the following:

- Poor work habits (tardy, undependable)
- Poor work attitude
- Work lacks quality (inaccuracies, wasteful)
- Work lacks quantity (low output)
- Inability to accept advice and supervision

These are each areas about which career counseling and career guidance can make a difference. However, for many young persons going through the school-to-work transition, they find little support from schools, community services, or from their employers to deal with such issues.

Issues in Employer Responsibility for Induction to Work

The third, or final, phase of a continuum of school-to-employment processes has to do with the services and the support systems that occur in workplaces and in advocacy by employers. Work force development in these terms has to do with how new employees are oriented to their jobs, to the culture of the workplace, and to their contributions to the mission of the enterprise, as well as the degree to which new or younger workers and older workers receive employer-provided training and the nature of that training. It has to do with how human resource development processes and systems are provided by an enterprise, the mentoring and information they provide to employees, the encouragement and training provided to have workers develop loyalty and commitment to long-term mobility within the firm, incentives to improve their competencies, and the ability to find ways to improve how their jobs are done and how the individual worker can relate as a team player to co-workers and as a person of service to his or her customers, however they are defined. It has to do with whether or not individual enterprises make a connection between their human resource policies and business strategy (CPC Foundation/Rand Corporation, 1994, p. 59).

There are many other issues involved in the unfolding of the school-to-work process that relate to employers. These vary from nation to nation in their importance but one of them has to do with whether or not employers actually pick up human resource development of employment-bound youth from the point where schools stop such development. In other words, is there a continuity of expectations, messages, skill development, and training that is connected to the knowledge and skills that schools have provided students?

Within this context, one of the issues of particular importance is the degree to which employers are involved in job training. In a recent report to the U. S. Congress (Hilton, 1991), the U. S. Office of Technology Assessment concluded that only a few U. S. firms use training as part of a successful competitive strategy, in contrast to firms in Germany and Japan.

However, it must be noted here that the United States has begun to develop new models of training and a variety of other nations are also pursuing training systems to help insure international competitiveness and rising living standards. For example, "skill intensive Singapore obliges big companies to set up training systems, then measure their success. The French [in response to Germany's ability to produce skilled workers] have made a sustained attempt to improve their vocational education. In its most recent budget, the British government unveiled a scheme for reintroducing apprenticeships....other British spokespersons on the economy are advocating creation of a university for industry, which would link workers and trainers electronically in a sort of permanent technology seminar" (*The Economist*, 1994, p. 20).

But, as many have noted in a variety of contexts, "Improved training is not the royal road to success in all places at all times, what works for a manufacturing dominated economy like Germany does not necessarily work for services-oriented economy like the United States. What works for computer makers does not necessarily work for discount stores. Heavy investment in training cannot compensate for poor management or misguided product strategies, as IBM has found to its cost."..."Above all, the pro-training camp highly overstates the ability of training to curb long-term unemployment for a growing number of people, the real problem lies not in a lack of job-specific skills but in a surplus of social pathologies—too many people with too little self-discipline, self-respect, and basic education to fit easily into any workplace" (*The Economist*, 1994, p 20).

One of the tasks of the employer in inducting or orienting new workers and of career counseling in the school, during the school-to-work transition, or at the point of entry into a job is to help youth and other workers recognize both their own reasons for working and the expectations employers have for the worker's contribution to the productivity and climate of the workplace. That such reconciliation of worker and workplace needs does not always occur is seen in the dismissal of workers, in jagged early labor market experiences, and in other problems of work stability or adjustment.

Among all of these issues of employer responsibility in the induction to work, what is not clear is the degree to which employers actually provide direct training and supervision of the entry-level skills such as those identified above by Hulsart and by Ashley, et al. Employer responsibilities in behalf of their role in the school-to-work transition is particularly critical based upon studies that show that the quality and availability of supervision of work experience has an important impact on the school-to-work transition (Silberman, 199 4; Stern, McMillan, Hopkins, and Stone, 1990). It is likely that more such training and supervision is provided by large firms than by small firms. But it is also true that though they are frequently not pleased with the quality of training schools are providing, many employers expect that the common schools, K to 12, will provide most such training. For example, in a joint study of the Wisconsin Department of Public Instruction and the Parker Pen Company (Oinonen, 1984), it was found that only 3 to 10 percent of the employers thought that high schools were preparing students at a "good" or "excellent" level in the following areas:

- understands U. S. economic system
- recognizes, solves problems by self
- understands career ladders, advancement
- writes well
- demonstrates spelling and grammar skills
- applying and interviewing for a job

While one can take the position that the degree to which schools are providing students the knowledge, skills, and affective competencies that they need to make a successful school-to-work transition is uneven and often incomplete, it seems fair as well to argue that schools should not have to achieve these goals in a vacuum. Combinations of schools, businesses and industries, and government should provide transition schemes to insure that every student who leaves the high school makes a successful passage to work. As seen elsewhere in this book, other nations have acknowledged the importance of investments in training by industries, trade associations, and government. They have provided career counseling and information systems in strategically placed job centers to help persons decide about and find work opportunities; they have created work-based learning schemes—apprenticeships, cooperative education, work shadowing, work-study—that have provided a clearly defined transitional structure as employment-bound youth leave their secondary school, of whatever type, and proceed to full-time employment.

It needs to be acknowledged here that there have been changes in the vocabulary and the process associated with support services provided within many workplaces and corporations. As many large organizations have transformed from simply doing personnel management to the more encompassing spectrum of personnel development, they have increasingly emphasized such components as human resources management, employee assistance programs, and career development systems for employees. As Leibowitz, Farren, and Kaye (1986) have suggested, a career development system is best defined as "an organized, formalized, planned effort to achieve a balance between the individual's career needs and the organization's work-force requirements.... It is an ongoing program linked with the organizations human resource structures..." (p. 4). In discharging such a system, work organizations may have career counselors on site or under contract from community resources for selected purposes. They may also have these career development specialists engage in a wide diversity of roles including designing and operating a company's career resources center, providing individual career assessment and counseling, and maintaining a job posting system for the company, providing workshops and seminar of career development topics (e.g., career ladders available, promotion requirements, the use of educational benefits), they may initiate support groups for women or minority employees, coordinate a firm's educational and training programs or wellness programs, they may work directly with plateaued workers or serve as mentors for other populations.

The point is that if the school-to-work transition is to successfully culminate in the successful induction into work, employers, managers and supervisors, and career counselors in work organizations will need increasingly to view employment-bound youth new to a workplace as a constituency needing special support as these youth go through the dynamics associated with induction and work adjustment.

Indeed, youths, young adults, and adults entering or re-entering the work force will need to be seen as engaged in both the uncertainty and the promise that characterizes transition at any point in life and their needs should be seen and planned for within the expanding understanding of career development as a subset of human resource development.

Thus, career counseling and other human resource mechanisms must deal not only with the smoothness or jaggedness of individual career development, but also the sub-set of career development issues which occurs as one anticipates, is inducted into, and progresses through the particular transitions required of persons in particular organizations. These are questions of person-situation fit as well as of employability skills; they are also human resource and work force development issues.

Because of a complex network of factors—the impact of advanced technology, corporate mergers, changing demographics of the work force, trends toward later retirement, growing concerns by workers about the quality of life, economic competitiveness—the views held by business and industry of workers is steadily undergoing change in the United States and in many other industrialized nations. Workers are being seen increasingly as people who do not leave their family and personal problems at the door when they enter the workplace nor leave problems on the job when they go home. Thus, terms such as Employee Assistance Programs, Human Resource Development, and Career Services are rapidly entering the vocabulary of business and industry as workers are seen as corporate resources to be nurtured, not used up and cast away, as human capital which needs its own preventive maintenance in the forms of education, training, counseling, information about mobility within the firm and how to prepare oneself for such opportunities rather than being encouraged to go from one job to another across corporations.

These conditions have led to a steady, although uneven, rise in career services for young and older adults in industrial and corporate settings. The foci of these services vary; they include work with young workers to facilitate their induction and adjustment to work; with plateaued workers; women re-entering the work force or as a part of dual career families; workers selecting training and education programs; assisting workers to identify career ladders and career paths of interest to them and the ways to progress through them; dealing with substance abuse problems; promoting physical and mental wellness; outplacement counseling; retirement planning; and planning for geographic or international transfers. Thus, there are a wide range of contributions which counselors and other career guidance specialists can make in the workplace, that augment the effects of training and retraining, the supervision of technical performance or the implementation of other human resource development processes.

While not addressing the role of counselors in the workplace, Hamilton (1990), an advocate of new models of youth apprenticeships and the expanded use of such mechanisms to help youth more effectively prepare for the adult work world, has advocated dividing the tasks of career development for youth apprentices between the school or education system and the employer at the worksite. For example, he suggests that guidance counselors in the school advise apprentices, their parents, and their teachers about the apprenticeship program, while coaches at the worksite develop the competencies of the apprentice, and mentors at the worksite counsel the apprentice about career directions and life goals and initiate him or her into the norms of the workplace and its culture. While it would be hoped that the counselor in the school would do more in helping youth apprenticeships acquire career development knowledge and skills than simply advise potential apprentices about the program, this paradigm of shared support for employment-bound youth, whether or not they are youth apprentices, is a positive direction in helping resolve the need for shared support services between schools, workplaces, and other available transition services.

It seems important to acknowledge in U. S. policy and legislation the need for life span approaches to career counseling and guidance that cover the period of schooling, the school-to-work transition, and the period of initial work adjustment as well as subsequent career changes throughout the period of adult working life. While elements of such a system are in place in many parts of the United States, they tend not to be integrated in policy or in practice. They tend as well to be selective in terms of populations that are served. Thus, while the Carl D. Perkins Vocational and Applied Technology Education Act, the Joint Training Partnership Act, and the U. S. Employment and Training Administration are each in place, they do not coordinate systematically with schools nor with workplaces, nor does existing policy deal comprehensively with such needs.

What needs to be addressed in such policy in the future is that preparation and career development of employment-bound youth occurs in three phases which need to be systematically understood and accompanied by career services that focus on the 10 or 12-year period from the elementary, junior or middle, and senior high school, through the school-to-work transition, and into successful work entry. This period needs to be seen as first characterized by a sifting and sorting of individual priorities that begin in the late elementary or middle school and continues through the high school. Second, there is the interim period described as the school-to-work transition in which a variety of patterns, needs for service, graduated learning, and mastery of entry-level job skills and attitudes need to be achieved. Third is the employment entry period when employment-bound youth must make the multiple adjustments required by employers in job-specific technical skills, learning skills, interpersonal skills, adaptations to the work culture and to supervision, personal economics, and affective competencies. The responses to the competencies required by employment-bound youth need to be seen in *structural* terms—who will deliver what competencies, when and how—*conceptual*—what is the content to be included and/or reinforced at each of these periods—and *economic*—who will pay the bill? A further requirement is to define the roles of career counselors in the different settings that have or should have the primary responsibility for career counseling and guidance at each phase of the development of employment-bound youth. These will undoubtedly overlap but there will be distinctions in them as well, as the questions and issues to be addressed shift from those appropriate to the junior high school child in the throes of early exploration of a career identity and the relationship of subject matter to its applications in different occupations or workplaces; to the student in the senior high school making specific course choices and beginning to systematically plan for alternatives following high school; to the young person at the threshold of the school-to-work transition and attempting to find a career pattern to which to make a long-term commitment; to the young person trying to successfully execute his or her job entry-level skills.

Conclusion

The school-to-work transition is not an event but, rather, a process that unfolds over an extended period. Rooted in the concepts of self and of opportunity that begin to be acquired in the early life of the child and advanced through whatever career relevant activities and planning processes occur in the school, the adolescent or young adult ventures into the short or long transition period that bridges the journey between school and employment, which ultimately culminates, in the most positive sense, in the successful induction into a job. At each of these periods, the questions to be answered and the needs to be met for employment-bound youth differ and require the availability of career guidance, career counseling, and other support services. Unfortunately, the sustained availability of such services by school counselors, counselors in the Employment Services, Job Training Partnership Act Programs, or other initiatives targeted to employment-bound youth are often uneven, underfunded, and vaguely defined.

National reports recommending new paradigms of career counseling and new collaborative schemes of employment-bound learning and transitions from school to employment suggest that policy makers are taking the complexity of the needs of employment-bound youth more seriously and are committed to new approaches to addressing such needs. At each of the phases—in school, the transition period between school and full-time employment, and the induction to work—counselors have extraordinarily important contributions to make to facilitating the career planning, the sorting and sifting of job and educational alternatives, and the acquisition of information and skills by which employment-bound youth can progress to productive and purposeful employment.

Chapter Five

Career Counseling
of Employment-Bound
Youth

Any analysis of career counseling with employment-bound youth must begin with an acknowledgment that career counseling is only one of an array of career interventions (Spokane, 1991) that can be used to assist these youth to explore, choose, prepare for, make the transition to, or adjust to work. Whether career counseling is the most appropriate intervention, should be used alone or in combination with academic advising and other career interventions (e.g., labor market information, work shadowing, computer-assisted career guidance, job search strategies), or with academic advising and other program elements (e.g., part-time work, apprenticeship training, financial incentives) depends on what type of assistance a particular counselee needs, the setting in which the help is given, and the resources available.

Typically, career counseling is the centerpiece of the relationship between the counselor and an employment-bound youth but it is rarely the only form of assistance offered. This is true, in part, because most persons who need help with their career planning or transition to work have several concerns that need to be addressed and in part, because career counseling is frequently used to help the counselor and counselee decide upon other types of career interventions that might be helpful in this particular situation: e.g., anger management, stress reduction, interest and values clarification, the development of job search strategies. Thus, career counseling allows the counselor and counselee to evaluate and personalize the information, feedback, and skill development that come from these other career interventions, set and reset goals to be pursued in the counseling relationship, and for the counselor to support the counselee as he or she explores and tries on new roles and relinquishes old ones.

In the next chapter, we will examine in greater depth other career programs and practices that might be used with employment-bound youth. However, in this chapter, we will focus principally on career counseling as a special form of career intervention.

Career Counseling Defined

There are many definitions of career counseling from which one can select. They vary in emphasis and in the process implied but if these were all to be synthesized into a common form of definition, it would probably be something like the following:

Career counseling is a purposeful relationship between a counselor and an employment-bound youth in which the specific processes and information used vary with the counselee's needs and in which the counselor and counselee collaborate to facilitate self-clarification, evaluation of opportunities available, decision making, planning and action by the latter.

The basic content of career counseling is the possibility of choices which society permits an individual to consider as these are defined by age, particular setting, economic and personal characteristics, and psychological circumstances. In addition, the content of career counseling encompasses the anxieties, information deficits, and confused perceptions persons experience about their abilities, preferences, and the opportunities available. These include both rational and irrational beliefs, and the behavioral and emotional impacts that are experienced as a result of such structural barriers as racism, sexism, or ageism.

Such views emerge from the reality that adolescents and young adults, as well as older persons, vary in their self-understanding and in their understanding of the problems to be explored. Thus, while no two career counseling processes are precisely the same in content or emphasis, individual counseling is frequently necessary between the counselor and the employment-bound youth so that the latter can personalize the implications of information they have, determine the information they need, identify the content of choices available to them, evaluate alternatives, clarify their values, develop decision-making skills, learn about and develop skills (e.g., social skills, stress reduction) that are likely to improve their current situation, or cope with other such dilemmas.

The perspectives on career counseling advanced above incorporate many of the insights of major theorists in the field. For example, Crites (1981) uses the term career counseling to refer specifically to an interpersonal process focused upon assisting an individual to make an appropriate career decision. He states that, "Ideally, it involves active participation in the decisional process, not simply passive-receptive input of information" (p. 11)".career counseling often embraces personal counseling but it goes beyond this to explore and replicate the client's role in the main area of life—the world of work" (p. 11).

Brown and Brooks (1991) offer the following definition: career counseling is an interpersonal process designed to assist individuals with career development problems. Career development is that process of choosing, entering, adjusting to, and advancing in an occupation. It is a lifelong process that interests dynamically with other life roles. Career problems include but are not limited to: career indecision and undecidedness, work performance, stress and adjustment, incongruence of the person and work environment, and inadequate or unsatisfactory integration of life roles with other life roles (e.g., parent, friend, citizen). (p. 5).

During the past decade, the definition of career counseling has frequently been expanded to directly embrace the processes of personal counseling or, indeed, psychotherapy as they are applied to career content. Rounds and Tinsley (1984), for example, contend that "Career intervention is simply a form of psychological intervention designed to affect vocationally related feelings, attitudes, cognitions, and behaviors. Thus, it is a form of psychotherapy and should be viewed as a method of behavior change and tied to psychotherapy theory... We believe that a conceptual shift in which career interventions are understood as psychological interventions (and career counseling as psychotherapy) would foster advances in the understanding of vocational behavior change processes" (pp. 138-39).

While the view of Rounds and Tinsley is not at odds with many of the emphases defined in Crites' earlier view of career counseling, it goes a bit further than some other observers believe is appropriate. Spokane (1991), for example, views career counseling as a particular types of career intervention that should be distinguished from psychotherapy. Indeed, he believes that there have been misapplications of psychotherapy to career situations. Although Spokane allows that while career counseling overlaps psychotherapy as a one-on-one or dyadic intervention, career counseling is not simply psychotherapy as traditionally practiced, nor are career problems simply personal or interpersonal problems.

Indeed, it is likely that each of these theorists and the definitions of career counseling they propose is right for some segment of the career issues and concerns that employment-bound youth or adults bring to counselors. These concerns and issues are on a continuum from determining what information one needs and where to get it, clarification of self or career identity, identifying personal traits and work preferences, exploring work possibilities, establishing present-future relationships in connections between education and work options, achieving planfulness, acquiring general employability skills (e.g., job search and interview skills, effective work habits), to coping with generalized indecisiveness or resolving work adjustment problems (e.g., unwillingness to take constructive supervision, fighting with co-workers, chronic absenteeism, or job dissatisfaction). As one moves across these problem areas, the overlap of career counseling with personal counseling or psychotherapy becomes increasingly apparent particularly in those emphases related to indecisiveness and chronic work adjustment problems.

In seeking to define the competencies counselors need to possess to engage in career counseling, the National Career Development Association both in 1982 and in 1991 also defined career counseling. In the 1991 document, "career counseling is defined as counseling individuals or groups of individuals about occupations, careers, life/career roles and responsibilities, career decision making, career planning, leisure planning, career pathing, and other career development activities (e.g., resume preparation, interviewing and job search techniques), together with the issues or conflicts that individuals confront regarding their careers." (p. 1). The National Career Development Association further contended in 1991 that the minimum competencies necessary for a professional to engage in career counseling can be identified in some 10 areas of knowledge and skills. They include: career development theory, individual and group counseling skills, individual/

group assessment, information/resources, program management and implementation, consultation, special populations, supervision, ethical/legal issues, and research/evaluation.

Clearly, career counseling is not a singular process, nor can it be defined in a limited manner. Some career counseling is developmental and educative; some is aimed at facilitating decision-making; some career counseling is directed at eliminating or improving dysfunctional or maladaptive behaviors.

Within such contexts, the career counselor employs a repertoire of diverse processes in order to meet the needs of a diverse group of counselees. These processes tend to emanate from the existing models or theories of career counseling that are articulated in the next section.

Models and Theories of Career Counseling

However one considers models or theories of career counseling, their likely use by any particular counselor will depend on how that person defines himself or herself as a career counselor, how he or she views the skills and processes to be embodied in career counseling practice, and the kinds of problems and populations with whom that counselor typically works or prefers to work. How the counselor distinguishes the type of career counseling practice to be implemented and with whom will be major factors in determining whether the therapeutic approach used will focus upon intrapsychic changes, as in personal counseling or psychotherapy, or on altering the work environment or choosing another work environment through career counseling, or on assisting the individual to manage the stress induced in such an environment, or on dealing specifically with career exploration and planning about a specific job, an occupation, a post-secondary major in a vocational school or college, or a training opportunity. While it is likely that most career counselors will confront all of these challenges and others, the view one takes of the career counseling theories available will likely constrain or enlarge the range of problems to which one is sensitive and willing to engage.

While theories of career counseling or of career interventions tend to be classified into what appear to be essentially independent conceptions and processes, in fact most counselors tend to practice some form of eclecticism or differential treatment, in which the counselor either uses scientific data about which intervention is likely to be most effective for a particular process or they act more intuitively using a repertoire of counseling interventions that, as a result of the counselor's experience, have been found to be useful in similar problem situations. While it is to be hoped that the counselor will rely on available research data to determine what interventions are likely to be useful in a particular instance, it is also clear that there are many potential ways to provide career counseling and other career interventions that yield positive results. Substantiation of such perspectives come from several different reviews of the relevant research literature. For example, in one of the classic reviews of the research literature on the outcomes of career counseling, Holland, Magoon, and Spokane (1981) provided the following conclusions:

"The experimental evaluations of counselors, courses, career programs, card sorts, interest inventories, workshops, and related treatments imply that the beneficial effects are due to the common elements in these divergent treatments: (a) exposure to occupational information; (b) cognitive rehearsal of vocational aspirations; (c) acquisition of some cognitive structure for organizing information about self, occupations, and their relations; and (d) social support or reinforcement from counselors or workshop members. In addition, the strong tendency to find some positive effects for both diffuse interventions and specific interventions... occurs because the average client knows so little about career decision making and career problems that a small amount of new information and support makes a difference" (pp. 285-286).

These powerful observations of Holland, Magoon, and Spokane (1981) essentially suggest that whatever approach to counseling or other interventions one uses, of fundamental importance is helping persons develop some organized way to think about their personal characteristics and the relationship between these and some organized way to think about their opportunities (i.e., jobs, occupations, courses, curricula, training emphases); to formulate, verbalize, clarify, and evaluate the types of occupational and educational aspirations they hold for themselves; and, to do these things within a context, the career counseling relationship, which is supportive and provides reinforcement of the importance of such processes. The other important insight that stems from the observations of Holland, Magoon, and Spokane (1981) is that most clients do not need personality restructuring, they need information, help with sorting out its relevance to them, and assistance in putting together a plan of action that will help them secure employment, improve their work performance, or alter conditions that currently trouble them. More recently, Oliver and Spokane (1988) also conducted a comprehensive analysis of career interventions and the outcomes achieved. They reported refinements on the types of observations reported by Holland, Magoon, and Spokane (1981). They found, for example, that increasing the number of hours or the number of sessions of contact between a counselor and a client appears to increase the chances for a favorable outcome from career counseling. Such findings would suggest that one or two sessions of career counseling are less likely to yield favorable outcomes than are, for example, five or more sessions. Second, individual treatments tended to be more effective than workshops and structured groups but also less cost effective. Even so, workshops and structured groups were found in the aggregate to be effective and very useful.

Given the above observations, the broad outlines of approaches to career counseling tend to fall into several predictable categories. They were classified by Crites in 1981 and with refinement have continued to describe the broad emphases of career counseling in the United States. Using Crites' comparisons of career counseling models, the next sections will discuss trait-and-factor, client-centered, psychodynamic, developmental, and behavioral or cognitive behavioral approaches.

Trait and Factor Approaches

Although there are refinements in assessment devices and in the quality of information, this approach still reflects the essence of the original Parsonian model of vocational guidance. Emphasis is placed on appraisal or diagnosis of the students' or clients' presenting problems. This process involves extensive data collection about the attitudes, interests, aptitudes, family background, work history, and other characteristics of the counselee by the counselor. This material is converted by the counselor into a set of interpretations about possible future actions the counselee might take. The counselee is helped to sort these actions out or match them with available alternatives and then to act upon some choice among them.

The trait and factor approach is essentially a matching approach which attempts to evaluate and clarify individual characteristics (e.g., aptitudes, interests, preferences, values, needs), particularly strengths and weaknesses, organize them in some comprehensive manner and relate them to some classification of information about the person's alternatives so that choices can be made among available options. This approach essentially arose from the work of Frank Parsons, considered by many as the "Father of Vocational Guidance," whose studies of adolescent choice making from 1895 to the posthumous publication of his book, *Choosing a Vocation*, in 1909, led to the model which continues to define the elements of a trait and factor approach to career counseling.

Parsons's formulation consisted of three steps:

First, a clear understanding of yourself, aptitudes, abilities, interests, resources, limitations, and other qualities. Second, a knowledge of the requirements and conditions of success, advantages and disadvantages, compensation, opportunities, and prospects in different lines of work. Third, true reasoning on the relations of these two groups of facts (1909, p. 5).

From 1909 until the present, Parsons's formulation has spurred research and developmental efforts flowing from each of his three steps. The first step has stimulated efforts to identify and measure individual characteristics, particularly through the use of various types of tests. The second step has stimulated attention to the acquisition and use of occupational information. Together, the use of tests and information with clients has had a continuing effect upon vocational guidance practices. The third step has stimulated a growing body of research on the decision-making process, choice-making styles, risk-taking, and other elements embedded in the process of individual choice.

The trait and factor approach to career counseling continues to have considerable utility as a paradigm by which to consider how to connect or match individual characteristics with those required or expected in a job, occupation, or career. The approach has received continuing vitality from psychometric (or measurement) theory and the psychology of individual differences which combine to identify the factors by which people differ and the degree to which these factors are important in learning or in job performance.

The logic of the approach is that individuals can be conceived of as being comprised of a constellation of traits (e.g., aptitudes, interests, values, psychomotor abilities, energy levels, temperaments) which can be observed and reliability measured. It is further assumed that these patterns of personal traits are more or less unique to each individual. The further assumption is that the individual, if he or she understands the personal characteristics possessed, can order these in some priority ranking and choose in accordance with them. Such a view suggests that choice is primarily conscious and cognitive rather than psychological and emotional as some other approaches assert. However, it is also possible to apply the matching model to such psychological characteristics of the individual as are found in the psychodynamic approaches on needs and drives characterized by the work of such persons as Bordin, Nachman, and Segal (1963) or Holland's typology of occupational personalities: Realistic, Investigative, Artistic, Social, Enterprising and Conventional. Holland's approach (1966, 1973, 1985) gives explicit attention to behavioral style or personality type as the major influence in career choice development. Holland's theory has been described as structural-interactive by Weinrach (1984) "because it provides an explicit link between various personality characteristics and corresponding job titles and because it organizes the massive data about people and jobs" (p. 63). Holland's contributions to a trait and factor approach are apparent in his conceptualizations of how people choose and the instruments or assessment devices that assist in this choice process: e.g., the Self-Directed Search, My Vocational Situation, and the integration of his theoretical structure of occupational typologies—Realistic, Investigative, Artistic, Social, Enterprising and Conventional—as the framework for the Strong Interest Inventory. The tangible mechanisms to implement a trait and factor process are augmented conceptually by Holland's many important theoretical insights about career choice, including his analysis (Holland, 1980), of the common themes characterizing a structural-interactive approach:

"(1) The choice of an occupation is an expression of personality and not a random event, although chance plays a role;

(2) The members of an occupational group have similar personalities and similar histories of personal development;

(3) Because people in an occupational group have similar personalities, they will respond to many situations and problems in similar ways;

(4) Occupational achievement, stability, and satisfaction depend on congruence between one's personality and the job environment" (p. 2).

Thus, trait and factor approaches assume that different occupations or learning situations can be described in terms of their unique requirements for different combinations, patterns, or "quantities" of individual characteristics. In this sense, different occupational or educational options can be profiled in terms of those levels of individual behaviors which are assumed to be essential to performing whatever is required in such situations. The information about such requirements comes from such sources as employee interviews, trade competency examinations, job analysis, occupational aptitude profiles, and work sampling.

Finally, trait and factor approaches to career counseling assume that occupational choice is primarily a function of matching the person's profile of characteristics with that set of occupational or educational requirements most closely related to it. The general prediction is that the closer the congruence between individual characteristics and the requirements of occupational or educational options available, the more likely it is that adjustment and success will result (Brown 1984, p. 12).

It has been argued that vocational psychology, from its beginnings at the end of the nineteenth century until about 1950 was a psychology of occupations, not of careers (Super, 1974). The occupation was the subject and the persons in it were the sources of data on the occupation. Therefore, from a trait and factor, actuarial, or matching frame of reference, predictions can be made using individual traits as predictors and the degree to which these traits are possessed by successful persons in different occupations as the criteria. The techniques and results of the many studies combining different traits and different occupational requirements (factors) also provide a means of appraising an individual's possibilities. Such concepts underlie the system of occupational analysis and job analyses from which results the Department of Labor's *Dictionary of Occupational Titles* Occupational Aptitude Profile System, the *Occupational Outlook Handbook, the Guide to Occupational Exploration,* and other tools by which to match persons and work opportunities.

The counselor assisting employment-bound youth by using a trait and factor or matching approach will need to be familiar with measures of the youth's "competitiveness" (e.g., aptitude, achievement) as well as the youth's "resemblance" (e. g., interests, psychological typology or other characteristics) to persons in particular occupations as these can be related to the characteristics or requirements of alternatives available or under consideration. The counselor will need to help youth consider the "odds" or probabilities of getting into and being successful in various options available. The counselor will need to help the employment-bound youth to organize or classify information about himself or herself and about available options using the various directories or descriptions of jobs that can be obtained from governmental, commercial, or local sources. This information can be helpful to facilitate the "reality testing" and exploration of self and occupational characteristics by employment-bound youth as well as for purposes of career planning and job choice.

Given the characteristics of many employment-bound youth, as identified in Chapter One, as persons who are essentially specialty or technically oriented, not particularly interested in the humanities, classics, or more abstract ideas, not particularly interested in the humanities, classics, or more abstract learning, and from families of lower socioeconomic background than many college-bound students, where information about their opportunities is more limited and role models less abundant, trait and factor approaches offer ways to make information concrete. Trait and factor approaches help to provide classification systems of information about the self and about opportunities that can broaden an employment-bound youth's language of possibilities while also providing specific methods of exploration and analysis. Such approaches can help to neutralize or off-set the lack of information which many employment-bound youth experience in neighborhoods or families in which such information is not readily available and the access to or visibility of opportunities seen as likely outcomes to be pursued by a particular youth are limited. In many such circumstances, persons without knowledge about how to translate information about opportunity into realities for themselves tend to take on an external locus of control, attributing what happens to them as in the hands of others or as a function of "fate." Possessing information, knowing how to gain access to other information and resources, knowing what information is relevant to oneself, and how to plan on the bases of self-knowledge about skills, and preferences, is much more likely to lead to an internal locus of control, to a sense of power to affect and shape one's personal future.

Client-Centered Approaches to Career Counseling

It is probably fair to contend that most of the major approaches to career counseling other than trait and factor either emphasize counseling process variables or specific types of content. These perspectives can frequently be blended with or extend the notions of trait and factor approaches although in some cases observers would argue that they are sufficiently disparate to be considered as competing approaches to career counseling. One such approach is that which has been described as "Client-Centered" or "Rogerian."

This approach, which is essentially the counseling paradigm of Carl Rogers, (e.g., Rogers, 1961), argues that if a client becomes well-adjusted psychologically, then he or she will be able to solve whatever career problems are encountered without specifically attending to them in career counseling. This approach to counseling primarily emphasizes the quality of the relationship between the counselor (as defined by creating such conditions as unconditional positive regard, empathy, genuineness, congruence, understanding, acceptance) and the counselee as the major variable in freeing the latter to become actualized, able to make choices, gain in self-understanding, and so on. Little importance and, indeed, some negative connotations are attached to testing or the use of information during counseling except as these are clearly desired by the client. If occupational information is used, it must follow certain client-centered principles. Among them are 1) occupational information is introduced into the counseling process when there is a recognized need for it on the part of the counselee; 2) occupational information is not used to manipulate or influence the counselee; 3) the most objective way to provide occupational information, and a way which maximizes counselee initiative and responsibility, is to encourage the counselee to obtain the information from original sources, that is, publications, employers, and people engaged in occupations; 4) the counselee's attitudes and feelings about occupations and jobs must be allowed expression and be dealt with therapeutically.

One can also argue that the conditions defined as client-centered—which emphasize the respect of the counselor for the counselee, the need for both counselor and counselee to collaborate in identifying and dealing with the process and content of counseling—are necessary in any therapeutic alliance regardless of the specific counseling approach used. The client-centered elements described above create a relationship that is safe and facilitative of the employment-bound youth to explore, to try-on and try-out different possibilities, to consider decisions without fear of ridicule or judgment. It is a relationship which emphasizes the counselee's goals, not the counselor's.

Unlike a trait and factor approach which emphasizes the importance of information external to the individual as powerful and important (e.g., job information, the relationship of test scores to normative or reference groups of other persons who the youth may or may not resemble), the client-centered approach to career counseling is much more focused on internal perspectives. As a derivation of self, individual or phenomenological psychology, a client-centered approach would suggest that what is of fundamental importance is how the individual perceives himself or herself and his or her environment. Collaborating with the employment-bound youth to examine these perspectives, to reduce feelings of threat or defensiveness, to free the individual to be active in pursuit of his/her own self-actualization or excellence, would be seen in this approach as the ingredients that would likely lead the individual to seek relevant information and alternative possibilities on his or her terms not as imposed or coerced.

From a technique perspective, a client-centered approach to the career counseling of employment-bound youth would emphasize listening and clarifying. In this context of understanding, the counselor listens to the employment-bound youth's feelings, values, perceptions, ambitions, dilemmas, distress, and disillusionment non-selectively; that is, all cues or information provided by the employment-bound youth are attended to, reflected, clarified. The counselor in such a circumstance is sensitive to what is the employment-bound youth's world and how he or she wishes to change it rather than to simply impose on the youth what that world should be.

To engage an employment-bound youth within such a paradigm, the counselor must help the youth piece together information about content *and* feeling provided by the counselee in order to help the counselee develop both insight into their meaning and to integrate them into a plan of action. Again, the counselor will likely restate and reflect feelings and paraphrase what is discussed to attempt to insure that accurate understanding is achieved.

To bridge generations, gender, racial or educational differences between the employment-bound youth and the counselor, the latter using client-centered techniques will attempt to reduce the static in the communications between them. To do so, the counselor responds with acceptance and empathy to examples of circumstance and aspiration, confusion and disappointment, and to values. The counselor needs to facilitate openness in expressions of behavior or problems as well as to hopes and wishes. In this journey toward greater self-understanding and freeing up of new behavioral options, the counselor who fails to perceive feeling and value as well as the content of what is discussed by the employment-bound youth often misses the message. Listening involves not only hearing, but interpreting and evaluating the information heard and then responding. Subtle nuances of value, feeling, and meaning in counselee's statements are exceedingly important to how the counselor shapes his or her behavior. Appraisal, clarification, verification, and summarization are often needed to improve the quality of communications.

These same skills—listening, clarifying, reflecting, interpreting, linking (relating one person's comments to those of others), and summarizing are equally important in working with groups as they are with individuals (Amundson, Borgen, Westwood & Poliard, 1989). In either case, such skills are valuable when counseling individuals who are attempting to come to terms with such diverse issues as occupational choice, career plans, transition to work, or work adjustment. When the counselee's interests, backgrounds, values, and ambitions are amorphous or unknown, and when the counselee's clarity of statement and openness are questionable, use of listening and clarifying skills take a paramount importance. The counselor who will engage an employment-bound youth or group of youths in discussion, attend to what the counselee(s) says, help the person(s) elaborate and clarify meanings, and assist in the weighing of actions and possibilities is more likely to help counselees reach a successful conclusion to the counseling process. Such an approach is in basic opposition to pre-judging, misunderstanding and possibly misdirecting the individual(s) due to racial or sexual bias, directing the counseling process to goals that are unrelated to the counselee's needs at this point in his or her development, or dispensing information that is inaccurate or irrelevant.

Listening and clarifying skills, the elements of a client-centered therapeutic relationship, create an environment in which other counseling techniques can be used to facilitate the counselee's understanding of self or work characteristics and how such information may be employed in decision-making.

Psychodynamic Approaches

Fundamentally an application of psychoanalytic (Freudian and Neo-Freudian) conceptions of human behavior and use of diagnostic categories flowing from such a theoretical base, this approach to career counseling emphasizes counselor interpretations of the roots of counselee decision-making problems. Various diagnostic and testing strategies are used. Occupational information is used which primarily emphasizes the need-gratifying qualities of different forms of work. This approach is also a matching person and job approach but uses personal psychodynamic needs and potential occupational gratifications as the basis for interpretation and discussion rather than the more common conception of interests, aptitudes, and occupational requirements.

It is probably fair to suggest that the professional literature rarely talks about psychodynamic approaches to career counseling. While psychonomic concepts are sprinkled throughout the language of counseling—e.g., defense mechanisms, unconscious, the affects of early childhood experiences shaping adult work life—there is not a major career counseling approach now extant that systematically and explicitly uses psychodynamic concepts as its conceptual structure or the bases of its techniques.

The most prominent American approach to using psychodynamic concepts in career counseling was that developed by Bordin, Nachman, and Segal (1963) in the early 1960s. These researchers were originally focused on identifying the types of gratification that various types of work offer to meet certain individual impulses. For the more commonly described traits such as interests and abilities, Bordin, Nachman, and Segal substituted individual modes of impulse gratification, the status of one's psychosexual development, and levels of anxiety. Specifically, they maintained that connections exist between the early development of coping mechanisms and the later development of more complex behaviors. They believed that adult occupations are sought for their instinctual gratifications (e.g., anal, oral nurturing, exhibiting, flowing-quenching, manipulative) as need for these is developed in early childhood, and that in terms of personality formation, the first six years of life are crucial. More recently, Bordin (1984; 1990) has reformulated the original theory. The newer version speaks much more directly to the factors shaping ego development and ego identity. He also defines seven propositions that represent the major emphases of the reformulated theory and in so doing gives considerable attention to the role of spontaneity, the spirit of play, self-expression and self-realization as these are related to the role of personality in work and career.

The seven propositions advanced by Bordin (1990) include the following:
1. This sense of wholeness, this experience of job, is sought by all persons, preferably in all aspects of life, including work (p. 105).
2. The degree of fusion of work and play is a function of an individual's developmental history regarding compulsion and effort (p. 108).

3. A person's life can be seen as a string of career decisions reflecting the individual's groping for an ideal fit between self and work (p. 109).
4. The most useful system of mapping occupations for intrinsic motives will be one that captures life-style or character styles and stimulates or is receptive to developmental conceptions (p. 115).
5. The roots of the personal aspects of career development are to be found throughout the early development of the individual, sometimes in the earliest years (p. 116).
6. Each individual seeks to build a personal identity that incorporates aspects of father and mother, yet retain elements unique to oneself (p. 116).
7. One source of perplexity and paralysis at career decision points will be found in doubts and dissatisfactions with current resolutions of self (p. 117).

These propositions are descriptive of the factors that influence career behavior and the choices made rather than of career counseling techniques. Nevertheless several technique observations can be extrapolated from this approach to career counseling. One is that the original conception of this theory was much more a matching approach, attempting to connect the possibilities in occupations that allowed the matching of individual gratifications with occupational possibilities to meet these needs, than the current developmental approach to ego identity. Perhaps because the gratifications possible in the vast array of occupations were never fully mapped, this technique of matching has not been possible nor will it ever likely be. On the other hand, the emphases on development of individual identity and the early shaping influences of experiences in the family weave in and out of many conceptual models of career counseling that do not profess to be psychodynamic in origin.

From a career counseling standpoint, it seems appropriate to acknowledge that the kinds of content that counselors often would want to discuss with counselees is their motivation to work, who influenced them, what goals or expectations their parents hold for their work life or career and how they, the counselee, agreed or disagreed with their parents about work, about appropriate jobs, and further education-related matters. In pursuing such a line of discussion, counselors are quite likely to affirm that the counselee's interests, knowledge of job or further education, and willingness to consider some occupations and not others are directly linked to the values or stereotypes held by parents. Further, in dealing with work adjustment problems of employment-bound youth or indeed adults, it is not unlikely to find that at least some of the problems involved have to do with a replaying of the family drama (Chusid & Cochran, 1989). Youths who come from homes in which they had difficult and unresolved relationships with their father or mother may transfer such difficulties to their relationships with their supervisors and these authority or power relationships also become problematic and often the source of work adjustment or even dismissal. The research of Kinnier, Brigman, and Noble (1990) has indicated that family dynamics and the process of career development are not simply reflected in issues of work adjustment but also in career decisions made. Their research has indicated that family enmeshment, where families are undifferentiated from or overly dependent on each other, was found to be related to difficulty in making decisions about their careers and to career indecision. Other research has shown that parents of different socioeconomic status levels not only differ in their ability to provide resources, information, and models of occupations and education but they tend to differ in the socialization patterns to which their children are exposed. (Friesen, 1986; Schulenberg, Vondracek & Crouter, 1984). For example, Kohn's (1977) research has shown that middle-class parents tend to value self-direction in their children and lower SES parents tend to value conformity.

While these phenomena deserve further elaboration, they do suggest the sources of and the evaluation of many types of decision-making and behavioral issues that come before counselors in their interactions with employment-bound youth. Frequently, these issues emanate from the influences of family dynamics in the socialization patterns of the counselee. As such, they carry with them psychodynamic implications that often pervade career counseling, even if not so identified.

Developmental Career Counseling

This approach has been primarily stimulated by the extended research and theoretical contributions of Super (e.g, 1957; 1990), although others have been influential in shaping the approach as well (e.g., Crites, 1981; Gottfredson, 1981; Ginzberg, Ginsburg, Axelrad, & Herma, 1951). In an overly simplified way, a developmental approach to career counseling suggests that as individuals grow or mature they confront and cope with developmental tasks or, in contrast, are continuously bothered by unresolved developmental tasks. Diagnosis, or more precisely appraisal, is conceived in terms of understanding the patterns of behavior the counselee has displayed in the past and examining the meaning they may have for future behavior. Super has provided a number of models that portray how one might conceive of the developmental tasks that affect employment-bound youth. These would essentially occur in the first two life stages of his five stage model. The total model includes: Growth, Exploration, Establishment, Maintenance, and Decline, life stages also known as maxi-cycles.

In the *Growth Stage*, which essentially occurs from birth to approximately age 14, the young person's self-concept begins to develop through identification with key figures in the family and in the school. Needs and fantasy job possibilities are dominant early in this stage with interests and capacities becoming more important in the later years of this stage as increasing social participation and reality testing occur. The major tasks of the Growth Stage are to (1) develop a picture of the kind of person one is; (2) develop an orientation to the world of work; and (3) develop an understanding of the meaning of work.

In the *Exploration Stage,* which encompasses the period from approximately 14 to 24 years, the individual is likely to engage in considerable self-examination, role try-out, and occupational exploration in school, in leisure activities, and in part-time work. The sub-stages of the Exploration Stage include tentative, transition, and trial-little commitment. The respective tasks for each of the three sub-stages include crystallizing a vocational preference, specifying a vocational preference, and implementing a vocational preference. Thus, as the individual moves through the Tentative sub-stage, needs, interests, capacities, values, and opportunities are each considered, choices are tentatively made and tried out in fantasy and in discussions with significant others in the family and peer group and tested in experiences in school, courses, part-time work, etc. As a result, possible appropriate fields and levels of work are identified. In the second sub-stage, Transition, reality considerations (for example, the values society applies to certain kinds of work, one's capacity to do certain kinds of work or enjoyment of it) are weighed as the person enters the labor market or professional training and, in particular, as one attempts to implement one's self-concept. In this sub-stage, the earlier generalized choice is converted to a more specific choice. In the third sub-stage, Trial-little commitment, a seemingly appropriate full-time first job is located and tried out as a potential type of life work. At this point, however, commitment to this job or any other is likely still to be provisional and if the job is not appropriate for some reason, it is likely that the person will reinstitute the processes of crystallizing, specifying, and implementing a preference. Throughout these sub-stages of the Exploration Stage, the tasks, in summary, are to implement a vocational preference, to develop a realistic self concept, and to learn more about more opportunities.

Such a process is much more simply described than lived. The actual developmental process is comprised of a large number of factors, internal as well as external to the individual, that influence the choices made. These factors continue to narrow the array of options the individual considers as he or she focuses on self and on situations. Super (1990) describes "a career as the life course of a person encountering a series of developmental tasks and attempting to handle them in such a way as to become the kind of person he or she wants to become. With a changing self and changing situations, the matching process is never really completed" (pp. 225-226). To describe the status of one's development through the various tasks comprising career development, Super has typically used the term career maturity, for adolescents and young adults, and, more recently, career adaptability for adults. Such notions give prominence to the individual's mastery of increasingly complex tasks at different stages of career development. Super (1990) has defined career maturity as the "individual's readiness to cope with developmental tasks with which he or she is confronted because of his or her biological development and because of society's expectations of people who have reached that stage of development. This readiness is both affective and cognitive" (p. 213).

In his factor analyses and other research studies designed to clarify the nature of career maturity or career adaptability, Super has suggested in various contexts that involved are such affectively laden variables as career planning, or planfulness, and career exploration, or curiosity. Also involved are such cognitive characteristics as knowledge of the principles of career decision making and ability to apply them to actual choices; knowledge of the nature of careers, occupations, and the world of work; and the knowledge of the field of work in which one's occupational preference falls. In speculating about career maturity in adolescence or career adaptability in adulthood, Super (1977, 1985) has postulated that the same five factors are important in mid career as are important in adolescence: planfulness or time perspective, exploration, information, decision making, and reality orientation.

The wide-ranging view of Super suggests that in a developmental approach to career counseling, many factors are involved. Some employment-bound students may not have progressed systematically through the stages or sub-stages of growth and exploration. They may not have formulated a clear picture of whom they now are or want to be; they may not have learned the elements of planfulness, or of what information is relevant to their career or to planning; they may not have developed an understanding of the relationship between current behavior and future behavior, between school subjects and adult work requirements, between planning now and outcomes later; they may not have learned the technical aspects of decision-making or the importance of choice in shaping a career or accepting the consequences of decision or of being willing to choose independently, of what others want you to do or become; they may not have developed a language of self or occupations or of interests, values, abilities; they may not have reality tested what they anticipate doing; they may be plagued by indecision or indecisiveness.

In such an approach the emphasis is upon counseling the client for planfulness for readiness for choice. The process involves reality-testing information which the person has assembled about himself or herself and about various options under consideration. It is assumed that people are both rational and emotional and that career counseling must provide an opportunity for both to be explored and considered.

Questions such as the following represent much of the direction of this approach to counseling: What sort of person do I think I am? How do I feel about myself as I think I am? What sort of person would I like to be? What are my values and needs? What are my aptitudes and interests? What outlets are there for me with my needs, values, interests, and aptitudes? Testing, problem appraisal, interviewing, and occupational information are each used interactively to facilitate the outcomes of this approach.

One of the corollaries of Super's theoretical perspectives on career development is his attempt to operationalize his assumptions and propositions by creating assessment instruments that measure them. They include such instruments as the Career Development Inventory. In order to integrate this appraisal information effectively he developed a developmental model of Emergent Career Decision-making that describes the processes that occur when one is about to take on a new role, give up a role, or make significant changes in an existing role (Super, 1980, p. 291). The model that is depicted in Figure 1 (page 180) suggests its applicability whether the cycling and recycling identified occurs over a period of days, weeks, or years.

Super has also formulated a Developmental Assessment Model which combines the type of information available from the instruments mentioned above with the steps of emphases in counseling which might address topics of relevance. Figure 2 (page 181) depicts this model.

Behavioral Career Counseling

A final approach to career counseling will be discussed under the general rubric of a behavioral or learning model. Since its early description by Crites (1981), there have emerged several variations which have emphasized not just a behavioral approach but a cognitive behavioral approach as well.

Conceptually based in learning theory, behavioral career counseling uses such techniques as counselor reinforcement of desired client responses, social modeling and vicarious learning, desensitization, and discrimination learning to assist counselees achieve certain specified goals. Diagnosis in this approach is less related to the use of standard measurements and more concerned with analyzing the characteristics of the individual's environmental interactions to identify behavioral cues and reinforcers. In addressing themselves to vocational problems, behavioral career counselors are likely to analyze quite specifically the behavioral deficits of the client and to create conditions or experiences which will provide appropriate learned responses or skills. This specific analysis of client needs vis-à-vis some set of goals extends to the use of occupational information and its potential for helping the client learn specific concepts or experience certain material important to goal attainment.

Figure 1
A Developmental Model of Emergent Career Decision-Making

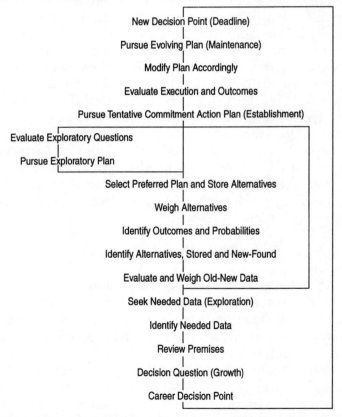

New Decision Point (Deadline)

Pursue Evolving Plan (Maintenance)

Modify Plan Accordingly

Evaluate Execution and Outcomes

Pursue Tentative Commitment Action Plan (Establishment)

Evaluate Exploratory Questions

Pursue Exploratory Plan

Select Preferred Plan and Store Alternatives

Weigh Alternatives

Identify Outcomes and Probabilities

Identify Alternatives, Stored and New-Found

Evaluate and Weigh Old-New Data

Seek Needed Data (Exploration)

Identify Needed Data

Review Premises

Decision Question (Growth)

Career Decision Point

SOURCE: Life-Span, Life-Space Approach to Career Development by Donald E. Super, *Journal of Vocational Behavior*, pp.282-298, Figure 4, p. 295. Orlando, FL: Academic Press, 1980.

Figure 2

A Developmental Assessment Model for Career Counseling

Step I. Preview
    A. Assembly of data
    B. Intake Interview
    C. Preliminary assessment
Step II. Depth-view: further testing?
    A. Work salience
       1. Relative importance of
         diverse roles
         a. Study
         b. Work and career
         c. Home and family
         d. Community service
         e. Leisure activities
       2. Participation in each
         role
       3. Commitment to each
         role
       4. Knowledge of each role
    B. Values sought in each role
    C. Career maturity
       1. Planfulness
       2. Exploratory attitudes
       3. Decision-making skills
       4. Information
         a. World of work
         b. Preferred occuptional
         group
         c. Other life-career roles
       5. Realism
    D. Level of abilities and
       potential functioning
    E. Field of interest and
       probable activity
Step III. Assessment of all data
    A. Review of all data
    B. Work salience
    C. Values

    D. Career maturity
       1. Individual and
         occupations
       2. Individual and
         nonoccupational roles
    E. Planning communication with
       counselee, family, etc.
Step IV. Counseling
    A. Joint review and discussion
    B. Revision or acceptance of
       assessment
    C. Assimilation by the counselee
       1. Understanding the
         present
       2. Understanding the
         meaning
         of work and other life-
         roles
       3. Exploration for maturing?
       4. Exploration in breadth for
         crystallization?
       5. Exploration in depth for
         specification?
       6. Choice of preparation,
         training, or jobs?
       7. Searches for jobs and
         other outlets?
       8. Exploring self and
         situation for self-
         realization?
    D. Discussion of action implica-
       tions and planning
       1. Planning
       2. Monitored execution
       3. Follow-up for support
         and evaluation

SOURCE: The Values Scale: Theory, Application, and Research Manual, Research Edition by D.D. Nevil and D.E. Super, Palo Alto, CA: Consulting Psychologist Press, 1986.

Behavioral counseling tries, among its purposes, to amplify the counselee problems being addressed and to break them into specific goals for learning or relearning. As indicated above, primary techniques include social modeling and vicarious learning. Each of these techniques represent methods of helping a counselee understand the behaviors or skills to be learned by viewing another person performing them and by experiencing vicariously the positive consequences that accrue to being able to produce such behaviors or skills in appropriate settings. Within such contexts behavioral counseling has undergirded such techniques as psychoeducational models. Psychoeducational models are comprehensive approaches to producing behavioral change by using various educational procedures combined with a range of psychological techniques. The former would include planned or structured curricula, didactic teaching, and specific content, exercises, and homework. The latter include such psychological techniques as simulations, role playing, behavioral rehearsal, modeling, feedback, and reinforcement.

Psychoeducational models differ in their emphases, but they typically include the teaching of target skills, assignment of homework and practice, the use of audiovisual materials, simulations or similar approaches. In a typical psychoeducational training session, employment-bound youth who need to acquire specific skills that are critical to job search or to work adjustment are shown examples of competent skill behavior, given opportunity to rehearse what they have seen, provided with systematic feedback regarding the adequacy of their performance, and encouraged in a variety of ways to rehearse and practice these skills in their daily life. Skill emphases which use psychoeducational models as their principal structure are as diverse as career education, deliberate psychological education, stress management, decision-making training, anxiety or anger management, job-search strategies, parent effectiveness training, assertive training, social skills development, communications skills (Herr, 1989).

In some instances, psychoeducational models are used to help students or employment-bound youth acquire skills they will need in the future as a preventive approach to learning behavior before they are needed; in other situations, psychoeducational models are used as remediation or treatment of problems that already exist. For example, an employment-bound youth may be referred to a counselor because of apparent inability to get along with peers or a supervisor. Using behavioral counseling techniques, the counselor and the employment-bound youth may decide that the problem for this particular youth is anger management. In this case, the employment-bound youth may not have developed a behavioral repertoire from which to select behaviors that are likely to be appropriate, socially acceptable, or interpersonally sound as they are applied in different settings and situations. Thus, if this individual's existing behavioral repertoire is limited to physical violence or verbal aggression whenever he or she experiences frustration on the job, in working with others, or in receiving supervision, he or she is essentially going to be enmeshed in an endless cycle of school, job, or social maladjustment. Therefore, to produce a different behavioral response under selected conditions, the counselor using behavioral techniques may recommend a psychoeducational approach such as coping skills training. In such an approach, a first counseling goal may be to help this particular employment-bound youth identify and better understand what cues or situations precipitate his or her anger, a second goal may be to help this counselee learn how to interrupt the flow of cognitions and automatic responses in order to exert more self-control in anger-producing situations, and a third goal may be to help counselees learn effective communication patterns, positive assertiveness, or other skills that allow them to express anger in a constructive manner.

Many of the behavioral counseling techniques and psychoeducational approaches previously discussed have been effectively captured in what Olson, McWhirter, and Horan (1989) describe as "A Decision-making Model Applied to Career Counseling." Table 3 (page 184) depicts the general goals of the process, the relevant assessment questions, and the intervention strategies used.

Cognitive Behavioral Counseling

Inherent in the decision-making model described in Table 3 are some of the newer concepts linked to behavioral counseling, but identified primarily under the rubric of cognitive

Table 3.

Assessment Questions and Intervention Strategies in Decision-Making Counseling

Summary Model	Assessment Questions	Intervention Strategies (when the answer is no)
Conceptualization	(1) Is affective arousal low?	Listening(extinction) relaxation training desensitization and variations cognitive restructuring
	(2) Can client correctly define problem as one of choice?	paraphrasing probe (cuing and reinforcing) socratic dialoguing
	(3) Can client explain the decision-making paradigm?	cognitive restructuring emotional role playing cognitive modeling verbal reinforcement
Enlargement of repetoire	(4) Has client avoided an impulsive response?	Thought-stopping-substitution covert sensitization outcome psychodrama emotional role playing cognitive restructuring skill-building interventions
	(5) Has client identified all alternatives known to counselor?	creative instructional set originality training brainstorming metaphorical thinking modeling
	(6) Will client search for additional alternatives?	Verbal cuing and reinforcement modeling simulation strategies
Identification of discriminative stimuli	(7) Has client identified all discriminative stimuli known to counselor?	outcome psychodrama modeling
	(8) Will client search for additional discriminative stimuli?	Verbal cuing and reinforcement modeling simulation strategies
Response selection	(9) Does client support adaptive utilities and probability estimates?	Cognitive restructuring emotional role playing outcome psychodrama induced cognitive dissonance awareness of rationalizations peer modeling
	(10) Can client explain a response-selection paradigm?	modeling variations
	11) Are client's skills sufficient to implement the selected response?	Comprehensive behavioral programing stress inoculation emotional inoculation

From *A Decision-Making Model Applied to Career Counseling* by C. Olsen, E. McWhirter and J.J.Moran, Journal of Career Development, 1989, Vol. 16, pp. 107-117.

behavioral therapy. Stemming from a variety of perspectives including self-efficacy theory, attribution theories and other cognitive theories, cognitive behavioral therapy is concerned with the internal monologue, the self-talk, by which people construct their reality. Such a cognitive approach assumes that a primary problem for the counselee lies with his or her faulty assumptions, irrational beliefs, or misconceptions about characteristics of the self, other persons' intentions, opportunities available, and life events. Since it is assumed that cognitive structures trigger or sustain behavior, cognitive behavioral approaches are concerned with helping the individual to modify the inaccurate or maladaptive cognitive set about self, others, and life events by which he or she constructs reality and acts accordingly. The therapeutic process includes different methods and goals but fundamental to cognitive behavioral counseling is helping counselees understand the cognitive bases of their needs, anxieties, or depression and the direct linkage between their thoughts and their feelings: how they acquire and accept automatic thoughts and cognitive distortions about themselves, others, and life events that often lead to negative feelings and actions. Among the major techniques involved in cognitive behavioral approaches are cognitive restructuring or reframing. These are attempts to help a counselee identify maladaptive thinking and reconstruct it. Once counselees identify and understand distortions in their thinking, they are often provided homework as well as techniques by which to interrupt and rebut negative cognitions. More specifically, some counselees may need assistance to build self-esteem and eliminate feelings of worthlessness, or they may need help with tendencies to overgeneralize a problem or cast it into very rigid all-or-nothing dichotomies. Sometimes counselees are assigned the reading of selected books that describe irrational beliefs and assist the individual to engage in self-monitoring of negative automatic thoughts. With specific application of these concepts to career counseling, several theorists have offered helpful perspectives.

Krumboltz (1983), for example, discussed the private rules of decision-making which individuals use and how these can be affected by cognitive distortions. He suggests that because of faulty self-observation generalizations or inaccurate interpretations of environmental conditions, a number of career problems may arise. Examples he suggests include:

1. Persons may fail to recognize that a remediable problem exists.
2. Persons may fail to exert the effort needed to make a decision or solve a problem.
3. Persons may eliminate a potentially satisfying alternative for inappropriate reasons.
4. Persons may choose poor alternatives for inappropriate reasons.
5. Persons may suffer anguish and anxiety over perceived inability to achieve goals.

Krumboltz recommends a range of interventions that address such career counseling problems including several that have already been discussed, for example, cognitive restructuring, use of psychometric instruments, positive reinforcement and role models. He also suggests the use of imagery, structured interviews, use of films illustrating problem-solving techniques, teaching task approach skills or belief-testing, use of computerized career guidance systems, and the use of the Career Beliefs Inventory to identify presuppositions that may block people from achieving their career goals.

Like Krumboltz, Nevo (1987) has also been concerned about the faulty thinking and distracted beliefs that frequently are implicated in the problems that people bring to career counseling. They include:

1. There is only one vocation in the world that is right for me.
2. Until I find my perfect vocational choice, I will not be satisfied.
3. Someone else can discover the vocation suitable for me.
4. Intelligence test will tell me how much I am worth.
5. I must be an expert or very successful in the field of my work.
6. I can do anything if I try hard, or, I can't do anything that doesn't fit my talents.
7. My vocation should satisfy the important people in my life.
8. Entering a vocation will solve all of my problems.
9. I must sense intuitively that the vocation is right for me.
10. Choosing a vocation is a one-time act.

Many employment-bound youth experience irrational beliefs such as those cited. Unless these are confronted and restructured using behavioral or cognitive behavioral techniques suggested above, such beliefs are likely to constrain the options considered or the behavioral maturity acquired by such youth.

Perspectives on Decision-Making

Most counselors who engage in career counseling can add to the list of Nevo or Krumboltz or others. Employment-bound youth are not immune to irrational beliefs or cognitive distortions about their circumstances, their worth, or their opportunities. Indeed, because of the potential pejorative connotations of terms like "the forgotten half" or the "non-college bound," they may internalize and include in their self talk such negative attributions as, "I am a loser. There is no real future for me since I am not going to college," or distorted perspectives on self-efficacy, "I am not bright enough to do advanced mathematics so I better stay out of electronics or computer assisted drafting." As a result of such negative thinking, many young people settle for far less than they could accomplish and/or carry with them feelings that they are less worthy or valued than other youth that distort the decision making process in which they engage. Decision-making is really the tip of the iceberg, the part that can be observed, of the individual's internal dialogue about his or her philosophy of life, feelings about self-worth or self-efficacy, knowledge of opportunities and how or if they might be pursued.

A considerable body of research has accumulated about individual decision-making strategy or its lack and how different groups of persons can be classified with regard to their decisiveness, indecision, or indecisiveness. In one such study of the status of high school student decision status, Fuqua, Blum, and Hartman (1988) used techniques of cluster analysis to distinguish the status of decision-making and its effects among four identified groups of students. According to these researchers:

Group One (42%) seems to represent a career decided group, relatively free of excessive anxiety and relatively effective in terms of attribution and identity formation. Group Two (22%) appears to possess at least moderate career indecision, increased anxiety, less identity formation, and a fairly internalized locus of control. Groups Three (28%) and Four (8%) seem to suffer fairly serious career indecision, are more external in their attribution and show poorer identity formation. Group Three has moderate levels of anxiety with Group Four alone showing excessive anxiety relative to their peers (pp. 369-370).

While it is not possible in their research to know which of the students in these four groups are represented by employment-bound youth, it is likely that the latter appear in all four and that counselors need to be attentive to how any given employment-bound student may experience decision-making, anxiety, lack of control, and attributions.

Jepsen has conducted research on adolescent decision-making styles over nearly twenty years. In his early research (1974), he suggested that individual differences in decision making can be classified in terms of strategy types used by adolescents. He found twelve types of adolescent decision-makers based on how they organized data about themselves and career options. These clusters essentially reflect differences in planning activity. Three of the 12 types represent examples of adolescent differences in planning. They include:

Strategy-type 3. Adolescents in this group, sought little career information; considered only a few occupational alternatives and few reasons for considering either occupations or post high school actions.

Strategy-type 6. These adolescents named many alternative occupations and post-high school activities and reasons for each. Many possible outcomes were anticipated and many intrinsic and self-appraised reasons were given. Planning activity was very high.

Strategy-type 9. Adolescents in this group took very few actions on plans and they sought very little information. Vaguely stated and low-level occupational alternatives were reported, and a single class of reasons was given for considering them.

In more recent research, Jepsen (1989) discussed the ability of adolescents to cope successfully during important career decision points. He suggested that such ability includes mastering decision-making *processes* as well as finding satisfying *content*. In particular, he has stated that decision-making in adolescents "involves learning effective ways to decide in addition to finding actions that lead to pleasing outcomes. Failure to master the challenges of career decision points during this age may leave the person with dampened hopes, self-doubts, regrets, and confusion and his/her identity" (p. 78). Jepsen, in these perspectives, has also discussed the factors in the social context that prompt the adolescent to deal with a career decision point and the internal mechanisms by which such messages are received and processed. He suggests that the adolescents' social environment includes several reference groups which are the principal agents of socialization and the purveyors of messages about expectations for action: the family of origin, classes and activities in school, peer friend groups, the extended family, the coworker group on a job, a religious group, or the group of families constituting a neighborhood. These groups send intermittent powerful messages, not delivered to all adolescents in the same way or with the same power, but with a general expectation for the adolescent to take actions necessary to enter productive work roles. Adolescents, then, respond with both overt responses (statements or actions) and covert responses (private thoughts and feelings) that may or may not be consistent with each other. This inconsistency may be in other areas discussed in this chapter, e.g., self-efficacy conflicts, incomplete developmental tasks, feelings of doubt about one's work, lack of confidence, feelings of vulnerability, lack of information that shapes the adolescent's internal or covert self-talk.

Jepsen's model connects adolescent decision-making to the social environment that shapes the content and strategies likely to be employed. While, again, it is important to note that the model is not expressly focused on employment-bound youth, its attention on the covert and overt messages adolescents receive is certainly relevant to the factors influencing the decision-making they employ and to counselor actions related to them. Jepsen suggests such counselor activities with adolescents.

"First, counselors can help adolescents to distinguish and clarify the powerful messages communicated by the particular groups in their social environment"...

*"Second, counselors can help adolescents to focus on their
covert responses and thus reveal what they are telling
themselves"...*

*"Third, counselors can help adolescents to appraise the
content of powerful messages"...*

*"Fourth, counselors can help adolescents to inventory
their resources for meeting the demands of the decision"*
(pp. 77-79).

While other studies of adolescent decision-making could
be described here, the important issues have already been
described. Choice is clearly a multidimensional concept that
varies widely in the certainty, risk, self-knowledge and knowledge of alternatives, the degree to which relevant information
is known or used, the choice factors on which individuals try
to maximize or optimize their gain and minimize their loss.
The factors of importance in a decision are likely to be differently weighted by individuals. But individuals can be taught
how to make career-related decisions in counseling and in
decision-making programs. It is likely that once taught, a
decision-making strategy and skills in decision-making have
transfer value.

Decision-making is a complex interaction of internal and
external variables. Personal attributes and characteristics,
value structures, opportunity factors, and cultural forces are
important aspects of decision-making, although the combination, weighting, and content of these vary from individual
to individual.

In a sense, different models of career counseling emphasize different elements of decision making and its facilitation.
Each such approach either assumes motivation for choice or
tries to establish readiness on the part of the person doing
the choosing to take responsibility for career decision-making. However defined in a specific career counseling model,
the end result is likely to be a particular form of problem-
solving and to be seen in terms of a series of stages defined
essentially as follows:

1. Defining the problem.
2. Generating alternatives.
3. Gathering information.
4. Developing information-seeking skills.
5. Providing useful sources of information.

6. Processing information.
7. Making plans and selecting goals.
8. Implementing and evaluating plan (Bergland, 1974, p. 352).

As suggested by Herr and Cramer (1992), all of the "decision-making models for use in individual counseling are action-oriented. By whatever terminology they are called, they address choice in a staged, systematic manner. They are intended to assist individuals in filtering objective data through subjective systems of risk taking, emotionality, utility determination, and so on... no single model has been determined to be superior to any other; yet each implies its own unique success. They suggest to counselors that virtually any model of assisting an individual in career decision making—extant or yet to be invented—can be successful if based on sound theoretical and research findings, and if operationalized in logical, consistent ways" (pp. 609-610).

What has been little discussed here but implicit at several points is that the career counseling models and the perspectives on decision-making are generally as applicable to group career counseling as to individual career counseling.

Of perhaps the most importance to these deliberations about career counseling techniques to be used with employment-bound youth is the particular reality in which employment-bound youth exist in the United States. Many of them enter vocational education at ninth or tenth grades; others enter part-time work at age 16 or so. Others of them because of the overt messages to which they are exposed in their families, or schools, or mass media decide early in their adolescence what they are going to do or what they are not going to do. Indeed, many employment-bound youth are figuratively swept up (Herr, Weitz, Good, & McCloskey, 1981) into vocational curricula or work without benefit of the extended exploratory processes to which other adolescents are exposed and have the opportunity to contemplate. As tech-prep and systematic approaches to work-based learning in U. S. schools are more firmly embedded, the extended opportunities for exploration for employment-bound youth may be increased. A number of studies and reports have indicated such career development of employment-bound youth, particularly for disadvantaged youth, does not now occur with sufficient quality and coverage as is needed in the nation (Employment and Training Administration, U. S. Department of Labor, 1993; Sarkes-Wircenski & Wircenski, 1994).

Other Career Interventions.

Although this chapter has talked primarily about approaches to the one-on-one approach to individual career counseling, while extremely important for a variety of purposes, such approaches to career counseling are almost always embedded in a program of counselor activities which goes beyond the one-to-one interaction of counselor and employment-bound youth. For example, comprehensive career guidance programs are likely to include such elements as assessment, individual counseling, group guidance or workshops on such topics as anger management, communication skills, job search skills, and decision-making; placement of students into part- or full-time employment and follow through and support while students are getting settled in a new job or adjusting to it. The development or planned experiences in didactic or simulated modes to teach clients certain information about themselves or occupational alternatives or skills in decision making or values clarification has become reasonably commonplace. Consultation about student development or employability by counselors with teachers, employers, and others, the use of group processes, the use of simulation and gaming, as well as computer-based systems of information retrieval and analysis, each represent other current emphases in the provision of program aspects which complement career counseling.

Although Chapter Six will address program planning and components more fully, it is useful to conclude this chapter by identifying techniques/components frequently used in a comprehensive program of career guidance. In this context, career guidance is seen as a systematic program of counselor-coordinated information and experiences (Herr & Cramer, 1992), the ultimate goal of which is to provide individuals with the knowledge and skills needed to develop realistic career plans and make the appropriate decisions to carry out these plans (Employment and Training Administration, U. S. Department of Labor (1993).

The Employment and Training Administration of the U. S. Department of Labor (1993) suggests that there are a myriad of processes that can be combined in various ways to serve the career guidance needs of persons engaged in career planning and decision-making. They include the following:

- **Outreach** alerts students to services.
- **Classroom instruction** provides an integrated set of planned and sequential curricular activities.
- **Counseling** helps students explore personal issues and apply information and skills to personal plans and may be offered individually or in small groups.
- **Self-assessment** provides students with a clearer understanding of their values, skills, abilities, interests, achievements, aspirations, and needs.
- **Career information**, easily accessible, current, relevant, and unbiased, provides a solid framework on which to base decisions.
- **Exploration activities** are experiences designed to broaden horizons, test interests and stimulate career planning.
- **Work experience** offers opportunities to test decisions and develop effective work abilities and behaviors.
- **Career planning** activities help youth learn the skills needed to make decisions and understand the future impact of choices.
- **Placement** services help youth make the transition to school, work, or the military.
- **Referrals** to other professional services allow youth to obtain assistance beyond the scope of the program.
- **Follow-up** activities provide opportunities to maintain contact and track progress (pp. 6 and 7).

Within this perspective, however vital career counseling is seen to be, there are other important techniques that need some clarification.

Group Processes of Career Guidance and Counseling.

Group processes will also be valuable adjuncts to individual counseling. Such experiences have various purposes. Several reasons for implementing group approaches have been identified (Herr & Cramer, 1992, pp. 613-614). They are included here in paraphrased form:

1. **Information Dissemination.** Providing and clarifying for students or adults information about personal, occupational, educational alternatives available to them and the ways by which such information can be obtained and processes for personal purposes.
2. **Motivation.** Readiness to consider the importance of personal options, that choice is available, etc.
3. **Teaching.** While much of choice-making and planning is emotional and not really susceptible to a teaching approach, much of career guidance and clarification of personal alternatives rests on a cognitive base and is appropriately treated in this manner.
4. **Practice.** Fundamentally, group processes of counseling are opportunities to test in simulated ways one's own characteristics in relation to different possibilities for action. Through role playing, case studies, selected audio-visual devices, discussion, resource people, an opportunity can be created for employment-bound students to project themselves figuratively into a given situation and analyze how they, personally, would feel in that situation.
5. **Attitude Development.** Although most attitudes are learned within family and peer groups, group processes represent an important tool to discuss and clarify attitudes and values as well as self-understanding.
6. **Counseling.** Groups can be used to provide a secure and supportive environment in which developmental growth and the emotional characteristics of personal and career dilemmas can be assessed and acted upon.
7. **Exploration.** Groups can use the presence and security of several people at similar developmental levels to stimulate exploration or to provide feedback and mutual analysis of exploratory experiences.

Obviously, these seven purposes are not mutually

exclusive but rather represent emphases, sometimes acting together, which group processes of career guidance and counseling can serve.

Amundson, Borgen, Westwood, and Pollard (1989), Canadian psychologists, have written extensively about employment group, their meaning and processes. In so doing, they remind their readers that groups work opens "up a way to offer clients an efficient and secure environment in which to make career and employment decisions, to master the skills required to find and keep a job and even to find a new world of work" (p. 1). These authors describe groups related to helping persons find employment or cope with unemployment in much the same way that psychoeducational models are described in this chapter and in other places in the book. Psychoeducational groups emphasize what employment-bound youth or others dealing with employment issues need to learn or relearn. They are typically structured to focus on exploration, learning job-search skills, and developing the sense of self-confidence necessary to carry out and maintain a prolonged and effective job search.

In this context, Amundson, et al, contend that in employment groups, as in psychoeducational groups, there are typically two major emphases: "acquisition of relevant skills and information, which is the 'education' element, and the development and/or maintenance of a constructive attitude (so often impeded by emotions which must be recognized: anxiety, fear, and depression). The development of this attitude, the 'psycho' part of 'psychoeducative' can greatly facilitate the task at hand" (p. 3).

Finally, for our purposes here, Amundson and his colleagues remind us that the "bases which underlie positive and negative factors can be understood by considering the fundamental human needs which have been identified by Alvin Toffler (1980), namely, the need for community: a sense of belonging, being part of a larger whole (family, friends, and, of course, work); meaning; making a contribution, being valued (and, sometimes, in our day, having money), and structure: a guaranteed schedule for the day, predictability consistency in day-to-day living and the sense of safety which goes with these" (p. 9). These needs for community, meaning, and structure are no less important for employment-bound youth than for any other subpopulation. While employment groups or psychoeducational groups are not the only way for the counselor to assist in meeting such goals or facilitating gratification of such needs, they are nevertheless extremely important elements of the counselor's professional repertoire.

Appraisal

Sometimes considered synonymous with testing, appraisal is a somewhat broader term referring to the analysis of personal characteristics—aptitudes, interests, values, temperaments—as well as the ways they might be modified or strengthened in relation to various options available to the person. Appraisal sometimes deals with an analysis of predictor variables pertinent to some choice or more broadly with an analysis of the viability of goals held by the person. Appraisal data include previous achievement and behavior patterns as well as the more commonly understood use of tests related to educational and job or occupational decisions, e.g., General Aptitude Test Battery, Ohio Vocational Interest Survey, Strong Interest Inventory, the Differential Aptitude Test Battery, the Armed Services Vocational Aptitude Battery, The Bennett Test of Mechanical Comprehension. Increasingly, appraisal involves both the *process of choice* (whether or not a person knows how to make decisions, can collect and evaluate pertinent data, is independent and mature enough to choose) and the *content of choice* (what is to be chosen). The process of choice is likely to include such instruments as the Career Maturity Inventory, the Career Decision Scale, the Career Development Inventory, and the Career Beliefs Inventory.

Information Retrieval

Throughout the career counseling process, accurate and relevant information is the fuel necessary to effective decision making; thus it is a central element of a career guidance program. There are many sources of information to which the counselor will have occasion to turn in individual counseling or in the group processes of career guidance. The source used will depend upon the purpose to be achieved and the readiness or the educational level of the student or adult to be served.

Sources such as the *Occupational Outlook Handbook*, the *Guide to Occupational Exploration*, and the *Dictionary of Occupational Titles* (U. S. Department of Labor) are excellent starting points from which to obtain information about the occupational structure, specific occupations and requirements, or the relationship of vocational education courses to occupational alternatives. Depending upon the needs of the student or adult, however, it may be more useful to turn to the wide variety of commercial or professional print or audio-visual material designed to explore different personal, social, occupational, or educational domains. It is typically necessary to use appraisal or other forms of information first to help the counselee gain a personal frame of reference from which can be evaluated information about the personal, educational, or occupational options available.

Given the wide-range of information available and the need to individualize it as fully as possible, a major trend in support of career counseling is the incorporation of computerized career guidance systems. Depending upon the purpose, such computer systems may aid the counselor and the employment-bound youth in many ways. For example, if the software available is from a State Occupational Information Coordinating Committee (SOICC), it is likely to include the types of occupations and educational opportunities available within a particular state and provide interactive methods to help the user determine which opportunities fit his or her abilities and interests. Commercial computerized career guidance systems are likely to incorporate theoretical concepts and to implement them in decision-making exercises by which the user can retrieve information which is specific to some set of values, reinforce career awareness, and process choices. While the computer does not and cannot replace the counselor's role, it certainly extends the capability to individualize information retrieval and to provide current and timely input to decisions to be made. Although computers focused on the content and processes of career guidance have added to the counselor's repertoire, they also add expectations that counselors will integrate such tools into a program of career relevant activities not simply allow the computer to be an isolated, independent piece of hardware. In addition, they require that the counselor become a planner, an applied behavioral scientist, and a technologist in order to effectively use computers in a meaningful way and to know why he or she is doing so.

Environmental Treatment

Counselors have increasingly been implored to help to change the environments of their employment-bound students to make them more psychologically wholesome and supportive. In that sense, counselors treat not only employment-bound youth or other counselees but also the environmental characteristics affecting them. In some instance, this means that the counselor should be a source of information about the needs of a student or adult to aid the development of an educational program for that person; in other cases, counselors should stimulate the school to create educational experiences which comprehensively respond to the range of human talent rather than only some small sample of it (e.g., abstract verbal ability, numerical reasoning); in still other instances, counselors and vocational educators need to communicate with and assist employers in bringing about realistic employment requirements.

Remediation and Development

These five categories of techniques used in career guidance are used in two ways. First, they are used for remedial purposes when a particular person's career development is somehow blocked, the individual is in conflict, or the person's behavioral repertoire is inadequate to resolve the choice-making or work adjustment dilemma he or she is facing. A remedial approach to career counseling or career guidance takes place after a person already gives evidence of experiencing a problem which he or she cannot resolve or cope with effectively. Second, these techniques are used for developmental purposes. Increasingly, counselor efforts are being focused on helping students and adults acquire self-understanding, exploratory and decision-making skills, knowledge of ways to sort out available educational and occupational alternatives, job application, and employability skills before they are required. In a sense, career counseling and career guidance are conceived of as facilitating the acquisition of survival skills known to be necessary in a complex society in an effort to counter the need for remediation later in the life of employment-bound youth.

Conclusion

While only one of the major methods of facilitating the career planning and work adjustment of employment-bound youth, career counseling is perhaps the process that best epitomizes what counselors are trained to do to personalize the experience of their counselees. As with most therapeutic processes, career counseling can be conceived through different lenses or theoretical models; in this chapter some six major approaches were described which tend to undergird the existing variations in technique which now characterize the field. The oldest approach to helping employment-bound youth or young adults deal with problems of job choice or change is that set of processes described as trait and factor, actuarial, or matching. The newest approach is that of cognitive-behavioral counseling. In fact, however, the different approaches to career counseling are not truly independent, discrete, or appropriate for all needs of employment-bound youth. Rather, it is probably fair to suggest that each of the six approaches have particular contributions for particular types of concerns and therefore can be combined into a counselor's repertoire of responses that allows him or her to be systematically eclectic in providing assistance to employment-bound youth. Table 4 (page 205) illustrates emphases in different career counseling approaches that can guide counselor use of individual approaches or their potential combination in systematic eclecticism.

Systematic eclecticism assumes that specific treatments or counseling approaches are effective for some career problems and not for others, and that persons come to counselors for many different reasons. Rather than assuming that the same approach is useful for all youth or adults, the counselor tailors the counseling response to the unique needs of an individual counselee or to a group of persons sharing similar concerns. In this view, counselors need to understand and be trained in an array of career counseling approaches—trait and factor,

Table 4.

Examples of Potential Contributions of Six Approaches to Career Counseling for Employment-Bound Youth

Approach	Major Contributions in Career Counseling
Trait and Factor	• Matching of individual traits to the requirements of a particular job, occupation or training opportunity. • Helping employment-bound youth to examine the range of jobs for occupations or which their abilities, achievement, aptitudes, interests would qualify them. • Assisting employment-bound youth to understand the elasticity or transportability of their current knowledge or skills across jobs, occupations, industries. • Providing employment-bound youth a classification system of self characteristics and language (e.g., interests, values, aptitudes, achievements, skills) and of jobs, occupations, and careers by which to facilitate identification of possible options to explore and information to secure. • Facilitating individual assessment of the probabilities, the odds, of gaining access to and being successful in different jobs, occupations or educational opportunities.
Client-Centered	• Providing a safe and accepting environment in which to explore career planning and work adjustment issue. • Encouraging employment-bound youth to take control of their lives and to set goals for action that can be rehearsed and tried out in counseling.

• Helping employment-bound youth develop insights into their personal priorities, personal patterns of behavior, and barriers to their achievement of goals.

• Establishing a sense of hope that conditions which brought the counselee to the counselor can change in positive ways.

• Reinforcing that the counselor views the counselee as a person of value who has the ability to identify issues and barriers in his career life and ways to change them.

Psychodynamic

• Providing a connection between past experiences and present behavior that is relevant to career choices or work adjustment.

• Assisting the counselee to understand unresolved conflicts in the family or in other past relationships that may be hindering current interactions with co-workers or supervisors.

• Facilitating the employment-bound youth's understanding of messages from and expectations of others that have been incorporated into the individual's negative view of self, senses of self-efficacy, or feelings about opportunities.

• Helping the individual to examine past educational, employment, or social experiences that may clarify needs or gratifications to be sought from work.

Developmental

• Providing insight for employment-bound youth about developmental tasks that they may need to explore, complete, or anticipate in their career planning process.

• Helping counselees to clarify and integrate the role of work and its importance in comparison with other life roles: family, parenting, leisure, community service, and student.

• Assisting counselees to acquire awareness that work and occupation serve to provide a focus for personality organization for most men and women, although for some persons this focus is peripheral, incidental or even non-existent.

• Facilitating clarification of the counselees' self-concept and ways to implement it in work.

• Assisting counselees to identify and act on their work values, resources, self-concept in fashioning possible career patterns they wish to pursue.

• Facilitating counselee understanding of the process of change across time and the ways to anticipate and cope with such change.

• Helping counselees understand that success in coping with the demands of the environment and of the person at any given life/career stage depends on the readiness of the individual to cope with these demands. In particular, this means helping the individual to understand and acquire the elements of career maturity or career adaptability: planfulness or time perspective, exploratory skills, relevant information, decision making skills, and a reality orientation.

• Providing counselees awareness of the important roles played by feedback and reality-testing in the development of self-concepts and the translation of these into occupational self-concepts.

• Assisting counselees in understanding and acting upon knowledge that work satisfactions and life satisfactions depend on the extent to which the individual finds adequate outlets for abilities, needs, values, interests, personality traits, and self concepts. They further depend on establishment in a type of work or work situation, and a way of life in which one can play the kind of role that growth and exploratory experiences have led one to consider congenial and appropriate.

Behavioral

• Helping to demystify employment-bound youth's concerns about or problems with career planning or work performance.

• Facilitating clarification of goals that counselees hope to achieve in counseling, in work, in social interaction and breaking them into ncrements that can be learned or relearned.

• Analyzing with counselees their environments to identify cues and reinforcers that are important in triggering and sustaining their behavior.

• Providing opportunities for social modeling, vicarious learning simulations, role playing, behavioral rehearsal, and feedback so that counselees can be helped to accurately understand and learn desirable behaviors or skills important to their goals, improved work performance or adjustment, job choice, and career planning.

• Assisting counselees to specifically identify behavioral deficits and create conditions or experiences which will provide reinforcement of appropriate learned responses important to goal attainment.

Cognitive Behavioral

• Helping employment-bound youth to modify inaccurate or maladaptive cognitive sets about self, others, and life events.

• Assisting counselees to understand the cognitive bases of their moods, anxieties, or depression and the direct connection between thoughts and feelings.

• Facilitating counselee analysis of their automatic thoughts and irrational beliefs about their abilities, worth, work opportunities or performance.

• Providing employment-bound youth help in cognitive restructuring or reframing their concern about career planning, the school-to-work transition, or work adjustment.

• Identifying with counselees' tendencies to overgeneralize or use cognitive distortions as they assess problems, issues, or barriers related to the choice of and implementation of work.

client-centered, psychodynamic, developmental, behavioral and cognitive behavioral—as well as techniques that augment or extend these approaches—appraisal or testing, group processes, psychoeducational models, computer-assisted career guidance programs, education and labor market information, collaboration and consultation, referral. Thus, while it is possible to talk about career counseling as a one-on-one process between a counselor and a counselee, it is unlikely that individual counseling will occur independent of other program elements or techniques. This is true because most young people or adults who come to counselors do not have only one question or problem; typically they have several to address or overcome if they are going to plan, prepare for, make the transition to and adjust to work effectively.

More approaches to career interventions for employment-bound youth will be discussed in the next chapter. Also given further attention will be the role of counselors with employment-bound youth.

Chapter Six

The Counselor
and Related Career
Interventions

Chapter Five has discussed approaches to career counseling in some depth and indicated that, ordinarily, career counseling is used in conjunction with other processes or techniques and, often, as one component of a comprehensive program of career guidance activities designed to meet the needs of persons in a particular setting. The latter perspective will be discussed further in this chapter.

Counselor Roles in Career Intervention

However a program is developed to assist employment-bound youth or any other population of adolescents or adults, there are implications for what counselors do and the conceptions they hold about their professional role. These perceptions are shaped by the types of problems that persons bring to counselors, by the interaction of such problems and federal or state legislation designed to respond to them, and by role statements of professional organizations. Each of these dynamics changes in emphasis across time but clearly the importance of career counseling, career guidance, or career services has remained a constant and important aspect of the role of counselors throughout the twentieth century. Under the stimuli of the international economic competition and related trends discussed in the early chapters of this book, the role of counselors in dealing with career-related issues of choice and planning has expanded to attend to concerns experienced by persons throughout the life span. Therefore, while this book is principally concerned with employment-bound youth and, because of the age and setting which describe most employment-bound youth, with the role of school counselors, many of the implications of the context, content, and processes of relevance to school counselors also have utility and application for other counselors dealing with career content in settings and with populations other than described here.

The American School Counselors Association (ASCA) has been instrumental in defining and, indeed, shaping the role of school counselors. In their various role statements, resolutions, and position papers, they have made a variety of observations about how to think about what counselors do and why. For example, in one role statement adopted by the Board of Directors of ASCA in July 1990, it is asserted that "School counseling programs are developmental by design, focusing on needs, interests, and issues related to the various stages of student growth. There are objectives, activities, special services and expected outcomes, with an emphasis on helping students to learn more effectively and efficiently. There is a commitment to individual uniqueness and the maximum development of human potential. A counseling program is an integral part of a school's total educational program" (p.22). Later on in that same role statement, the following comments are made: "In a comprehensive developmental counseling program, school counselors organize their work schedules around the following basic interventions:"...Individual Counseling, Small Group Counseling, Large Group Guidance, Consultation and Coordination (American School Counselor Association, 1992, p. 22). In another position statement directly related to The School Counselor and Career Guidance, a rationale describing career guidance includes:

"Career guidance is a delivery system which systematically helps students reach the career development outcomes of self awareness and assessment, career awareness and exploration, career decision making, career planning and placement. It has consistently been seen as a high priority needed by youth, their parents, school boards, the private sector, and the general public. Such expectations are at an all-time high. As these expectations have risen, so, too, has the difficulty of the task facing the professional school counselor. The certain rapidity of occupational change, coupled with the uncertain nature of the emerging service/information oriented high technology society have combined to change career guidance practices in significant ways. The school counselor's role covers many areas within the school setting and career guidance is one of the most important contributions to a student's lifelong development" (p. 30).

These perspectives are wide-ranging, accenting, as was done in the previous chapters, that individual counseling is only one of the elements of a planned program to shape and facilitate student outcomes related to their ability to engage in career planning and choice. There are other important perspectives on the role of the school counselor relative to the delivery of career guidance or counseling. However, before returning to this matter in a specific sense, it is useful to acknowledge that counselors in settings other than the schools also deal directly with employment-bound youth and as the national attention to the school-to-work transition accelerates, it is likely that professional career counselors in industry and the community as well as counselors in the U. S. Employment Service or affiliated with Private Industry Counselors will collaborate with school counselors more comprehensively in delivering career guidance services. To that end, it is useful to examine the perspective of the National Career Development Association (1985) in assessing the role of the career counselor as these persons function in private practice, in community agencies, and in workplaces. According to NCDA:

The services of career counselors differ, depending on competence. A professional or Nationally Certified Career Counselor helps people make decisions and plans related to life/career directions. The strategies and techniques are tailored to the specific needs of the person seeking help. It is likely that the career counselor will do one or more of the following:

- Conduct individual and group personal counseling sessions to help clarify life/career goals.
- Administer and interpret tests and inventories to assess abilities, interests, etc., and to identify career options.
- Encourage exploratory activities through assignments and planning experiences.
- Utilize career planning systems and occupational information systems to help individuals better understand the world of work.
- Provide opportunities for improving decision-making skills.
- Assist in developing individualized career plans.

- Teach job-hunting strategies and skills and assist in the development of resumes.
- Help resolve potential personal conflicts on the job through practice in human relations skills.
- Assist in understanding the integration of work and other life roles.
- Provide support for persons experiencing job stress, job loss, career transition (pp. 1-2).

There are also changing perspectives on the role of employment counselors that are useful to the topic at issue. With respect to change, both in the expectations of employment counselors and in the characteristics of clients during the previous decade, the National Employment Counselors Association adopted an official definition of employment counseling as the "process whereby an employment counselor and client work together in order that the latter may gain better self-understanding and knowledge of the world of work and more realistically choose, change, or adjust to a vocation" (National Employment Counselors Association, 1975, p. 149). This statement then identified four types of counseling assistance required by different kinds of clients:

- Assisting the inexperienced person to explore career alternatives, to make satisfactory vocational choice, and to develop a realistic vocational plan.
- Providing pre-employment or employment development services.
- Assisting the experienced worker wishing or needing to make occupational changes.
- Helping the worker encountering barriers to entering, holding, or progressing in a job discover, analyze, and understand the vocational and personal problems involved and make and implement necessary plans for adjustment.

Historically, a major goal of employment counselors has been to serve clients who are nearly job ready who can be matched to existing jobs or training programs by finding positions in which they might fit with little or no need for change in behavior or personality (Fletcher, 1971). In addition, however, employment counselors also serve disadvantaged clients and those who have experienced jagged employment or unemployability because of personality and behavioral problems and who must undergo change to be acceptable or to have the skills required by the available job openings. In such instances, the employment counselor's role is likely to involve teaching the client about general employability skills and helping them to rekindle or sustain their motivation to move through the preemployment process and, hopefully, into full, competitive employability (Herr, 1990). The skills that the employment counselor has, including expertise in local and original labor market information, job placement, and direct employer contacts, are each important assets as they can be brought to bear on the needs of many employment-bound youth. If the employment counselor, the counselor in private practice or in business and industry, and the school counselor could be brought into greater interaction and common focus in behalf of employment-bound youth, many of the issues now related to the school-to-work transition for this group of youth could be resolved within the capabilities of existing counseling delivery systems available in many parts of the nation.

In any case, each of the perspectives about the goals and functions of counselors in various settings casts the counselors into a role which is complex and multi-dimensional; one in which the individual counselor typically must plan and organize as well as tailor what is done to meet the specific needs of those with whom he or she works. To return to the role of the school counselor with employment-bound students, and again from a role statement of the American School Counselor Association, counselors directly *teach* students relevant content or *consult* with and *coordinate* with others (e.g., vocational teachers, community-based role models) who teach the content. School counselors also guide students as they process information about themselves—their career interests, aptitude and values—the work world—its makeup, opportunities, and requirements—and their personal plans—the means for making and implementing them. They ensure appropriate provision of career and job-specific *information*, provide *assessment* opportunities for students to gather information about themselves, and *consult* with and coordinate the resources of the students/parents, advisers, mentors, and potential and current employers.

In their activities for employment-bound youth, school counselors *counsel* students as they approach obstacles to successful school completion, transition-to-work, or both. Such obstacles might be students' own lack of goal clarity, lack of success at a school or work endeavor, or non-school/work-related problems that threaten to interrupt their progress. There might also be external obstacles such as bias and stereotypes of race, ethnicity, gender, sexual orientation, disability, or age. Specialized *assessments* might be provided. Counselors, again, consult with relevant other adults who might be interfering with or might be able to help the youth achieve their goals, or they might refer the youth and their families to other agencies that provide the assistance needed—financial, psychological, or job-finding assistance.

Finally, professional school counselors develop and *manage* their guidance programs to ensure career development assistance to all students, particularly to those who will begin their work-centered life upon completion of high school. They collaborate in the development of other programs designed to assist students' successful transition from school-to-work, such as vocational education and apprenticeship programs. They also accept the responsibility to *maintain their competence* as career guidance professionals (American School Counselors Association, 1984).

Within this school counselor role statement as it is pertinent to interaction with employment-bound youth are the expectations that these professionals will perform at least the following functions:

- Provide access to information.
- Provide instruction in career guidance topics and, possibly, in a guidance curriculum.
- Provide career counseling.
- Provide advocacy by interpreting the special needs and characteristics of employment-bound youth to administrators, employers, and training and employment policymakers.
- Provide consultation to persons in and out of the school who can provide support, mentoring, and information for employment-bound students.
- Provide program development and management (Herr & Associates, 1993).

Each of these functions has many competencies and sub-elements that could be described here but, for most of this chapter, we will concentrate on the latter: program development and management, planning, and the content of programs that are illustrative of those relevant for employment-bound youth. At a fundamental level, program development and management suggests that counselors need to go beyond one-to-one individual counseling or a random set of activities to a conception of program, or a cohesive set of services, that is planned and has a set of expected results or outcomes. Such a program is likely to go beyond what counselors can do alone and include teachers, parents, representatives, employers, counselors in community or employment settings, and other persons who can make a contribution to the career development of employment-bound youth. Such programs must be coordinated, evaluated, and managed as well as planned (Herr & Cramer, 1992; Gysbers & Henderson, 1988). And they may take on a variety of forms.

One major delivery system within the school is the integration or infusion of career development content, for example, information about the relationship of academic subject matter to occupations which rely on such knowledge to solve problems throughout academic courses. This type of infusion, which was accented in the 1970s and early 1980s during the prominence of career education in legislation and federal policy, continues to be an important way to: make all schooling more career relevant; to connect what students are learning in school with how it will be used in the future in the world of work; help them relate and reality-test their abilities and preferences in academic subject matter to occupations or career patterns they might pursue; emphasize the similarity between the rationale for effective study habits in school and the need for and content of successful work habits on the job; convey the importance of learning planning and problem-solving skills as ways to identify and make plans to pursue how one will deal with the school-to-work transition or other possible options after high school. The attempts to make school content more career relevant by interspersing academic subject matters with examples, exercises, or concepts that answer such So what? questions asked by students as why am I taking the course? are subtle but important reinforcements that school and work are interdependent and that one needs to see course selection, learning, and planning as intermediate steps toward an effective school-to-work transition, toward entering the adult world of responsibility and commitment.

The goal of infusing the content of courses with career relevant experiences and concepts is applicable to any discipline or knowledge base (e.g., social studies, mathematics, sciences, music, vocational education). This goal can be reinforced in many ways. School counselors and teachers can co-teach selected career guidance units in the academic classroom as a form of large group guidance. Counselors can offer workshops or guidance units on selected topics (e.g., career planning skills, the choice of curricula as career choices, job search skills, expectations of employers, the language of self, the types and characteristics of post-secondary education, the pros and cons of tech prep or apprenticeship, stress reduction, time management, anger management, study skills). Such units can be offered during an activity period, or in a group guidance curriculum, in selected class periods and in many other approaches. For example, they may be developed in self-directed modules, or as the foci of video or audio tapes made available to students to borrow. They may be tied directly to the outcomes of the school's testing program, particularly to aptitude, interests, values and career maturity assessments. Resource persons from the industries and businesses of a local community may be brought into the school to describe their work, how they prepared for it, and its relation to particular academic subject matter. Students can be involved in assignments to interview workers about such content and report back to class about their findings. They can engage in work shadowing of workers or field trips to workplaces. They can be assigned to read biographies and books about occupational content. They can engage in computerized career guidance programs developed either by their State Occupational Information Coordinating Committee or by commercial organizations (e.g., DISCOVER, GIS, Choices).

Many employment-bound youth, particularly those enrolled in vocational education, will have the opportunity to be involved in cooperative education, high school apprenticeship programs, or other situations in which academic study and work in a job with adult norms and supervision are combined.

These programs have the added advantage of helping students so involved to have access to both the career oriented resources of the school as well as those of the community.

Vocational education curricula add other advantages to those of cooperative education or entry to apprenticeship or tech prep. In most instances, the content of vocational education is an integration of academic and vocational skills, it is typically problem focused (how to diagnose and repair an engine, how to design and build a particular structure, how to estimate the electrical requirement of a building, order the supplies for and wire it appropriately) which requires the application of academic content (e.g., mathematics, applied science) to the problem at hand and then solving the problem, usually through some form of cooperative learning where more than one student works together to get the job done. Often the tasks to be achieved (e.g., structures to be built, vehicles to be repaired) are part of community projects that expose students to the resources of the school and to the resources and, indeed, the criteria or expectations of the community for acceptable work.

Employability Skills for Employment-Bound Youth

In many cases, the skills that students learn from making schooling more career relevant are not just performance skills, how to do a particular job task or run a machine or solve a work problem, they are general employability skills. Indeed, most observers believe that readiness for employment or employability can be broken into subsets of skills (Herr & Johnson, 1989; Herr & Long, 1983) and the knowledge and skills in these subsets can be used as the content by which to assess the work readiness or adjustment of individuals as one of the bases for career counseling of employment-bound youth. The content of such skills also can be used as the conceptual frames of references for planning career counseling or career guidance programs.

The three types of skills typically included as the content of employability include occupation-specific, firm-specific, and general. The first two types of employability skills refer to those required to perform the technical aspects of a job either as defined by occupational requirements (e.g., accountant, machinist, heavy equipment operator) or by those of a particular firm (e.g., the rules and procedures under which we operate heavy equipment in x firm). Both the occupational and firm-specific employability skills differ for specific type of professional, managerial, skilled and unskilled jobs and by specific workplaces. General employability skills, however, are more elastic and less likely to become quickly obsolete because they are the psychological, personal, and behavioral skills that mediate how one applies his or her technical skills. They include such emphases as work habits, dependability, honesty, punctuality, goal directedness, and flexibility. General employability skills comprise the knowledge, attitudes, and behaviors that permit one to plan for, gain, and adjust to work in any setting. These behaviors are more likely to be a principal concern of counselors in career counseling or as the substance of career guidance programs than are the technical content of occupational or firm specific skills. An exception to this general rule, however, is the situation where an employment-bound youth is clearly having problems learning or performing the technical skills of an occupation or required by a firm and is becoming anxious, rebellious, or confused about the situation. Obviously, in such a case, where the counselee may need to reinstitute an exploratory process related to choosing other more congenial jobs or sets of technical skills or reassessing his or her career goals, this content would be of specific concern to the career counselor whether the incident that brought the employment-bound youth to the counselor occurred while in vocational education, during the school-to-work transition, or after induction to a job.

To return to the counselor's major concern with counseling or nurturing the acquisition of general employability skills by employment-bound youth, it must be acknowledged that there are many forms of conceptual content that are relevant. Chapters Two and Three included a number of such examples. One set of such concepts that can be used as the objectives for programs aimed at increasing employability has been offered by Herr (1989) and by Herr and Johnson (1989). In this view of general employability skills needed by employment-bound youth, it is contended that general employability is comprised of three emphases: work context skills, career management skills and decision-making skills. In brief, each of these emphases can be summarized as follows:

Work Context Skills relate to the psychological aspects of the organization or environment in which work activity is carried on. Included are the skills which underlie employer-employee relations, supervisory relationships, interpersonal skills, willingness to follow rules, work habits, adaptability, adjustment to co-workers, pride in work, self-discipline, efficiency, and understanding of life in an organization. These skills parallel what tends to be called "industrial discipline" in Europe, what Kazanas (1978) has called "affective competencies." Haccoon and Campbell (1972) described the need for sich skills as work-entry problems of youth, and Crites (1981) termed a lack of such skills as "thwarting conditions."

Career Management Skills are those skills by which one brings self information and career information together into a plan of action. Included are both career planning and job search and access skills. Career planning involves the ability to use exploratory resources and to reality-test alternative choices, understand the constructive use of leisure, implement personal economic skills, acquire and apply self- and career-knowledge, and the ability to match personal characteristics to those required in preferred curricula or occupations. Job search and access skills include knowing how to find relevant employers, effectively implement job applications and interviews, and positive follow-up.

Decision-making skills overlap career management skills but focus primarily on learning the skills of decision making and the process of choice, rather than on making career choices. Relevant skills include systematic methods of processing information, predicting and weighing alternatives, clarifying values, examining risk-taking styles, and projecting action consequences. Also important is the need to understand the importance of choice as the mechanism by which one forges a career, creates personal realities, integrates family, work, and leisure roles, and translates desires and potential options into activities.

In Table 5 is an illustration of how both in-school and out-of-school resources and interventions can be used to help employment-bound youth develop general employability skills. It is important to note here that while the left column talks of in-school resources, one could readily substitute JTPA or Job Corps or any community agency program designed to assist employment-bound youth through the school-to-work transition process.

Table 5

Examples of Interventions for Developing General Employability Skills in Employment-Bound Youth

	IN SCHOOL	OUT OF SCHOOL

WORK
CONTEXT
SKILLS
	Role Models
	Skill-centered Curricula
	Enhancing Self-concept
	Group Counseling
	Exploring Work Values
	  • Interpersonal
	    skills training
	  • Assessing/Modifying
	    Self-Efficacy
		Role Models
		Interview parents/
		relatives
		Utilize community
		resources
		Work Visits
		Work Participation
		Work Shadowing
		Mentoring

CAREER
MANAGEMENT
SKILLS
  • Career
    Planning
	Infusing Coursework
	with Career Concepts
	Work Study
	Career Counseling
	Career Libraries
	Career Information and
	Planning Courses
	Countering sex-typing
	Career Awareness Programs
	Work Simulation
		Work Visits
		
		Work Study
		
		Work Shadowing
		
		Mentoring
		Utilize family and
		community role models

• Job Search & Access	Job Search Training Job Finding Clubs Interview Skills Training Stress Management	Job Clubs Stress Management

DECISION-
MAKING
SKILLS
	Distinguishing Indecision
	& Indecisiveness
	Testing for decision-making
	Group Guidance Programs
	Decision-Making Programs
	Group counseling/exercises
	in problem-solving
	Values and Needs Clarification
		Information-gathering
		Career Decision-Making
		  for Parents
		Family and Community
		  Role Models
		Reality-testing

SOURCE: Table 1, page 20, Herr, E. L., & Johnson, E. (1989). General Employability Skills for Youths and Adults: Goals for Guidance and Counselling Programs. *Guidance & Counselling, 4*, 4.

While what has been suggested above is one type of approach to career guidance content for employment-bound youth, there are, in fact many examples of such content available. The perspectives on developmental tasks discussed under developmental career counseling in Chapter Five and the content discussed in Chapters Two and Three are others. Examples of these are identified in Table 6 (page 220). Many state departments of education have created career development models or plans for use by counselors to implement systematic career guidance programs at each educational level and for adults. In 1988, the National Occupational Information Coordinating Committee (NOICC) published *The National Career Counseling and Development Guidelines*, which give, in multiple volumes, examples of how to plan career guidance programs for adults in human service agencies, for students in post-secondary institutions, and for students in elementary, middle/junior, and high schools. The guidelines suggest relevant content at each of these levels and for the populations served at those levels and settings. The NOICC guidelines provide recommended competencies and indicators for each competency. The former represent general goals, the latter include the specific knowledge, skills, and attitudes that individuals should master in order to deal effectively with each of the lifelong career development tasks specified by the guidelines. In broad terms, *The National Career Counseling and Development Guidelines* are classified into three areas: Self-knowledge, Educational and Occupational Exploration, and Career Planning. The competencies for each of these areas are then divided into competencies that have been developed by level. For example, the career development competencies for the high school level include the following:

- understanding the influence of a positive self-concept
- skills to interact positively with others
- understanding the impact of growth and development
- understanding the relationship between educational achievement and career planning
- understanding the need for positive attitudes toward work and learning

- skills to locate, evaluate, and interpret career information
- skills to prepare to seek, obtain, maintain, and change jobs
- understanding how societal needs and functions influence the nature and structure of work
- skills to make decisions
- understanding the interrelationship of life roles
- understanding the continuous changes in male/female roles
- skills in career planning

The first three of the competencies relate to self-knowledge, the next five to educational and occupational awareness, and the last four to career planning. Each of these competencies includes, in addition, what are called indicators that represent particular types of knowledge or skills that in combination would indicate that the student had acquired the competency. To illustrate how indicators appear, it might be useful to list those associated with competency 12: Skills in Career Planning. The indicators relevant to this competency include the expectation that the student will:

1. Develop career plans that include the concept that a changing world demands lifelong learning.

2. Acquire knowledge of postsecondary vocational and academic programs.

3. Validate or revise the career and educational plan developed in middle school/junior high to coincide with developing career and educational plans and actual educational attainment.

4. Demonstrate an understanding of how constant changes in the world of work require frequent retraining and updating of employees.

5. Use school and community resources to explore education and career choices.

6. Describe the costs and benefits of self-employment.

7. Acquire occupationally-related skills through volunteer experience, part-time employment, and/or cooperative education programs.

8. Develop skills necessary to compare education and job opportunities in terms of occupational, training, and continuing education benefits.

Table 6

Guidance Needs Across Time

Children Elementary School Major Guidance Tasks	Young Adolescents Middle School Major Guidance Tasks	Later Adolexcents Senior High School Major Guidance Tasks
Formation of basic attitudes and information about self and life opportunities	Exploring and reality testing attitudes and information about self, others and opportunities	Specific planning related to imminence of making the transition from school to work or college
Sub-tasks (examples) • Developing a sense of personal competence, self-worth, self-acceptance • Developing a sense of life opportunities, their breadth and their characteristics • Developing the rudiments of a sense of academic readiness, self-efficacy, and college consciousness • Developing a sense of personal identity, uniqueness, a self-concept system • Developing social relationships with peers and adults Beginning to understand and take responsibility for actions, understand the role of choices and decisions • Understanding preferences and their linkages to opportunities	Sub-tasks (examples) • Testing and refining aspirations • Sustaining motivation • Organizing and testing one's knowledge of social and physical reality • Learning to work well in the peer group • Engaging in a wide variety of experiences and opportunities in academic, career, and personal domains • Using and testing their skills and reflecting upon their meaning • Acquiring the life skils related to planning and choice of curriculum and career • Learning about the connections between academic choices and future choices of education and work; learning how to keep options open • Sharpening self-identity, feelings of self-efficacy. • Exploring and reality testing subject-matter and occupational skills and preferences	Sub-tasks (examples) • Preparing for the transition from school to young adulthood • Becoming self-reliant and achieving psycho-logical independence from their parents • Expanding peer relationships achieving the capacity for intimate relationships • Learning to handle heterosexual relationships, dating, and sexuality • Making plans to pay for college or other post–secondary education • Learning how to manage personal health • Learning to manage time • Formulating a personal value system • Assuming responsibility for career planning and its consequences • Keeping one's options open as fully as possible by taking courses to qualify for postsecondary education • Developing skills important to life as a consumer and to effective use of leisure time

SOURCE:
Herr, E. L. (1989). *Community-based approaches to guidance.* Indianapolis, IN: Lilly Endowment.

Obviously, these competencies and indicators for the high school population are virtually all of importance to employment-bound youth. As such, they can serve as the focus of career counseling with individuals or as the content of career guidance programs designed for this population. While most of the competencies and indicators cited for high school populations are applicable to employment-bound youth engaged in the school-to-work transition or in the throes of adjusting to job entry, it is also possible to extrapolate from some of the adult competencies to suggest those that may be appropriate for employment-bound youth who have left the school context. They might include such competencies as:

- Skills to maintain effective behaviors.
- Skills to enter and participate in education and training.
- Skills to participate in work and lifelong learning.
- Skills to prepare to seek, obtain, maintain, and change jobs.
- Skills to make career transitions.

There are, as suggested previously, other lists of competencies, behaviors, knowledge, and skills that could be identified and used as the frame of reference for the design of programs for employment-bound youth whether they are infused into academic courses, counselor-led career guidance programs, compressed into JTPA training, special programs offered by the U. S. Employment Service or by career counselors in business and industry or in private practice. Wherever these programs take place, they will be tailored to the particular characteristics of the employment-bound population being addressed: those with disabilities, males or females, those with a background in vocational education or not. In whichever way programs must be developed or adopted for a special employment-bound group, much of the content remains the same, as does the planning process. However, since employment-bound youth are comprised of a large proportion of disadvantaged youth or at-risk youth, career guidance and career counseling programs must be designed "to help reduce the correlation between membership in disadvantaged social groups and failure in the workplace. At-risk youth already have one or two strikes against them (poverty, substance abuse, teen pregnancy, lack of motivation, lack of basic academic skills, etc.). Unlike the college-bound, employment-bound youth need immediate and realistic career plans for their lives after high school." (U. S. Employment and Training Administration, 1993, p. 13). Further, "Comprehensive career guidance programs may provide benefits that are of special importance to the development of at-risk youth. In particular, career guidance programs are designed to perform the following functions:

1. Provide youth with opportunities for personal growth by forcing critical examination of self-image and self-identity, and helping youth gain motivation, focus their ambition, and identify goals;

2. Increase cognitive information about education and occupations by highlighting the importance of education for one's future and by enhancing the number and quality of social experiences beyond the classroom and in the community and workplace; and

3. Provide positive relationships with adults that offer exposure to working role models and contribute to building networks of contacts" (p. 14).

The Counselor as Planner and Coordinator

Given the wide range of outcomes that might be achieved and the array of interventions that might be employed to facilitate the outcomes chosen, the counselor working withemployment-bound youth must be a planner and a coordinator. These roles reflect the need to orchestrate or integrate the work of others as part of a career guidance program or to bring together the resources—e.g., testing, labor market information, support groups, access to work-study opportunities—that a particular employment-bound youth needs in order to deal effectively with his or her particular career planning or work adjustment concerns. It is widely accepted that effective delivery of career guidance and counseling services requires a team approach involving school-based personnel, parents, government, community-based organizations, and the business community. Regardless of who is involved per se, such processes are labor-intensive, requiring extensive personal interaction and consultation as well as planning and coordination (U. S. Employment and Training Administration, 1993; W. T. Grant, 1988).

The counselor's role in planning or coordination also extends to the provision of planned programs designed to accomplish specific results. Increasingly, the federal government as well as professional sources are advocating comprehensive programs that have multiple services or elements included and which are planned. For example, one of the clearest statements ever made by government about this matter is that found in the original Carl D. Perkins Vocational Education Act which authorized grants for "programs (organized and administered by certified counselors) designed to improve, expand, and extend career guidance and counseling programs to meet the career development, vocational education, and employment needs of vocational education students and potential students." This legislation further states that: "Such programs shall be designed to assist individuals to:

1. acquire self-assessment, career planning, decision making, and employability skills;
2. make the transition from education and training to work;
3. maintain marketability of current job skills in established occupations;
4. develop new skills to move away from declining occupational fields and enter new and emerging fields in high-technology areas and fields experiencing skill shortages;
5. develop midcareer job search skills and clarify career goals; and
6. obtain and use information on financial assistance for postsecondary and vocational education and job training."

In addition, in Section 332b of the Act is elaborated the intention that programs of career guidance and counseling shall encourage the elimination of sex, age, handicapping conditions, and race bias and stereotyping (Carl D. Perkins Vocational Education Act of 1989, Title III, Part D of Public Law 98-524). Many of the possible goals or competencies to be served by the program specified by the Perkins Act or in other career guidance and counseling programs were identified in the previous section of the chapter. Planned approaches in any setting endeavor to specify clearly the ends sought and the specific methods by which such ends will be realized. Such planned programs allow counselors to be accountable for their contributions to, for example, the general employability skills acquired by employment-bound youth. In such planned counseling programs, the intervention strategies used can vary in relation to the intended outcomes, but such planned counseling programs can be evaluated and held accountable for the results achieved and the differences made in the lives of employment-bound youth, rather than on whether specific services are offered or functions are in place.

The impetus toward planned programs in counseling and in career guidance in schools, colleges, and universities has been evident for at least the past two decades and has accelerated in the 1980s. National reports (e.g., the Commission on Precollege Guidance and Counseling, The College Board, 1986) have argued for assessments of student needs in schools and then systematically planning about how best to meet these needs. Similarly, from the standpoint of employees in the workplace, Leibowitz, Farren, and Kaye (1986) contended that comprehensive, systematic career development programs have become essential to maximize employee productivity and meet the human resource needs of organizations. To that end, they developed a change and planning model to install career development systems in industry that includes 12 principles or tasks that can be classified into four planning phases. They include Needs: Defining the present system; Vision: Determining new directions and possibilities; Action Plan: Deciding on practical first steps; and Results: Maintaining the change. These stages roughly parallel those proposed by Herr and Cramer (1992) as applied to the design of comprehensive programs of career development in schools, colleges and universities, workplace or agencies. They include:

1. develop a program philosophy;
2. specify program goals;
3. select alternative program processes;
4. describe evaluation procedures; and
5. identify milestones (critical events) that must occur for program implementation.

Thus, as a counselor coordinates and plans systematic programs that include career counseling and other career interventions, in order to understand the complexities of the content that undergirds such roles, the counselor is likely to need to be an applied behavioral scientist, a technologist, and a program designer. In such roles, rather than confining himself or herself to one theory of practice or one process (e.g., individual counseling), the counselor will need to have a broad acquaintance with the characteristics of the populations to be served (in this case employment-bound youth, including those designated as at-risk), the theories, concepts, and ideas bearing on career development and the empirical evidence available on the effectiveness of the interventions that might be used for different purposes. It is in such perspectives that the counselor is an applied behavioral scientist. Since many of the interventions that might be used include computer-assisted career guidance systems, computers for administrative and scheduling purposes, simulations, games, videodisks and tapes, assessment centers and other technical devices, the counselor also needs to become a technologist. (Please see Table 7, page 226-227, for examples of Career Information Delivery Systems from which a counselor may choose appropriate interventions for a particular setting or population.) And, in bringing all of these knowledge bases and resource personnel into programs, the counselor becomes a coordinator, planner and a program designer.

Examples of Effective Career Guidance Programs

For many reasons, available information or evaluative data about the fully integrated, systematic comprehensive career guidance programs called for in national reports, the professional literature, or in this book is limited. This is true because many such programs are local or state models, the descriptions and evaluation of which do not find their way into the professional literature. In addition, since such programs often are tailored for specific local purposes or demographic profiles, they are hard to replicate or, indeed, documentation of the planning and implementation of such programs is unavailable. If evaluations of such program occur, they frequently suffer from methodological shortcomings that render the

Table 7

Types of Career Information Delivery Systems

Career Resource Center

Devoted to acquisition, storage, retrieval, dissemination of information

Technical assistances and coordination of community resources

Printed Matter

Directories
Occupational Briefs
Occupational Outlook Handbook
Vocational Biographies

Media Approaches

Bulletin Boards and Displays	Records
Television	Cassettes
Slides	Filmstrips
Films	Microfilm
Microfiche	Videodiscs

Interview Approaches

Career Day
Person-to-Person Interviews
Group Interviews
College Night
Interview Workers or Personnel Directors
Job Clinic for Immediate Job Placement

Simulation Approaches

Role-Playing	Problem-Solving Kits
Games (e.g., the Life Career Game)	Job Sampling
Role Models	Work Shadowing
Career Clubs	

Field Trips

Individual
Group

Formal Curriculum Approach

Subject Matter Information
Modules
Workshops

Direct Experiences

Part-Time Work or Summer Employment
Cooperative Education
On-the-Job Training

Computer-Assisted Approaches

Discover
Sigi
NOICC, SOICC, CIDS, Networks

---

results meaningless from an experimental design standpoint and, thus, are limited principally to only descriptive uses. Further, most program descriptions do not characterize themselves as addressed primarily to employment-bound youth, even if they are so focused.

Exemplary Programs

Given the above caveats, Public/Private Ventures of Philadelphia, Pennsylvania under funding from the U. S. Employment and Training Administration, Department of Labor, (U. S. Employment and Training Administration, 1993), engaged in an effort to identify potential exemplary programs by conducting a comprehensive search of data bases for materials related to career guidance for disadvantaged youth, and particularly of reports containing evaluation information; by reviewing summaries of all programs identified by the Department of Education's National Diffusion Network; and by pursuing recommendations made by experts in the field. From this very comprehensive process, the researchers found only four programs that met their selection criteria.

Each of the four programs selected were visited and a variety of information about them was identified and summarized. In the view of the researchers, "each of these programs has demonstrated success with its target populations.

In general, dropout rates declined, while attendance, motivation, life skills and future planning [by students involved] increased" (p. 33). The researchers found that the four exemplary programs share several traits described below in slightly abridged fashion.

1. **Career guidance is not compartmentalized and targets youth in ninth grade or earlier.** Exemplary programs utilize an integrated sequence of career development activities (self-exploration, information gathering, hands-on experience, and decision-making components) rather than one-shot approaches occurring late in the school career (i.e., late adolescence). They are built-in rather than added-on and consist of activities tailored to the age and status of participants.

2. **The connection between education and employment is emphasized.** According to the researchers, all programs visited seek to help students understand the relationships between their current status, their planned occupational futures, and their educational needs. They link education, knowledge, and skills to economic, personal, and social rewards. All four of the programs visited provide opportunities for youth to gain work experiences and reflect on these experience in a guided, controlled environment.

3. **A limited caseload for counselors, advisors, mentors, or coaches allows for individualized attention.** They have low adult-to-youth ratios and all four programs have mechanisms that provide for continuity of relationships between youth and individual members of the counseling staff; the programs assume that given the career development needs of the participants, easy and consistent access to counselors is critical. The delivery of the programs' other components is individualized to ensure both the quality of program content and youth's positive relationship with adult authority figures.

4. **Coalitions linking programs to businesses, parents, and community agencies are fostered**

and developed. Outreach to these partners help ease the load of counseling and guidance and connects youth to the adult worlds of work, family, and civic responsibility. Adults outside school settings play particularly important roles in guiding youth's career decisions. Each constituency contributes to the delivery of the program and has a stake in its success.

Table 8 (page 230) provides a summary of the career guidance programs visited as a part of this study. The descriptions show the variety of approaches that were considered to be exemplary in the perspective of the researchers involved. While the projects reviewed are focused on disadvantaged students, the four shared traits of the programs as described above undoubtedly have implications for career guidance programs for employment-bound youth, who are neither disadvantaged nor at risk. The four findings identified in this project also overlap with two other perspectives that deserve brief mention.

During the 1970s and 1980s, a considerable amount of evaluation and research on school-based career education projects was undertaken and discussed in several major reports. From these reports, Herr and Cramer (1992) report a synthesis of the ingredients that effective models tended to share. They include:

1. They have visible and continuing administrative support.
2. The goals of career education are seen as major commitments of a school district, a higher education institution, or a work setting. In this respect, they are seen as central to the institutional mission and to the facilitation of specific behaviors to be attained by graduates or by employees.
3. Career education is a planned, integrative dimension of an education or work setting, not a random add-on or by-product relegated to the responsibility of only one group of specialists. Representatives of all the groups of educators, industrial personnel, and community persons affected by and making a contribution to career education are involved in the planning and selected advisory groups are used effectively.

Table 8.

Summary of Exemplary Career Guidance Programs Visited

PROJECT	CLIENTELE

Maryland Tomorrow/Project Sucess
Prince Georges County, MD
 	
   Located in six P.G. County schools
 	
   School-Within-A-School Model
	Academically disadvantaged
	at-risk ninth-graders
	
	Program Year 1991-92
	90 students served per school
	85% black
	<10% economically disadvantaged

DeLaSalle Education Certer
Kansas City, MO
 	
   Replicated at over 45 sites nationwide
   including a satellite program located in
   predominatly Hispanic neighborhood
   across town.
 	
   Alternative School Program
	Academically disadvantaged at-risk, inner-
	city school dropouts
	
	Program Year 1991-92
	660 enrolled
	83% between 14 and 18 years old
	90% economically disadvantaged
	95% academically disadvantaged
	83% black

City-As-School
New York, NY
 	
   Original sites located in Manhattan,
   Brooklyn and the Bronx, New York, but has
   been replicated in over 35 sites nationwide
   as a school-within-a-school model or stand-
   alone program.
 	
   Alternative School Program
	Inner-city youth at-risk of academic failure
	Grades 9-12
	
	Program Year 1991-92
	1,000 enrolled in NYC
	90% economically disadvantaged
	83% minority
	38% black
	40% Hispanic

PRO-100
Indianapolis, IN
 	
   Worksites located on a dozen public golf
   courses and school grounds across the
   city.
 	
   Summer Work/Education Program
	Out-of-school, inner-city youth age 14-18
	
	Program Year 1991-92
	100 open slots per year
	87% black
	73% male

SOURCE: Table 8, Page 34. *Finding One's Way: Career Guidance for Disadvantaged Youth.*
Reasearch and Evaluation Report Series 93-D. Washington, D.C.: U.S. Department of Labor,
Employment and Training Administration, 1993.

Table 8. (Continued)
Summary of Exemplary Career Guidance Programs Visited

DESCRIPTION
Beginning in the summer before ninth grade, selected students participate in a year-long program that includes counseling, education, vocational jobs and social skills training. Each cohort is taught within a team structure and receives intensive attention from teaching and counseling staff. Curriculum includes class units on careers and vocations. Weekend retreats focus on employment and social skills. Counseling caseload is limited to 90 and shared by a team of two. Professional staff are supplemented by a corps of mentors who volunteer to meet with kids on school site. Follow-up activities allow teacher-teams to stay involved with "their" students through graduation.
De LaSalle, an accredited alternative school, is distinguished by its adherence to a student-centered approach that includes a comprehensive array of support services and individualized case management. Personal, family, substance abuse, and vocational counseling supplement DLS's concentration on providing at-risk youth alternative educational opportunities leading to a high school diploma or postgraduation plans. Students negotiate individualized courses of study on a contractual basis with each teacher, then pursue them at their own pace. Comprehensive assessment of student needs is conducted at Intake. Students are assigned a counselor who tracks student progress for their duration at DLS. Counselor case load is limited to 60 students. Career education coursework and guidance are supplemented by hands-on vocational training and JTPA sponsored pre-employment training.
C-A-S is designed to reconnect young people to school, the community, and the world of adult authority and responsibility based on the idea that "many institutions educate." Students gain academic credit through multiple structured and supervised experimental learning activities with the community, and gain career guidance and exploration through one-on-one contact with school-based counselors and adult mentors in internship-like experiences. They maximize choice and learn responsibility through the process of negotiation involved in entering the placement and fulfilling the customized curriculum known as Learning Experience Activity Packet (LEAP). Specialized small classes in combination with weekly seminar groups serve as forums for discussion of academic, social, and occupational issues. Maximum advisor caseload is 50 students.
A seven-week summer program involving paid work experience and career development coursework. Interns interact with eight trained coaches, who supervise work teams of 12 to 14, provide counseling, and lead structured career development exercises and activities. Work experience revolves around supervised public beautification projects. Daily coursework includes work maturity and career guidance curriculum. Returnees can stay in the program for up to four years. Interns, coaches and evaluators perceived different but overlapping gains: Improvements in work habits, life skills and job search skills were identified by all groups.

4. Resources are provided for planning and for staff development, and these emphases are matters of systematic effort. The planning and the staff development are based on theory and research in career behavior so that there is concern about not only the how of career education but also the why.

5. Field experiences (whether internships, planned field trips, career shadowing, or something else) are planned to extend and to reinforce curriculum infusion and other career education instruction. They are not independent of the latter. The community is seen as a large learning laboratory that has responsibility to be in partnership with the schools in creating the most effective educational and occupational opportunities available.

6. Career education is not seen as something so different that the school system, teachers, counselors, and others must start from ground zero. Rather it involves the acknowledgment that experiences already in place have career education implications and further career education can be built on them. Organizational changes are planned and developed to facilitate the career education effort, but they are not dramatized as so new as to be threatening to participants.

7. Career education and vocational education are not confused. Career education is seen as being for all children, youth, or adults within the educational level or setting in which it is implemented; it is not confined in its scope to only the development of occupational task specific skills.

8. An evaluation process is built into the planning and implementation of career education so that its results can be examined and advocated as appropriate to policy-making bodies or other decision makers. (pp. 39-40).

It is also useful to further discuss a concept that is inherent in the fourth finding of the survey discussed above: the importance of collaboration with adults in the community as mentors, collaborators, and stakeholders in the success of the program. This possibility has also been advanced by Herr

(1989) in an analysis funded by the Lilly Endowment and now being studied in some 10 communities. In essence, while not confined to career guidance, but addressed to guidance programs in their totality, the model discussed by Herr is concerned with the need to link school-based programs with youth-serving organizations that essentially begin to function when the school day ends at 3:00 or 3:30 p.m. These organizations include Boys and Girls clubs, Boy and Girl Scouts, YMCA, YWCA, 4-H, Junior Achievement, church, youth groups, etc. They provide continuity of support and supervision of students from early morning when school begins until mid-evening and they provide a range of adult models with whom students can identify. Perhaps as important as any of these issues is the potential for such interactions and linkages to be seen as community-wide responsibilities.

For communities to assume their responsibilities for adolescent development, or for the school-to-work transition or any other emphasis of such a magnitude, extensive planning and cooperation is required among many special interest groups. In the model proposed by Herr (1989), it was suggested that the following would be essential elements:

1. A community-wide steering council, or similar mechanism, to design the philosophy, outcomes and resources for the program.
2. Systematic networking between the school and existing youth-serving organizations and/or business and industry in the community to articulate their mutual purposes and resources effectively.
3. Systematic collaboration between the school, business, and industry, and other civic organizations in behalf of guidance outcomes for different groups of children and adolescents.
4. Systematic collaboration between the school and parents in behalf of the guidance needs of children and adolescents.
5. A redesign of school counselor roles in ways to empower coordination, organization, orchestration, maximizing of multiple resources in the community and the schools in behalf of student needs. In effect, the result would be differentiated staffing.

While the steps just suggested for community involvement for adolescent development would need to be augmented to include steps designed to provide support for employment-bound youth and young adults if that were the intent, steps to network counselors across the community to focus information sources and community level resource centers, to provide support groups as youth move through the school-to-work transition process, to mobilize civic and economic development organizations to provide lectures, mentoring, and direct interventions in the lines of employment-bound youth would all be relevant to community-wide efforts to facilitate the transition of these persons.

In addition to the exemplary programs just discussed, there are other options that are worthy of mention as they address specific populations and as they have implications for employment-bound youth.

Elementary/Junior High/Middle Schools

One of the issues that originates in the early life of the child in the family, probably during the pre-school period, are gender differences in the stereotypes about what subject matter or type of occupations is appropriate for males and females. Many approaches have evolved by which counselors and/or teachers can combat sex stereotyping and the internalized concepts of boys and girls that they should not enter what are considered nontraditional occupations for their gender or, in the case of girls particularly, mathematics, science, or other technical academic subjects and occupations. One such approach that provided evaluation data about its outcomes was reported by Wilson and Daniel (1981) who use a role clarification and decision making workshop to help seventh and eighth students overcome sex role stereotypes. Using a variety of activities—such as considering the lives of famous women, songs illustrating social norms and social change in men's and women's roles, discussion of characteristics required for different occupations, interest inventories, analyses of nontraditional jobs—they found in comparing an experimental with a control group that a relatively brief workshop (five sessions) is effective in influencing traditional sex-role attitudes.

A frequent method of dealing with sex-stereotyped views of education and work is to use women in nontraditional occupations as guest speakers or as persons for students to shadow on the job. Such persons can also demonstrate the efficacy of multiple role planning. Beyond these types of direct interventions, counselors need to be alert to and consult with teachers and parents about how to recognize and counteract sex stereotyped activities and reinforcement in teaching materials and in educational policies and procedures.

Beyond programs emphasizing ways to diminish the effects of sex stereotyping on the career choices of young women and, indeed, young men, there are also comprehensive programs designed to integrate a variety of career interventions of importance to junior high school students. One such program, entitled Project Career Reach, was developed at West High School, Aurora, Illinois (Bollendorf, Howrey, & Stephenson, 1990). Combining a career development model of junior high school career needs, a model of guidance objectives for program planning, a generic individualized career plan, and a marketing scheme to stimulate students to make use of the program offered by the guidance department, the six high school counselors designed Project Career Reach. They used five steps to develop the program: mission analysis, market analysis, resource analysis, strategic planning, and measures of program outcomes. The result was a multifaceted program intended to be systematically delivered. Included in Project Career Reach were the following:

- College Night
- Achievement Testing
- Peer Counseling
- Registration
- School-Business Partnership
- Mini-Workshops (such as Financial Aid Seminars)
- Career Speaker Service
- Grade Boosters
- College Representatives
- Career Center
- Practical Composition (Career English)
- GIS searches of career-related information

After putting such program components in place, the counselors used all forms of media to reach students with different learning modalities and to encourage them to use the career programs. The school newspaper interviewed staff members and publicized activities for student readers. Signs were used as visual stimuli to publicize the career speaker series, the School-Work-Connection, the regional Career Fest, and other program emphases. Community newspapers and local radio and television announcements were also used to create visibility for the career guidance program.

As a result of the program, career information searches increased by 149 percent in the year following implementation of Project Career Reach. Nearly half of the students surveyed at the end of the program indicated their intent to be involved in other career development activities during the next school year. Students surveyed who were involved in the program indicated that they better understood careers and career information resources.

In another comprehensive approach to the provision of career skills and the understanding of work and of work organizations, the St. Louis Public Schools have developed extensive collaboration between the schools and resource persons from business and the community (Katzman, 1989). Examples of such collaboration include in abridged form:

- Traveling career panels in which seventh graders learn the importance of basic skills within the world of work and how these skills are applied by individuals on the job. A panel of two persons from business or industry visits a seventh grade classroom, bringing tools and a classroom activity that typifies their job. A math panel, for example, might include a chef who brings a chili recipe for 20 people that needs to be converted to serve 100 and a corporate budget director who brings ledger sheets and teaches the students to form a personal budget. The class follows up with career-related field experiences to view the panelists in their work environment.
- Career awareness fair in which eighth graders have an opportunity to watch career role models demonstrating their jobs.

• Business/school mentoring in which a business or community agency pairs with a middle or an elementary school to communicate with, provide career and motivational information for, and guide students over an extended period of time.

There are a variety of other techniques of relevance to employment-bound youth in the middle/junior high school period and earlier. For example, what have been labeled skill-centered curricula can foster knowledge about and acquisition of work context skills. Such curricula may be essential to prevent youths from psychologically dropping out of school by the junior high school years. Such students need to be helped to see how participation in schooling is relevant to their goals—for example, to getting a better job. As such, they need to experience the attitudinal and the affective as well as the technical requirements of work and the ways by which the content of schooling relates to these domains. Johnson (1980) has reported on one such program in the elementary school designed to integrate traditional school curricula (math, science, social studies, and language arts) with knowledge about the free enterprise system. In this program, students formed banking, retailing, manufacturing and farming teams. They set up and operated a simulated bank, a farm, and a factory, and made decisions regarding the sale of vegetables from the farm and goods from the factory. Among the emphases of such a program were ample opportunities to discuss and reinforce appropriate work values, adaptive interpersonal behaviors in the workplace, pride in practical skills, self-discipline, and teamwork.

Work participation programs have been described for junior high school students (Royston, 1970; Herr & Long, 1983). These programs can take many forms but they typically attempt to involve students in direct adult supervision and participation in community projects or actual job performances so that students can learn about adult work norms rather than those of peers. Such programs, however, must emphasize supervision and mentoring to be successful. Research has shown that work participation itself does little to foster general employability skills. Young workers in their first part-time employment typically receive little supervision, mentoring, and opportunity to learn work adjustment skills (Greenburger, Steinberg, &

Ruggiero, 1982). Success of work participation programs, therefore, depends upon guidance components in which work experiences can be discussed and problem solving undertaken.

Work shadowing is an underutilized resource for increasing work context skills (Herr & Watts, 1988). This term refers to "schemes in which an observer follows a worker around for a period of time, observing the various tasks in which he or she engages, and doing so within the context of his or her total role" (Watts, 1986, p. 1). Work shadowing thus provides the student with the opportunity to observe, participate, interact, and see the general context of a specific work environment, and fosters learning about the interpersonal environment of the workplace—work roles, power relationships, and other formal and informal mechanisms. The experience is much broader, therefore, than work participation alone, which focuses on the technical requirements of a job. Furthermore, brief experiences (one or two days) are effective (Watts, 1986; 1988). Many of the same benefits can probably be derived from mentoring programs (e.g., Borman & Colson, 1984), provided these programs are structured with work context skills in mind.

Training in job search and access skills, like that for other general employability skills, can begin early and is appropriate throughout a person's career. Programs have been instituted at elementary schools wherein students consider the requirements of, apply, interview, and are hired for jobs within the school (Leonard, 1972; Hedstrom, 1978). Similarly, youth employment services can be instituted for middle and secondary students in which students research available entry-level or part-time jobs in the community and actually match students with jobs. Local employment counselors can also be brought in to talk about jobs in the community. The purpose of these activities is not job finding per se, although this can be of considerable benefit, but teaching job search and access skills. Job-finding clubs can be particularly useful for both youth and adults (Wegmann, 1979; Johnson, 1981). In these groups, job search is considered a full-time job: the members meet daily until employment is secured, interview and telephone contact skills can be learned, family members are acquainted with the process, and emotional support is provided. Training in use of formal and informal job search techniques (Allen & Kearney, 1980), letters of application and resumes (Stephens, Watt, & Hobbes, 1970), interview skills

(Galassi & Galassi, 1978), and stress management techniques (Murphy, 1984) could become modular components of guidance and counseling programs since nearly all youth will sooner or later look for a job, and this process is frequently stressful.

As stated earlier in this chapter and in other parts of the book, in any of the programs suggested here, modifications may be necessary to address different populations. For example, it is likely that career guidance programs will need to be highly structured for emotionally disturbed secondary school students (Matthay & Linder, 1982). This type of program might include elements dealing with behavior management, social skills training, employment education, work adjustment training, occupational and career self-awareness activities, identification, management and reduction of stress, decision-making skills, and work-experience activities.

Finally, it is useful to reaffirm here that among the employment-bound populations are those of minority students, rural students, students of immigrant families, and students whose parents have not finished high school or have done so in a different culture. These sub-populations may have particular deficits in occupational information about the range of options available to them, the importance of serious attention to the course choices one makes as they close or keep options open, the support system of counselors, role models, summer work programs, or financial aid available to help them plan and realize their goals. Informational programs which help students become aware of work opportunities, duties, requirements, the various ways to prepare for them, how academic subjects relate to the work world, work visits, and observations of resource persons talking in personal ways about selecting, preparing, and entering specific jobs or occupations have been shown in several studies to be effective in increasing the span of career alternatives which these students are likely to consider (Herr & Cramer, 1992).

Minority or Culturally Different Students

Employment-bound students, whose background is culturally different from that of white, middle-class America, must be provided with opportunities to sort through the implications of these cultural differences for their own career development and to learn coping strategies for dealing with differences in cultural expectations. Culturally diverse and disadvantaged youth, disproportionately exposed to risk factors in school and in the work place, comprise the fastest growing segments of the work force. These students, too, need an effective integrated system of career guidance and career counseling that offers them the career education, the career resources and activities designed to help them develop and act upon their personal career development plans. Culturally different and disadvantaged youth need the competencies that career guidance programs described in this chapter seek to instill for all youth, though the needs of minority youth, the disadvantaged, and the at-risk for these competencies may be particularly acute. "Many employment-bound at risk youth are in critical need of immediate and realistic career plans. A key problem disadvantaged youth face is the lack of informal information sources and networks that other young people can access to help guide decisions about jobs and careers. Without sound information sources in their families and neighborhoods, disadvantaged youth may turn to unrealistic and misleading sources" (Employment and Training Administration, U. S. Department of Labor, 1993, p. 43).

Certainly not all minority or employment-bound youth from culturally diverse backgrounds are at risk or have diffi-culty negotiating their journey to a job and a productive life, but many are. For example, between now and the beginning of the twenty-first century, the work force will grow more slowly; become older, more female and more disadvantaged; be comprised of more people of color; and will absorb more immigrants (Johnston & Packer, 1987). A large proportion of these persons will be minority employment-bound males and females. Many of them will be facing the subtle forces of exclusion, racism, or other barriers and what are frequently the corollary effects of such treatment: a lowered sense of self-esteem, learned helplessness, and/or excessive distrust of the dominant culture (Sue, 1981). Such effects also act to preclude or diminish the benefits of job holding. For example, approxi-mately 25 percent of all African-American men have never held a job (National Alliance of Business, 1984) and available data suggest that many African-American youth engage in restricted vocational and self-identity exploration as a result of the negative self-images they have internalized as a function of the perceptions fed back to them by the larger society (Sewell & Hauser, 1975; Smith, 1975).

In other instances, students from immigrant families whose parents come from cultures where the work ethic and other value sets are different frequently have to straddle two cultures and try to fit comfortably within each. These students and other minority employment-bound youth must receive career guidance activities that expose them to culturally diverse role models representing a wide range of occupations; opportunities for racial awareness and ethnic identity; skills by which to cope effectively with racism; develop interpersonal skills by which to communicate effectively with potential employers, particularly when these communications are to be cross-cultural in nature; to develop a sense of commitment to the career planning process as a means for overcoming racial and ethnic barriers; and the acquisition of a comprehensive understanding of tentative occupational interests and how these would fit with cultural or family expectations. Career guidance activities relevant to these goals include identifying examples of prominent minority persons who have been successful in occupations related to a particular field of study, field trips to potential work sites to understand work organizations and environments and to see minority persons working on-site in different jobs, and participating in small groups to discuss concepts of career relevance as it relates to the influence of one's culture of origin and that of others on career decision making. These possibilities are obviously in addition to all of the other career guidance and counseling emphases available to all youth.

In some instances where students' parents are from quite different cultures and, therefore, unable or unwilling to serve as principal career guidance agents for their children as they begin to plan for work in the dominant culture, it is likely that the counselor will need to consider career guidance activities for parents. Conceived as a form of parent education to help parents become more informed about the services available for their children, such programs may focus on the educational and occupational options among which children may choose, the expectations, norms and characteristics of the American work culture, the notion that preparing and planning for work in the American culture is not to demean or forego the values or traditions of their cultures of origin, but rather to help their children gain an alternative set of cultural competencies that they will be expected to possess by the dominant culture as they implement their educational and occupational aspirations (Herr & Niles, 1994).

The Senior High School

Many of the issues of gender stereotyping, a lack of occupational information or effective role models, confusion about career planning, and other problems discussed in the junior high school continue for many employment-bound students into the senior high school. Indeed, it has been found in nationwide surveys of this matter that 70 percent of eleventh graders indicate their desire for help with career planning (Prediger & Sawyer, 1985). It has also been found that senior high students with low self-esteem have less explicit conceptions of themselves relative to career decision making, decideness, vocational identity, a sense of well being, and career salience than do students with high self-esteem. Thus, as suggested by Munson (1992), self-esteem, vocational identity, and career salience are important factors in career counseling interventions. Again, in many states and local areas, sequential programs of career guidance or programs that combine career guidance, career education, career counseling, and often experiential education are available. Most are not described in the professional literature but there are examples which are and can be cited.

The St. Louis Public Schools also have engaged at the senior high school level in collaborative activity with the business and industrial community of that city to provide experiential learning components in a sequential career education program that (Katzman, 1989) include the following in abridged form:

- Career Prep Club in which business and community persons team teach with the classroom teacher. This 12-lesson program draws upon business persons to present job-seeking and helping skills. Topics include career planning, how to find job openings, applications (college, armed services, and jobs), resumes, interviews, job attitudes, and how to advance on the job. Every student is responsible for completing a personal job/college portfolio.

- Decision-making seminars in which ninth graders learn from government and business speakers about individual and group decision making and how knowledge of social studies is used in public and private sector jobs.

- Shadowing in which a tenth, eleventh, or twelfth grader investigates his/her interests at a business site. These shadowing sites vary extensively in their focus and provide not only direct experience for the students engaged in shadowing at a particular site but also content for classroom sharing and the vicarious learning about the workplace for other students.

- Men and Women of Tomorrow Plan Today in which high school juniors are paired with professional role models in the community for a day in a conference setting outside of school. The adult role models and the students attend sessions together on self-esteem, goal setting, manhood and womanhood, and communication skills. The adult role model and the student spend the day together, developing a contract about goals the student hopes to achieve and designing a follow-up shadowing activity.

- Pre-employment skills work programs in which juniors and seniors have an opportunity to work as well as attend school. Designed as an after school program, students work two hours a day, five days a week in the private sector and attend a Career Prep Club class every two weeks. Funding is provided by the Job Training Partnership Act."

In another major city, a career development class was implemented and evaluated by Mackin and Hansen (1981). The population for the class was eleventh- and twelfth-grade students at an inner-city high school in Minneapolis where students were administered the attitude scale and three of the Competency Subscales of the Career Maturity Inventory (CMI) as part of a pre/post design. The Career Development Curriculum designed by the senior author served as the independent or treatment condition provided over 11 weeks. The Career Development program was based on development tasks for high school students drawn from the Career Development Curriculum developed by Tennyson, Hansen, Klaurens, and Antholz (1975). The goals of the curriculum were (1) to increase self-awareness; (2) to increase career awareness; (3) to increase decision-making and planning skills. Self-Awareness consisted of four units— self-concept, interests, abilities, and values and needs. Activities included student completion of a self-esteem measure, an adjective list, an occupational family tree, the Strong-Campbell Interest Inventory, Holland's Self-Directed Search, standard achievement and aptitude assessments, selected readings, values auctions, and a paper dealing with self and society.

Career Awareness included two units: Career Development and The Future. Activities included constructing personal life-lines, life-career rainbows, guest speakers, field trips, and occupational fantasy trips. Guest speakers included persons who would provide role models counteracting prevailing stereotypes of sex-typed or racially typed roles.

Decision Making and Planning was devoted primarily to "teaching decision-making skills and helping students identify goals and plans for the attainment of these goals. Emphasis is on learning a process of decision-making. Activities used include selected exercises from Decisions and Outcomes" (Gelatt, Varenhorst, Carey, & Miller, 1973), analysis of decision-making styles, a force-field analysis of student plans, and a career plans paper.

Although the sample size was small (N = 15) and there was no control group, the results were quite positive. Students were found to have significantly increased their scores on the attitude scale, self-appraisal scale, and goal-selection of the CMI. On class-evaluation scales, the students indicated that the class was helpful in the eight areas of intended effect: interests, values, skills, needs, occupational and school information, setting goals, making decisions, and making plans.

An additional example of a sequential approach has been designed to create a team effort to support career planning for academically disadvantaged students in East Lyme High

School, Connecticut (Matthay & Linder, 1982). The team included two special educators, two counselors, and two cooperative work experience coordinators. Fifty-one tenth-grade students comprised the population of students who were included. They were chosen because of lack of decision-making skills, lack of motivation toward finishing high school, and low academic test scores.

Participants in the program's career awareness classes met for 45 minutes every day for one semester, participated in weekly individual counseling with the school counselors, and received tutoring from the special educators as needed. The classes consisted of action activities, individual assessments of interests, aptitudes, and exercises, values clarifications discussions, activities, maintenance of journals, career decision-making exercises, audio-visual presentations, speakers, field trips, interviews with workers, assigned readings, and individual and group counseling. The content of the program included self-awareness, career awareness, and specific career discovery.

Based on pre/post testing, open-ended feedback from students, and the observations of students by teachers and counselors, the results of the program were found to be as follows:

1. Students became more familiar with regional career opportunities and trends and increased their job-search and decision-making skills.
2. Thirty-nine of the 51 students were found to have improved academic performance, improved class and school attendance, more positive self-images, more dedication to their school work, greater drive toward choosing career goals, and increased initiative to make meaningful choices about future goals.
3. Thirty-eight of the participating students planned to enter the cooperative work experience program in either their junior or senior year. Eight others felt the program was helpful in assisting them to consider entering vocational education programs.
4. Twenty-four of the students indicated that the program provided them an impetus to complete their high school education.

5. Students reported improved understanding of the relationship of school courses to specific careers and an understanding of the background knowledge and skills essential for successful job performance.

JTPA and Other Programs for Employment-Bound Youth

There tend to be few, if any, examples of programs, particularly those for more than a few sessions, of career guidance or career counseling in either the services provided by the Joint Training Partnership Act (JTPA) and, in turn, Private Industry Councils or by Job Service personnel in States as authorized by federal legislation and supervised by the U. S. Employment and Training Administration. The reasons are fairly straightforward. Schools have the ability to provide sequential, developmental, and longitudinal programs of career guidance and career counseling over extended periods of time. That they do not all do so is clear from the existing data. But, by the nature of their ability to affect and to shape the lives of children and youth over a period of approximately 12 years, schools are the most concentrated institutions in American society to address the needs of employment-bound youth. Therefore, most of the planned programs reported in this book and in the professional literature exist in schools.

That comprehensive programs of long-term career development of employment-bound youth do not now exist outside of the school is largely a function of federal policy and the prescribed mission of JTPA or the Job Service or other community agencies supported by governmental funds. In essence, both JTPA and Job Service personnel and programs are authorized to provide short-term responses to the needs of counselees identified by legislation as the appropriate constituency for each. Typically, throughout its history, the Employment or Job Service has expected the employment counseling in which it engages to be done with job applicants or employability program enrollees for limited purposes and for a limited time. Personnel in these roles frequently find themselves under pressure for case closures, positive terminations, and job placements (Herr, 1990). Similarly, JTPA programs "are mandated to provide short-term skill training leading to immediate job placement and earnings gain. Consequently JTPA programs tend to be shorter, more flexible, geared toward less academically proficient students, narrower in focus and staffed by trainers without the credentials or certification of typical vocational education teachers and career guidance personnel" (Employment and Training Administration, U. S. Department of Labor, 1993, p. 35).

There are also other differences between Job Service, JTPA, and in-school career programs for employment-bound youth. In-school programs, as suggested previously, can be comprehensive in their goals, sequential, and longitudinal. They include disadvantaged and minority youth but, in fact, tend to serve all youth. While not all in-school youth avail themselves of the career guidance resources or personnel available to them, such resources and personnel do address comprehensive goals and constituencies. Job Service personnel are primarily occupied with out-of-school youth and not only those who are disadvantaged. JTPA serves only economically disadvantaged and mostly out-of-school youth (Employment and Training Administration, U. S. Department of Labor, 1993). And, JTPA program goals tend to be more limited than those served by school counselors and, perhaps, even more limited than those served by Employment or Job Service counselors. JTPA programs place more emphasis on employment-related outcomes (e.g., relationship of training to job obtained, job status and ability to meet employers' needs) but focus mainly on the earning obtained by those being served. In comparison with the career guidance/ career counseling outcomes identified previously in this book and, more specifically, NOICC's *National Career Development Guidelines* discussed in this chapter, the JTPA Preemployment and Work Maturity Competencies are more narrowly defined. The JTPA Competencies are divided into those which relate to preemployment and those which address work maturity. The two sets of competencies include:

Preemployment
    Awareness of the world of work
    Labor market knowledge
    Occupational information
    Career planning and decision-making
    Job search techniques

Work Maturity
Punctuality
Regular attendance
Neat appearance
Good working relationships
Following instructions
Showing initiative and reliability (Employment and
Training Administration, U. S. Department of Labor,
1993, p. 38).

In contrast to the NOICC career development guidelines or those provided by many local or state departments of education, the JTPA competencies are more limited in their intent, do not focus on self-knowledge, on educational exploration other than local training, or on comprehensive models of career planning. These perspectives are not intended to belittle or negate the important role played by the JTPA legislation or the Job Service, or indeed, in-school programs for employment-bound youth. It is rather to suggest again that when employment-bound youth leave the school, there is not an integrated, comprehensive system of career counseling or career guidance activities that builds on the career development knowledge and skills they acquired in the schools, however positive, and helps them to extend and manage the personal career development process through the school-to-work transition process and into adjustment into the first job.

Conclusion

Chapter Six has examined the role statements of professional counselor organizations as well as federal policies as these define and shape the importance and the delivery of career counseling and career guidance in the United States. It seems clear that the most comprehensive approaches for employment-bound youth how exist within schools, although they are unevenly distributed and available from community to community and from school to school. As suggested in this chapter, beyond the process of career counseling itself as described in Chapter Five, there is a large array of career guidance activities that can be incorporated into programs for employment-bound youth. These include the infusion of career relevant information, examples, and exercises into academic subject matter as was advocated and implemented during the period of Career Education that was dominant in the United States during the 1970s and early 1980s. In addition, there is a large constellation of methods by which career information and other career relevant interventions can be provided by school counselors and by counselors in settings in the community. Selected examples of these career guidance activities are described. As career guidance activities are blended into comprehensive programs, they require the counselor to be a planner, coordinator, and technologist and to design such programs around concepts, knowledge, and skills that are pertinent to the needs of employment-bound youth. Some examples of such programs are given in the chapter as are comparisons between the potential contributions to the career development of school counselors, Job Service counselors, and the personnel and programs funded by the Joint Training Partnership Act.

Chapter Seven

Epilogue

Challenges to Career
Counseling and Guidance

Throughout this book, much of the emphasis in the content has been on doing better what is now done in career counseling or other career interventions: distributing the delivery of such services more evenly and more comprehensively to employment-bound youth; attending more fully to the current void in the provision of career counseling or career guidance during the period described as the school-to-work transition; and, during this period, strengthening the potential collaboration that exists among school counselors, Job Service counselors, counselors and specialists in Joint Training Partnership Act programs and other community based settings. In a major sense, such notions are evolutionary, not revolutionary. They accept what is and attempt to improve upon and tailor it to new challenges arising from the challenges of international economic competition or other social, political, and economic phenomena.

Implicit in such perspectives is an acknowledgment that the educational, occupational, and behavioral options for individuals, that become the content of career counseling and guidance are largely shaped by forces outside of the individual. Similarly, who does career counseling, where, and for what purposes is largely influenced by legislation and by school districts the sources and magnitude of resources for career counseling and guidance, and the guidelines and ethical standards from professional organizations that set boundaries on and create perceptions of what are, or are not, appropriate counselor behavior or areas of counselor intervention.

Thus, given the reality of the contextual factors—legislation, national and local policy, job creation mechanisms, economic development strategies—accelerating the availability and quality of career services to employment-bound youth in an evolutionary sense, or completely changing, and revolutionizing, the paradigms and the policies which govern how, where, and how much career counseling and career guidance will be provided to employment-bound youth depends upon forces outside of what counselors can do themselves. Significant changes in the availability of career counseling and other career interventions for employment-bound youth and in the choices open to them rely on new forms of collaboration across institutions and counseling practitioners, on new legislative and policy initiatives, on new forms of continuing support mechanisms that bridge the gap, however short or long, between the school and the workplace, and on new views of the importance to the economic development of the nation of employment-bound youth.

Previous chapters have talked about responses to many of the challenges cited above. Most of those responses will not be repeated here. Rather, this chapter will attempt to briefly summarize some of the issues and some of the possibilities that exist to strengthen the availability of career counseling, the continuity of such services across significant transitions like that between school and work, and the improvement of educational, governmental, and business and industrial collaboration designed to equip youth with the knowledge, skills, purposes, and attitudes required by the adult work world.

Federal Recognition of Employment-Bound Youth

As discussed elsewhere in this book, there is hope that a new recognition of the importance of employment-bound youth to the nation's future is gaining momentum. The federal government has produced a new work-based learning policy, advocated the development and extension of youth apprenticeship, and recently formulated "The Workforce Investment Strategy: A Comprehensive Proposal for Worker Adjustment Services and One-stop Career Centers," which outlines potential federal policies including (1) reemployment and retraining, (2) a One-stop Career Center network, and (3) information through a national labor market information system. Many of the concepts in these policies and initiatives have been embodied in the School-to-work Opportunities Act of 1994 discussed in some detail in earlier chapters of the book. The services provided in these initiatives will touch the lives of employment-bound youth by improving access to improved occupational and market information and the expanded availability of counselor support and career guidance, job search skills training, as well as in the specification and funding of school-based and work-based learning components and the activities that connect them.

The federal administration, the Congress and several state governments have underway or in discussion a variety of initiatives explicitly addressed to the school-to-work transition. At a National Conference, jointly hosted by the Departments of Education and Labor in September of 1993, a series of recommended strategies were discussed that were directly related to the Clinton Administration's School-to-Work Opportunities Act of 1993 introduced in September 1993 and adopted by the Congress on May 4, 1994. This Act is intended to stimulate the development of cooperative efforts between schools, business, and labor to upgrade skills of the American work force and to acknowledge the importance of providing complementary learning at school and work sites nationwide to achieve this goal. The Act made planning grant money available for the beginning of funding in spring 1994 to create state plans by which to achieve the Act's goals. These development grants were intended to serve as the basis for implementation grants beginning in late 1994. The grants required three components: (1) integration of work-based and school-based learning and occupational and academic learning, (2) work-based learning elements including a planned program of job training and experiences and instruction in general workplace competence, and (3) school-based learning including career exploration and counseling (*NTSC Bulletin*, Fall 1993). Specific aspects of such planning grant proposals included the provision that all students should develop a career plan and select a career major by eleventh grade. In addition, efforts are to be mounted that emphasize the integration and coordination of school learning and work-based learning, academic and vocational learning, secondary and post-secondary training, and education and training efforts. Also expected in such plans is the inclusion of counseling, the provision of work-place mentors, coaches, and instructors to increase the effectiveness of work-place learning for and the use of labor market information in the career planning and placement of students.

As described in the previous chapter, the School-to-Work Opportunities Act of 1994 has incorporated and, in some cases, exceeded the concepts and planning grant expectations that have preceded passage of the Act in May of 1994. The School-to-Work Opportunities Act has acknowledged that many states have already passed school-to-work legislation and therefore this federal legislation provides states and local partners support to design school-to-work systems that meet their specific needs or that exceed federal requirements. Given the comprehensiveness of the content and purposes of the School-to-Work Act as well as of the related state and local efforts underway, the components of *exemplary* school-to-work programs have begun to emerge and be identified. In addition to the broad categories of work-based learning, school-based learning, and connecting activities, according to Lyons (1994), additional components of exemplary programs are expected to focus on such areas as the following:

Organizational
- Formal agreement stating program goals and objectives;
- Clear administrative functions and staff assigned to the program;
- Regular supervision—scheduled and unscheduled—by the educational partner;
- Technical assistance to small businesses;
- Agreement of postsecondary partners to give priority to school-to-work graduates.

Work-based Learning
- Training plans followed at the work site;
- Students given the opportunity to learn broad, transferable skills as well as general workplace and employability skills;
- Planned program of training that leads to high-wage, high-skill jobs;
- Issuance of portable, industry-accepted skill certificate upon completion;
- Preference given to paid work experience, although non-paid experiences may be a part of the program;
- Careful assessment of work-based learning.

School-based learning
- Strong career guidance component;
- School-based activities and projects that directly relate to the work-based component;
- Integration of school-based and work-based activities
- Integration of core and technical skills.

Staff Development
- Training and ongoing support for staff at work site and school;
- Staff development for mentors.

Connecting activities
- Mentoring and counseling services to support student learning;
- Orientation and employability skills training for students.

Evaluation
- Continual assessment of program by all partners during the development and implementation stages;
- Assessment of program completers (p. 6).

The School-to-Work Opportunities Act obviously is not intended to simply support minor add-on activities to existing curricula. Rather, its support for programs requires integration of school-based and work-based learning activities that, in some cases, begin in the elementary school and which, in other cases, include major experiential, on-the-job, and work-based training segments that extend into the community. As such, the implementation of the School-to-Work Opportunities Act will provide the support and the substance by which to reform many dimensions of education and it will challenge employers to support and implement school-to-work objectives and systems, including providing more than a taken number of intensive work-based learning tasks for students. At a local or community level, as suggested above, school-to-work systems will need to incorporate three components into their plans and ensure all students equal access to them: career education and development (career exploration, instruction in both academic and technical skills, identification of employment and educational goals); work-based learning (on-the-job training and related experience); and connecting activities (coordination between the two components). Within the Act, there are both mandatory elements and those encouraged and permitted, but not mandated. Brustein and Mahler (1994) have summarized the content of the three components of the Act which for ease of reading have been placed by this author in columnar form as follows:

Work-based Learning	School-based Learning	Connecting Activities
Mandates:	Includes:	Includes:
• Work experience • A coherent sequence of job training and work experiences that are coordinated with school-based learning activities • Workplace mentoring • Instruction in general workplace competencies • Broad instruction, to the extent practicable in all aspects of an industry may include paid and non-paid work experiences, job shadowing, on-the-job training	• Career exploration and counseling • A sequential program of study with high academic standards that prepares students for postsecondary education and attainment of a skill certificate • Integration of academic and vocational training • Ongoing evaluations of student progress	• Coordination of work-based learning opportunities between students and employers • Good communication among students, parents, teachers, school administrators, and employers • Technical assistance for members of the partnership • Training for teachers, place mentors, school site mentors and counselors • Assistance to schools and employers to integrate academic and vocational education • Strong student counseling services • A system of following up on program graduates • Strategies for upgrading the skills of the workforce

These emphases in the School-to-Work Opportunities Act have been preceded by the actions of 13 states in mandating comprehensive school-to-work transition programs that are intended to be planned for all students, and that include a timely career education and development program which exceeds traditional career counseling. The four key components that are expected to be included in each of these comprehensive program designs include:

- processes for developing academic and occupational competencies
- career education and development
- extensive links between school systems and employees
- meaningful workplace experiences

There are other examples of federal legislation which continue to be important in their contributions to the training of selected segments of the employment-bound youth population. Probably the most prominent of these have been the Carl D. Perkins Vocational and Applied Technology Act, reauthorized in 1990, and the Joint Training Partnership Act. Both of these Acts tend to be restricted in impact to those groups that are the most economically disadvantaged or who have other significant problems that restrict or otherwise impair their preparation for and access to productive, full-time employment. Each of these Acts could, but probably will not, be expanded to include students beyond those anticipating entering or who are in vocational education, those who are disadvantaged or otherwise handicapped, or those with the most intractable employment problems. Nevertheless, these Acts do, in their own terms, extend the availability of comprehensive career guidance and career counseling programs to large numbers of persons preparing for entry or reentry into the American work force.

As hopeful as each of these recent initiatives are in expanding the career counseling and career guidance and related educational and transition mechanisms for employment-bound youth, there are additional and more specific initiatives that need to be considered by policy-makers, legislators, administrators and others influential in the support of or delivery of career counseling and related services. Before inventorying such possibilities, it is useful to make some observations about the historical and contemporary status of policies in the skill development of the work force as well as in career counseling and career guidance.

Employment Policy in the U.S.

By way of recent historical context, it seems useful to acknowledge that if the prime requisite of economic competitiveness is the skill level and preparation of the work force, it becomes necessary to know what the work force needs to know and to be able to do. But, once such insight is achieved and implemented in the common schools, it must be maintained and enhanced by continuous upgrading of skills over each worker's lifetime. Kuttner (1990) in addressing this issue contends "that the U. S. uniquely among industrial nations, has no systematic approach for continuously upgrading the quality of its workers and matching available human capital to industry's changing needs" (p. 21). Obviously, this lack of systemic approach affects how employment-bound youth are viewed and the availability or non-availability of systems to match them to appropriate job opportunities.

There is a parallel and perhaps much more significant question that tends not to be addressed very often. That question has to do with the willingness of employers to hire employment-bound youth for available entry-level jobs in the primary labor market where jobs are parts of a career ladder and training is available to help workers advance. If that is not so, then however well educated employment-bound youth are with technical skills or general employability skills, these skills will quickly become obsolete or reduced in value if they cannot be immediately used. The further question raised by such concerns is whether employers in the United States are willing to accept "part of the responsibility for helping youth make successful transitions from school to employment through partnership arrangements with the educational system" (Hoyt, 1994, p 192). If not, then much of the debate about improving the abilities of employment-bound youth are reduced to rhetoric about how schools are not effectively training youth for the work force, rather than a comprehensive solution to improving and using the skills of the American work force.

To talk in such terms immediately implicates other needs. One is long-term employment policy that is not fragmented, a by-product of other decisions, or the prerogative of each independent agency which touches the work force or the economy and then acts without coordination with other agencies. Comprehensive employment policy in the United States has tended to be aimed primarily at the 8 to 10 percent of the work force with the most jagged work histories, to the unemployed and the dislocated, to the disadvantaged and unskilled (Choate, 1984). While such groups clearly deserve attention and assistance, the other 80 or 90 percent of the work force is left to fend for itself. Although there are exceptions, employment policies typically have not looked holistically at the problems that need to be addressed or the support mechanisms critical to the preparation of workers, their access to the occupational structure, their adjustment to and their skill revitalization as the workplace and work processes change. For example, it is very difficult to know what to prepare workers for or to help them choose appropriate opportunities without a relevant, timely, and comprehensive base of labor market information. However, the United States is the only industrialized democracy that lacks a full-fledged labor exchange (Northeast-Midwest Institute, 1984). For example, the U. S. Employment Service receives information on only about 20 percent of job openings and accounts for only 5 percent of placements nationwide. While there are requests by the Department of Labor, or its state counterparts, to employers for information on likely or actual job openings, there is no sanction if that information is inaccurate or not forthcoming. As a result, in a nation which is awash in information, there is little or no systematic and direct sharing of information between business and industry and education, making it difficult for secondary schools and community colleges to know what training to offer and how best to prepare young people in a realistic fashion for the jobs available or anticipated in the community.

Therefore, without being overly negative, we have in the United States an aggregate of ideas, information, and mechanisms, many excellent foundations on which to build, but we do not yet have the policies or the processes that represent a deliberate integrated and comprehensive system to prepare people for employment in a historical period when individual career development, the need for job changes, and the characteristics of the occupational opportunity structure are increasingly shaped by the dynamics of a global economy. As a nation, we have not yet addressed an integrated set of life-span public employment policies that links the initial preparation of students for adult society and for employment, with those that address the transition from school to work, the induction and adjustment to work, the information and decision-making support that relates to the serial or mid-career change of jobs or occupations perhaps five or six times during a life-time, or pre-retirement and deceleration of commitment to the work force. As a result, we run the risk as a nation of leaving sectors defined by age, gender, and employment history uncovered by existing mechanisms, policies, or education and training.

These national voids in policy and practice have been seen with particular clarity in the last five or so years as attention has been focused on the lack of services available at the point when students leave high school, the school-to-work transition. As suggested throughout this book, unless high school graduates are going to college, or are in a special needs category, there are few, if any, transition services available to help them make the link between the school and work. They are figuratively cut adrift at high school graduation with few follow-up services, virtually no placement assistance or other direct help. Unlike the school-community-industry linkages in Europe—apprenticeships in Germany, or Careers officers in England, or other government schemes in Scandinavia, Ireland, and elsewhere—there are major gaps in the system of life-span services available in the United States, particularly as related to students who are immediately employment-bound after high school graduation and who do not attend vocational schools in which the connections with unions, craft councils, and employers are likely to be closer and more available to students than for those who graduate from comprehensive high schools in either academic or general programs.

Status of Policy in Career Counseling or Career Guidance

Since the early decades of the twentieth century, provisions for career counseling and career guidance services have been included in national policy formulations and, consequently, in the legislative translations of such policies into funding and action. However, counseling and guidance services have rarely been identified as the independent subject of policy formulations. Instead, career counseling and guidance services have been seen as having utilitarian goals that are a part of and integral to multi-dimensional programs of services and activities related to facilitating equality of access to education and training opportunities, creating human capital, rehabilitating those on the margins of society or economic productivity, or helping persons find purpose in and adjustment to work.

Each of these goals has taken on more or less urgency, depending upon events in the larger society that have arisen in different historical periods and that have varied markedly in their substance: for example, social reform in the late 1800s; the rise of individualism and cognizance of individual differences in the early 1900s; the concern for the handicapped and mentally ill in the 1920s; the economic exigencies and needs to match persons with available employment opportunities during the 'Great Depression' of the 1930s; national defense in the 1940s and 1950s; the democratization of opportunities in the 1960s; the concerns for equity and special-needs populations in a climate of economic austerity in the 1970s; and the transformation from an industrial to an information-based economy and the rise of the global economy in the 1980s and 1990s. Each of these historical periods spawned national social metaphors, achievement models, and rhetoric that have found their way into national or state policies affecting education, business and industry, and the identification of particularly vulnerable populations requiring specific forms of help to cope with changing social and economic conditions. Career counseling or guidance services have typically been included among the appropriate system of provisions supported by such governmental policies.

Viewed in terms of contemporary policy initiatives, the 1960s became the watershed decade for national legislation dealing with education and human resource development. An explosion of national "blue ribbon" reports, policy recommendations and legislative initiatives have continued since the 1960s to the present time, expressing growing concerns about unemployment rates, decreasing industrial productivity, the impact of automation on workers' skills, and the challenges of international competition. These policy-related processes have typically included various forms of career counseling or programs of career guidance services as aspects of national efforts to improve the economic equity of individuals of any age or group membership, to provide specific support for racial and ethnic minorities, and to strengthen the transition of individuals from school to work with general employability and workplace literacy skills.

The stimuli for the policies advocating the comprehensive needs for career counseling or guidance services have varied between the idealistic, the pragmatic, and the politically viable. Conceptual insights as well as economic demands have influenced policy initiatives. For example, national experience in diverse governmental employment and economic schemes, reinforced by research findings about career behavior, have supported the contention that the preparation of an effective worker requires more than technical skill training. The argument is that workers must be helped concurrently to develop a positive self-image, a valuing of work for themselves, and a repertoire of general employability skills (e.g., punctuality, self-discipline, job search and access skills, interpersonal and conflict-resolution skills, etc.) that allow them to choose, to adjust to work, and to apply the technical skills they possess within the goals of a work context and in effective interaction with other workers. Policies and legislation have assigned to career counseling and career guidance major responsibility for facilitating such outcomes (Herr, 1974; 1981; 1991).

Major Policy Challenges

Policy challenges to the universal availability across the life span of career counseling and career guidance services in the United States take several forms. The primary one is a lack of coherence and integration of the policies and legislation that provide for career counseling and career guidance services in the United States. Current national and state policies support-ing career counseling and career guidance services are a mosaic. There is considerable unevenness from state to state in whether career counseling and career guidance is a major expectation of schools and required in the training of school counselors. In some states, there are comprehensive state models of career guidance provisions at each educational level from the elementary school onwards. In such models, career guidance is often seen as one of the missions of the school and therefore as a central process to be implemented. In other states, the commitment to and implementation of career counseling and career guidance in the school is less apparent and given far less policy or funding support.

While the federal government has repeatedly produced policy, legislation, and funding support on behalf of career counseling and career guidance services in schools, states typically can avoid accepting such federal funds and thus can avoid the implementation of the policies and recommendations for practice that such funds promote and support. Therefore, the resources, availability of practitioners, and purposes of career counseling and career guidance vary dramatically for students, depending upon where they live and go to school. Some students can be considered to be very disadvantaged by a virtually complete lack of access to career guidance services, while students in other locations have a comprehensive set of opportunities for such help in school and in their community.

Hoyt (1994) has given an elegant analysis that bears upon the unevenness in school-to- employment transition services or the lack of other more basic attention to the career development of all students as a major part of the educational mission of the school. In essence, his view is that the current national emphasis on work-based learning, school-to-work transition services, and related processes have a more limited impact than necessary because these initiatives are not integrated into the current national emphasis on educational reform. Hoyt is undoubtedly correct in his view of this matter. This, too, is an issue of the coherence and integration of policies and legislation that provide for the availability of career relevant schools and of comprehensive career services for all students.

A second aspect of concern about policy coherence in career guidance services can be viewed in terms of implementation of policy at the federal level (Herr and Pinson, 1982). In the American system, national policy, legislation, and funding are highly interactive. Policy directly spawns and gives rationale to specific legislative enactments and to the authorization of funding for specific purposes articulated in policy.

However, there are many separate Federal Departments (e.g., Education, Labor, Health and Human Services, Defense, etc.). Each of these departments tends to have its own constituencies and the ability independently to recommend policies and levels of funding to the Congress for conversion into legislation. The practical effect is that as new population groups are identified as necessary recipients of career guidance and counseling, such services tend to be assigned to different federal departments and supported by many different pieces of legislation, rather than effectively integrated into an omnibus piece of legislation that encompasses and clarifies the responsibilities of career counselors in different settings and of schools and communities to provide career counseling.

Indeed, virtually all federal departments have some entitlement to support career counseling and guidance for children, youth, or adults or some specific subset of the population: economically disadvantaged, Native Americans, the elderly, migrant workers, the physically and mentally disabled, military veterans, ex-offenders, displaced homemakers, the unemployed, substance abusers, etc. Consequently, as separate policies and pieces of legislation originate in different governmental agencies, they tend to divide rather than make coherent the provision of career counseling and guidance services. As a result, several policies or pieces of legislation may be directed to the same population for different purposes, to be provided by different practitioners, in different settings. For non-school agencies in rehabilitation and employment counseling, for example, money flows directly from the responsible federal agencies to the offices funded in each state. In many instances, the career counseling specialist in one agency, e.g., the employment service, may work in isolation from those career specialists in rehabilitation counseling or, indeed, in the schools or the Veterans Administration, even though all may be receiving federal funds in support of career guidance services for similar purposes for the populations they serve.

Given such conditions, there is at present no specific location in the federal government from which can be obtained a global view of the needs for, provisions, or contributions of career counseling and guidance to national, state, local, or individual needs. One result of this condition is that national policy-making, and often that of state governments as well, regarding career counseling or career guidance, is often not fully informed about the ramifications of any specific legislative action; terms pertinent to career counseling—"vocational counseling", "elementary counseling", "career counseling", "career guidance", "career service", "employability service", "career development", "career education"—are used differently across policies and legislative titles; new programs and services are authorized without sufficient attention to the availability of services already in place; and authorization to employ counselors or career guidance specialists sometimes occurs without sufficient attention to the need for preparation or on-going training for such critical personnel. In sum, the argument can be made that without a coherent national policy about the need for and characteristics of career counseling or career guidance, such services continue to be vulnerable to social and political exigencies and to the possibility that resources for such services will be diluted through fragmentation and lack of co-ordination.

Recommendations for Future Policy Development in Career Counseling and Career Guidance

If future policy relevant to career counseling or to career guidance is to avoid some of the challenges now present in the United States, two recommendations seem in order.

Depoliticization. The first recommendation relates to the need for depoliticization. As described above, policy, legislation and the resources to support career counseling and guidance have been fragmented and frequently subject to the whims of a political and social agenda which is in considerable flux from one national administration to another. If the United States is to use its fiscal resources wisely in the face of the problems created by a large budget deficit and is simultaneously to provide the mechanisms by which its total work force will be equipped to cope effectively with the requirements of international economic competition, the nation will require long-term and comprehensive policy to give direction and substance to the delivery of career counseling and career guidance interventions for all populations, including employment-bound youth, and in a wide range of educational, community, and work settings.

The creation and implementation of long-term and comprehensive policy in career counseling and career guidance requires a bi-partisan or a depoliticized approach at the national level which can identify and support a core of career relevant services and activities that should be available for all citizens. In addition, such depoliticized support needs to provide for the possibility of sufficient flexibility in career services so that such services can accommodate the implications of an occupational structure in rapid transformation, the changing demographic structure (e.g., a rise in immigrants, more women, more minority group members) of the work force, cross-national mobility in a global economy, and educational and organizational shifts related to the implementation of advanced technology.

A *life-cycle approach.* A second recommendation is for a life-cycle approach to career counseling and career guidance policy. "Public policy often tends to segment problems artificially by age group or subject matter" (Research and Policy Committee, Committee for Economic Development, 1990, p. 6). To correct such a condition requires not only a depoliticization of human resource policy and a long-term strategy for providing the education, training, and career services necessary to a workforce that is literate, flexible, teachable and productive, but what has been described as a life-cycle view of policy. Such a policy links each stage of life and work to the next and takes into account the inter-related nature of needs and problems.

As recommended by the Research and Policy Committee of the Committee for Economic Development, a life-cycle approach to public policy in career counseling and career guidance would integrate such activities across the life cycle in ways which comprehensively reform, and bring into connection from one life stage to another, policies which are now piecemeal and fragmented. Such an approach to public policy would articulate the delivery of career counseling and career guidance services intergenerationally, based upon what is known about the salient needs for career maturity and adaptability from one life-stage to another. In essence, public policy would address the unique career guidance needs of children and youth as they explore and anticipate work, develop general employability skills, and engage in career planning; would provide programs that facilitate the transition from school to work; would facilitate worker adjustment, retraining, and career change; and would help older workers to plan for retirement or reduced labor-force involvement as they age. There is a wealth of knowledge about each career development life-stage and the transitions from one to the other which should inform a life-cycle approach to the locations and implementation of career counseling and career guidance and their need to be responsive both to cultural diversity in workers and to rapid change in the occupational structure.

A life-cycle approach to public policy including the role of counselors providing career counseling or career guidance should parallel and connect as appropriate with life-cycle policy approaches in education, industrial and economic development, job training, retirement, and other policies that affect the work force and the content of career counseling. In essence, what would result from a life-cycle approach to career counseling is a matrix of areas for public-policy intervention that would connect life stages, populations, settings and other relevant policy initiatives. This approach would also provide a case for investing in human capital throughout an individual's life, ensuring the cumulative flow of advantages of systematic support at all levels of students' and workers' lives so as to maximize personal purpose and productivity, not to mention the resulting benefits that would accrue to society. Such a life-cycle approach would also provide a structure for research that would have both summative and formative components as the impact of public policy on particular groups of persons or outcomes at selected ages is examined.

As suggested above, public policy in support of career counseling and career guidance in the United States has been frequent, abundant, wide-ranging, and variable in its coverage and intent. Career services are available in many settings and serve many groups of youths and adults. Many major needs remain, however, to bring such policies into co-ordination and cohesion to ensure greater evenness across populations and geographical entities in the delivery of such services, even if depoliticized and lifespan approaches to policy were implemented.

Among these challenges are the need to educate professional organizations, theorists, and practitioners of career services to the reality that from its beginnings in the United

States, the content and direction of career counseling and other career interventions have been shaped by sociopolitical purposes in the form of public policy, legislation, and statutes. The implementation of career services in the United States cannot be understood only as a set of evolving technical interventions in career behavior that have arisen in a political or economic vacuum. Instead, they must be seen in contextual terms as a function of political and economic forces that frequently change the levels of support and the focus of career counseling or career guidance in conjunction with political agendas.

As such, a fundamental need for the future is to affirm the long-term stability and importance of a core set of career services tailored to populations by gender and age across the life-cycle. These core activities must be seen as able to facilitate both individual purpose and productivity and, in turn, the aggregate economic development of the nation. The latter challenge will require greater use of available research about how the delivery of career counseling or career guidance services can be effectively articulated across settings and across a matrix of developmental and work-adjustment concerns. In addition, if available career services are to continue to be shaped and supported by public policy, such policies themselves must become more directly the focus of future research. The impact of public policy on the development of selected career attitudes, knowledge, and competencies in youth and adults needs to be a continuing target of empirical analysis rather than of only retrospective speculation. Within this context, the ultimate future challenge is to seek ways to set aside partisan political agendas in favor of a process of formulating public policy in support of the availability of career counseling and other career interventions based on research about the needs for coherence in the implementation of such services, and the potential outcomes and the importance of such processes as long-term national commitments to the preparation and maintenance of a literate, purposeful, and flexible work force.

Given the broad recommendations for the depoliticization of and a life-cycle approach to the provision of career counseling and career guidance for employment-bound youth and for other segments of the American work force, there are also additional especially recommendations specifically related to the strengthening of career services for employment-bound youth that deserve attention. Many of these reaffirm and advance themes that have been discussed in the previous section. One set of such recommendations has been proposed in a report funded by the Employment and Training Administration, the U. S. Department of Labor (1993). They include in an abridged form the following:

    1. Encourage and support joint ventures between the Department of Labor and Education.

        ..."Bridges with education could be strengthened by focusing JTPA resources on career guidance as the in-school service of choice. JTPA in collaboration with the Department of Education, could define the objectives and structure of in-school career guidance programs, to ensure compliance with standardized and comprehensive models." "The 1990 amendments to the Carl Perkins Act require the National Association of Vocational Education (NAVE) to describe and evaluate the Act's level of coordination with the Adult Education Act, the National Apprenticeship Act, the Rehabilitation Act of 1973, the Wagner-Peyser Act and JTPA (Grubb, 1992). DOL could require comparable assessments of cooperation with the Department of Education from the perspective of JTPA, the Job Service, apprenticeships, and work-based learning programs. Joint programs that intervene earlier may reach more youth while at the same time reducing the ranks of the hardest-to-serve population of the future" (p. 47).

    2. Explore the feasibility of developing career guidance projects for out-of-school youth. Programs available through JTPA for youth are essentially straight training and placement services. Little, if any, career guidance beyond the basic preemployment/work maturity competencies is offered through these programs"...There appears to be a definite need for more exploration into the ways career guidance can be offered to those youth who have abandoned the school system. DOL should consider piloting an extensive integrated program for out-of-school youth that

has career guidance as its centerpiece and combines other services that appear to offer significant benefits to disadvantaged youth (e.g., monitored work experiences). Such a pilot would be conceived as a sustained venture, exploiting the new opportunities through JTPA to work with youth over longer periods of time" (p. 47).

3. Incorporate into career guidance services as many elements of the comprehensive model as possible. For programs offered in both school- or non-school based settings, these elements include:

   a. Stimulation of Developmental Growth
      "Comprehensive career guidance activities recognize this by guiding youth through a sequence of stage-appropriate activities linked to a series of ever more sophisticated competencies that combine to form the skills needed to prepare for and succeed in the world of work. Given the acute needs of disadvantaged youth, these career interventions should be bundled with additional support services" (p. 48).

   b. Integrated Strategies and Interventions
      "Single strategies cannot be expected to address the diverse array of needs across the disadvantaged population. Nor can short-term, unintegrated, one-shot experiences meet the profound multiple needs of individual youth. Therefore, comprehensive programs integrate multi-pronged, multidimensional career interventions into fully formed programs (e.g., self-assessment, one-on-one counseling, group counseling, computer-assisted exploration, curricular integration, hands-on experiences, apprenticeships, etc.) with emphasis on career guidance, counseling, and planning."
      "Recommendations for action in schools have called for models in which counseling is central rather than peripheral to teaching and learning" (p. 48).

   c. Experiential Learning Opportunities.
      "Department of Labor should consider and develop mechanisms to coordinate and

strengthen youth's naturally occurring work experiences... "Currently, 5.5 million teenagers hold part- and full-time jobs, but these tend not to be monitored or integrated into their educational experience and may expose them to poor working models"... "Department of Labor should explore mechanisms to internally coordinate work-based learning and apprenticeships with career guidance" (p. 48).

d. Use of Multiple Mediums to Present Information. Given recent findings (Kirsch, Jungeblut & Campbell, 1992) "that 35 to 45 percent of high school graduates participating in JTPA, the Job Service, and Unemployment Insurance have literacy skills in the lowest two of five levels, it is imperative that the Department of Labor continue to expand the range and simplify the use of written, audio, visual, and computerized information concerning careers and planning" (p. 49).

e. Placement of Career Information in a Meaningful Context.
..."Guidance personnel, counselors, mentors, and others must assist youth in integrating career information into their own lives, thus providing them with the tools and skills to make meaningful decisions based on a personal understanding of themselves and an objective understanding of occupational and career information" (p. 49-50).

4. Modify and expand the Youth Employment Competencies [of the Joint Training Partnership Act] to more fully reflect the breadth of career guidance competencies.

5. Strengthen the Role of the Job Service in Providing Career Guidance.
..."In earlier years, Job Service Counselors visited the schools on a regular basis to counsel high school juniors and seniors about imminent career decisions, employment opportunities, training requirements and referrals. That practice, along with a complementary role for JTPA, could markedly increase the presence and

effectiveness of career guidance activities,
particularly in schools that serve large numbers
of disadvantaged youth" (p. 50).

While the recommendations for policy put forward in the research report published by the Employment and Training
Administration (1993) are principally addressed to the career counseling and career guidance needs of disadvantaged youth, the
substance of the recommendations, if implemented, would have
positive implications for all employment-bound youth. They are
strong affirmations of the need for the school counselor, the Job
Service Counselor, and JTPA personnel to use their unique
settings and competencies to jointly contribute to the career
development of students in schools and youth engaged in the
school-to-work transition, and to tailor the programs and experiences available to individuals based upon whether they are school
drop-outs, unemployed, or needing encouragement and support
as they pass through the school-to-work transition.

There are undoubtedly many other recommendations for
policy and for program initiatives that would be of particular
relevance to the career needs of employment-bound youth.
Many have been voiced elsewhere in the book; others can be
extrapolated into useful suggestions. Some examples follow:

- Place a Job Service counselor in a school district or in
  rotation to two or three school districts to work as a part
  of the school counseling team in providing occupational
  information, job search skills, assessment, and placement for every employment-bound youth.
- Require every high school to be accountable for
  providing a specific placement to a job, a training
  program, an apprenticeship for every employment-bound youth, just as is now the rule for
  students going to college.
- Have each high school provide a placement
  service, with community sponsorship, for every
  high school student legally eligible to participate in
  part-time work and monitor the learnings that
  individuals are acquiring from such work experiences as part of the career guidance program of the
  school. Provide access by school counselors to the
  information of the local Job Service office about
  local job vacancies and profiles of workers needed.

- Expect schools to have a specified career guidance
  component (e.g., selected workshops, courses,
  units) on career planning and transition to work or
  to further education as a graduation requirement.
- Require all schools, through the responsibility of
  school counselors, to have each student complete a
  career planning portfolio that will leave with the
  student at graduation and begin no later than
  grade six and continue throughout all subsequent
  years of high school.
- Request, through the National Alliance of Business
  or other related organizations, that they stimulate
  their local chapters of business persons to provide
  continuous resource persons on occupations,
  employer expectations of entry-level workers, and
  job search strategies to assist schools in providing
  students about such information.
- Request from the National Chamber of Commerce, the American Management Association,
  or related organizations the encouragement of
  employers to create systems of job coaches,
  mentors, and other induction and orientation
  mechanisms to support entry-level workers in
  their initial adjustment to work.
- Request that local employers, through the aegis of
  the Private Industry Council or Job Service, identify for schools the precise needs they have for and
  the number of new workers to fill available vacancies in their organizations and work directly with
  counselors to identify possible candidates among
  graduating employment-bound youth.
- Provide tax credits to employers who hire employment-bound high school students in the summer
  for jobs requiring specific types of subject matter
  expertise, e.g., Physics, Chemistry, Mathematics,
  Computer Literacy, Drafting, as a method of
  potential work-based learning and recruitment
  by employers.
- Provide funds through State Departments of Education and Labor to support summer training sessions/
  internships in workplaces for school counselors and

Job Service counselors to increase their knowledge of work environments and work processes.

- Develop community-based advisory committees of school counselors, Job Service counselors, JTPA and Private Industry Council personnel, and employers to structures and procedures by which to inform, place, and provide services to employment-bound youth upon graduation from high school and continuing until they are successfully centered into a job.

- Develop a Community Careers Council to develop a clearinghouse of information on all kinds of work experience, job placement, career counseling and related resources. Such Careers Councils might conduct local surveys of employers, government offices, and others to secure timely job relevant information for a community or a county. Such a Council might provide mobile displays of information for placement in schools, shopping malls, and other strategic locations, create video taped interviews with local workers as sources of career information, take part in the planning and execution of career days, job shadowing opportunities, and related activities. The Council might also house and assist employment-bound youth in using SOICC information about state-wide opportunities.

- Provide to employment-bound youth a system of local information about the availability of firm-specific training in the workplace or the community, the requirements of these, and their relationship to the content and level of educational attainment.

- Provide in schools a working-life course which provides information about and orientation to conditions in the labor market and work environments, occupational safety, the forms and uses of advanced technology, typical stages in the search for and induction into a job, personal economics, and related issues.

- Consider, as an integral part of the career counseling or career guidance of employment-bound youth, parental education. At whatever level of education or affluence, parents filter and reinforce images of work and work ethics to their children. They interpret, however accurately or inaccurately, the processes, content, opportunities, and activities of work. Efforts to include parents as active agents of career guidance resources and models need to be formulated by which parents can be informed about the career development activities and outcomes sought for their children, educated about the content of these activities and how parents can reinforce them, and their support and commitment solicited.

Conclusion

The intent of this chapter is not to be an exhaustive litany of policy recommendations or possibilities. Rather, the intent is to affirm that neither the shape and substance of career counseling and career guidance, the image and value attached to employment-bound youth, nor the content and problems that employment-bound youth bring to counselors occurs in a vacuum. Each of these phenomena is a function of forces and, more particularly, often of the comprehensiveness and substance of policies and legislation that address issues of relevance to employment-bound youth or other segments of the American work force.

While there are significant indications that more comprehensive national policy and legislative initiatives are underway and that many of these address both the needs of employment-bound youth and the general lack of career counseling and other career services during the period of the school-to-work transition, there are other broad, as well as specific, issues which need to counteract fragmentation and isolation of policy or legislative initiative. Unless bold new analyses of opportunities for collaboration among schools-employers-government agencies, redeployment of resources, and, indeed, recognition of the importance of employment-bound youth in the American Society, the efforts that ensue in behalf of this population will continue to be evolutionary, uneven, piecemeal rather than revolutionary, comprehensive and systematic.

References

Adams, A. V., & Mangum, G. (1978). *The Lingering Crisis of Youth Unemployment*. Kalamazoo, MI: Upjohn Institute for Employment Research.

Allen, R. E., & Kearney, T. S. (1980). The relative effectiveness of alternative job sources. *Journal of Vocational Behavior, 16*, 18-42.

American School Counselors Association (1984). *The School Counselor in Career Guidance: Expectations and Responsibilities*. Role Statement Adopted 1984.

American School Counselors Association (1992). *Guide to Membership Resources*. Alexandria, VA: The Author.

Amundson, N. E., Borgen, W. A., Westwood, M. J., & Pollard, D. E. (1989). *Employment Groups: The Counseling Connection*. Ottawa: Lugus Productions, Ltd. and Minister of Supply and Services, Canada.

Aring, M. K. (1993). What the 'V' word is costing America's economy. *Phi Delta Kappan, 74*(5), 396-404.

Ashley, W. L., Cellini, J., Faddis, C., Pearsol, J., Wiant, A., & Wright, B. (1980). *Adaptation to Work: An Exploration of Pocesses and Outcomes*. Columbus, OH: National Center for Research on Vocational Education.

Aubrey, R. (1985). A counseling perspective on the recent educational reform reports. *The School Counselor, 32*, 91-99.

Baker, S. B., & Popowicz, C. L. (1983). Meta-analysis as a strategy for evaluating effects of career education interventions. *Vocational Guidance Quarterly, 31*, 178-186.

Barton, P. E. (1991). The school-to-work transition. *Issues in Science and Technology, 7*(3), 50-54.

Barton, P.E. (1991). Odyssey of the transition from school to work 1960-1990. *In High School to Employment Transition Contemporary Issues* (pp. 3-12). Edited by A. J. Pautler, Jr. Ann Arbor, MI: Prakken Putlications, Inc.

Bergland, B. W. (1974). Career planning: The use of sequential evaluated experience. In E. L. Herr (Ed.) *Vocational Guidance and Human Development* (pp. 350-380). Boston: Houghton Mifflin.

Berlin, G., & Sum, A. (1988). *Toward a More Perfect Union: Basic Skills, Poor Families, and Our Economic Future.* (Occasional Paper Number 3). February. New York: Ford Foundation.

Bernstein, Aaron (1988). Where the jobs are and where the skills aren't. *Business Week, 3070,* September 19, 104-108.

Berryman, S. E. (1982). The equity and effectiveness of secondary vocational education. In *Education and Work.* Eighty-first Yearbook of the National Society for the Study of Education. (pp. 169-203). Chicago, IL: The University of Chicago Press.

Bhaerman, R. D. (1977). *Career Education and Basic Academic Achievement: A Descriptive Analysis of the Research.* Washington, D.C.: U. S. Office of Education.

Bollendorf, M., Howrey, M., & Stephenson, G. (1990). Project career REACH: Marketing strategies for effective guidance programs. *The School Counselor, 37*(3), 273-280.

Bordin, E. S., Nachman, B., & Segal, S. (1963). An articulated framework for vocational development. *Journal of Counseling Psychology, 10,* 107-116.

Bordin, E. S. (1984). Psychodynamic model of career choice and satisfaction. In D. Brown & L. Brooks (Eds.). *Career Choice and Development: Applying Contemporary Theories to Practice* (Chap. 5). San Francisco: Jossey-Bass.

Bordin, E. S. (1990). Psychodynamic models of career choice and satisfaction. In D. Brown & L. Brooks (Eds.). *Career choice and development: Applying contemporary theories to practice. 2nd Ed.*, (pp. 102-144). San Francisco: Jossey-Bass.

Borgen, W., & Amundson, N. *The Experience of Unemployment: Implications for Counseling the Unemployed.* Scarborough, Ontario: Nelson, Canada.

Borman, K., Izzo, K. V., Penn, E. M., & Reisman, J. (1984). *The Adolescent Worker.* Columbus: Ohio State University, National Center for Research in Vocational Education

Borman, G., & Colson, S. (1984). Mentoring—An effective career guidance technique. *Vocational Guidance Quarterly, 32,* 192-197.

Borman, K. M. (1991). *The First "Real" Job. A Study of Young Workers.* Albany, NY: The State University of New York Press.

Borow, H. (1989). Youth in transition to work: Lingering problems. *Guidance and Counseling, 4*(4), 7-14.

Brenner, M. H. (1973). *Mental Illness and the Economy.* Cambridge, MA: Harvard University Press.

Brenner, M. H. (1979). Health and the national economy: Commentary and general principles. In L. A. Ferman and J. R. Gordus (Eds). *Mental Health and the Economy.* (Chap. 3). Kalamazoo, MI: The W. E. Upjohn Institute for Employment Research.

Brown, D. (1984). Trait and factor theory. In D. Brown & L. Brooks (Eds.). *Career Choice and Development: Applying Contemporary Theories to Practice* (Chap. 2). San Francisco: Jossey-Bass.

Brown, D., & Brooks, L. (1991). *Career Counseling Techniques.* Boston: Allyn & Bacon.

Brustein, M., & Mahler, M. (1994). Doling the dollars: School-to-work grant requirements are lengthy and demanding. *Vocational Education Journal, 69*(7), 19-21.

Business Advisory Committee, Education Commission of the States (1985). *Reconnecting Youth*. Denver, CO: The Author.

Campbell, R. E. (1968). *Vocational Guidance in Secondary Education: A National Survey*. Columbus, OH: The Center for Vocational Education.

Carneval, A. P., & Gainer, J. (1989). *The Learning Enterprise*. Washington, D.C.: U. S. Department of Labor, Employment and Training Administration/The American Society for Training and Development.

Castells, M. (1985). High technology, economic restructuring and the urban-region process in the United States. In M. Castells (Ed.). *High Technology, Space and Society*, (Chapter 1). Beverly Hills, CA: Sage.

Center for Public Resources (1983). *Basic Skills in the U. S. Work Force*. Corporate Roles in Public Education Project. Washington, D.C.: The Author.

Cheatham, H. E. (1990). Afrocentricity and career development of African Americans. *The Career Development Quarterly, 38,* 334-346.

Chew, C. (1993). *Tech-Prep and Counseling: A Resource Guide*. Madison, WI: Center on Education and Work, University of Wisconsin.

Choate, P. (1982). *Retooling the American Work Force: Toward a National Training Strategy*. Washington, D.C.: Northeast-Midwest Institute.

Chusid, H., & Cochran, L. (1989). Meaning of career change from the perspective of family roles and dramas. *Journal of Counseling Psychology, 36*(1), 34-41.

Committee for Economic Development. (1988). *Strategy for U. S. Industrial Competitiveness*. New York: The Author.

Commission on Excellence in Education (1983). *The Nation at Risk*. Washington, D.C.: The Author.

Commission on Precollege Guidance and Counseling, The College Board (1986).

Commission on Workforce Quality and Labor Market Efficiency. U.S. Department of Labor (1989). *Investing in People, A Strategy to Address America's Work Force Crisis*. Washington, D.C.: The Author.

Commission on Work, Family and Citizenship (1988). *The Forgotten Half*. The W. T. Grant Foundation.

Commission on the Skills of the American Workforce (1990). *America's Choice: High Skills or Low Wages*. Rochester, NY: National Center on Education and the Economy.

Congressional Record, 101st Congress, 2nd Session (1990, August 2). The Carl D. Perkins Vocational and Applied Technology Act Amendments of 1990.

Council of Chief State School Officers (1991). *European Lessons from School and the Workplace*. Washington, D.C.: The Author.

CPC, Foundation/Rand Corporation (1994). *Developing the Global Work Force—Insights for Colleges and Corporations*. Bethlehem, PA: The College Placement Council, Inc.

Crites, J. O. (1969). *Vocational Psychology*. New York: McGraw-Hill.

Crites, J. O. (1974). Career Counseling: A Review of Major Approaches. *The Counseling Psychologist, 4*(3), 3-23.

Crites, J. O. (1981). *Career Counseling: Models, Methods, and Materials*. New York: McGraw-Hill.

Dayton, J. D., & Feldhusen, J. F. (1989). Characteristics and needs of vocational talented high school students. *The Career Development Quarterly, 37*(4), 355-364.

DeRidder, L. M. (1991). Integrating equity into the school. In R. Hanson (Ed.) (pp. 23-38). *Career Development for the 21st Century*, Knoxville, TN: The University of Tennessee, Department of Technological and Adult Education.

Dore, R. (1987). *Taking Japan Seriously: A Confucian Perspective on Leading Economic Issues*. Stanford, CA: Stanford University Press.

Drucker, P. F. (1986). *Innovation and Entrepreneurship. Practice and Principles*. New York: Perennial Library.

Drucker, P. F. (1989). *The New Realities. In Government and Politics/in Economics and Business/in Society and the World View*. New York: Harper & Row.

Drucker, P. F. (1993). *The Post-capitalist Society*. New York: Harper Business Books.

Duke, B. (1986). *The Japanese School Lessons for Industrial America*. New York: Praeger.

Dyrenfurth, M. I. (1984). *Literacy for a Technological World*. Columbus, OH: National Center for Research in Vocational Education. The Ohio State University.

Echikson, W. (1992, December 14). Europe's lessons for the future. *Fortune, 126*(13), 157-162.

Education Writers Association (1990). *Training for Work. What the U.S. Can Learn from Europe*. Washington, D.C.: The Author.

Education Testing Service (1990). *From School to Work*. Princeton, NJ: The Author.

Elbaum, B. (1989). Why apprenticeship persisted in Britain but not in the United States. *Journal of Economic History*, 337-349.

Employment and Training Administration, U. S. Department of Labor (1989, November). *Work-Based Learning: Training America's Workers*. Washington, D.C.: The Author.

Employment & Training Administration, U.S. Department of Labor (1993). *Finding One's Way: Career Guidance for Disadvantaged Youth*. Research and Evaluation Report Series 93-0. Washington, D.C.: The Author.

Fierman, J. (1994). The contingency work force. *Fortune*, *129*(2), January 24, 30-37.

Fletcher, F. M. (1971). The counselor of the future. *Journal of Employment Counseling*, *8*, 43-47.

Friesen, J. (1986). The role of family in vocational development. *International Journal for the Advancement of Counseling*, *9*(1), 5-10.

Fuqua, D. R., Blum, C. R., &, Hartman, B. W. (1988). Empirical support for the differential diagnosis of career indecision. *Career Development Quarterly*, *36*, 364-373.

Galassi, J. P., & Galassi, M. D. (1978). Preparing individuals for job interviews. Suggestions for more than 60 years of research. *Personnel and Guidance Journal*, *57*(4), 188-192.

Gelatt, H. B., Varenhorst, B., Carey, R., & Miller, G. P. (1973). *Decisions and Outcomes*. New York: College Entrance Examination Board.

Ginzberg, E., Ginsburg, S. W., Axelrad, S., & Herma, J. (1951). *Occupational Choice: An Approach to a General Theory*. New York: Columbia University Press.

Ginzberg, E. (1982). The mechanization of work. *Scientific American*, 247(3), 66-75.

Gittner, R. J. (1994). Apprenticeship-trained workers: United States and Great Britain. *Monthly Labor Review*, April, 38-43.

Glover, R. W. (1986). *Apprenticeship Lessons from Abroad*. Columbus, OH: National Center for Research in Vocational Education.

Gottfredson, L. S. (1981). Circumscription and compromise: A developmental theory of occupational aspirations. *Journal of Counseling Psychology, 28*(6), 545-579.

Gray, K. (1994). Firm size: The overlooked variable in school-to-work employment transition. Chapter 13 in *High School to Employment Transition: Contemporary Issues*, (151-156). Edited by A. J. Paulter, Jr., Ann Arbor, MI: Prakken Publications, Inc.

Greensberger, E., & Steinberg, L. (1986). *When Teenagers Work: The Psychological and Social Costs of Adolescent Employment*. New York: Basic Books.

Grubb, W. N. (1992). *Assessing the Coordination of Vocational Education with Other Federal Programs. Working Paper for the NCRVE*. Berkeley, CA: National Center for Research in Vocational Education.

Gysbers, N. C., & Henderson, P. (1988). *Developing and Managing Your School Guidance Program*. Alexandria, VA: AACD Press.

Haccoon, R. R., & Campbell, R. E. (1972). *Work Entry Problems of Youth: A Literature Review*. Columbus, OH: Center for Vocational Technical Education.

Hamilton, L. S. (1990). *Apprenticeship for Adulthood: Preparing Youth for the Future*. New York: The Free Press.

Hansen, L. S. (1981). New goals and strategies for vocational guidance and counseling. *International Journal for the Advancement of Counseling, 4*, 21-34.

Hansen, L. S., & Biernat, B. (1992). Daring to dream: Career aspirations and interventions in childhood and adolescence. In J. Lewis, B. Hayes, & L. Bradley (Eds.). *Counseling Women Over the Life Span* (pp. 13-54). Denver, CO: Love Publishing.

Hayes, C. D. (Ed.) (1987). *Risking the Future: Adolescent Sexuality, Pregnancy, and Childbearing.*

Hedin, D., Erickson, J., Simon, I., & Walker, J. (1985). *Minnesota Youth Poll: Aspirations, Future Plans, and Expectations of Minnesota Youth.* St. Paul, MN: Center for Youth Development and Research, University of Minnesota.

Hedstrom, J. E. (1978). Jobs for kids. *Elementary School Guidance and Counseling, 13*, 132-134.

Herr, E. L., Horan, J. J., & Baker, S. B. (1973). Clarifying the counseling mystique. *American Vocational Journal, 484* (April), 66-68.

Herr, E. L. (1974). Manpower policies, vocational guidance, and career development. Chapter Two in E. L. Herr (Ed). *Vocational Guidance and Human Development*, pp 32-62. Boston, MA: Houghton Mifflin.

Herr, E. L. (1977). *Career Education: The State of Research.* Columbus, OH: ERIC Clearinghouse for Career Education.

Herr, E. L. (1978). *Research in Career Education: The State of the Art.* Columbus, OH: ERIC Clearinghouse for Career Education.

Herr, E. L. (1981). Policy in guidance and counseling: The U.S. experience. *Educational and Vocational Guidance Bulletin, 37*, pp. 67-83.

Herr, E. L., Weitz, A., Good, R., & McLoskey, G. (1981). *Research on the Effects of Secondary School Curricular and Personal Characteristics Upon Postsecondary Educational and Occupational Patterns.* (NIE-G-80-0027), University Park, PA: The Pennsylvania State University.

Herr, E. L., Weitz, A., Good, R., & McCloskey, G. (1981). *Research on the Effects of Secondary School Curricular and Personal Characteristics upon Postsecondary Educational and Occupational Patterns* (NIE-G-80-0027) University Park, PA: The Pennsylvania State University.

Herr, E. L., & Pinson, N. M. (1982). *Foundations for Policy in Guidance and Counseling.* Falls Church, VA: AACD Press.

Herr, E. L., & Long, T. E. (1983). *Counseling Youth for Employability: Unleashing the Potential.* Ann Arbor, MI: University of Michigan, ERIC Clearinghouse for Counseling and Personnel Services.

Herr, E. L. (1984). Links among training, employability, and employment. In N. C. Gysbers (Ed). *Designing Careers, Counseling to Enhance Education, Work, and Leisure.* San Francisco: Jossey-Bass.

Herr, E. L. (1987). Education as preparation for work: Contributions of career education and vocational education. *Journal of Career Development, 13*(3), 16-30.

Herr, E. L. (1987). Comprehensive career guidance and vocational education. Natural allies. *Vocational Education Journal, 62* (1987), 30-33.

Herr, E. L., & Cramer S. H. (1988). *Career Guidance and Counseling Through the Life-Span: Systematic Approaches.* Glenview, IL: Scott, Foresman.

Herr, E. L., & Watts, A. G. (1988). Work shadowing and work-related learning. *The Career Development Quarterly, 37*(1), 78-86.

Herr, E. L. (1989). *Community-based Approaches to Guidance.* Indianapolis, IN: Lilly Endowment.

Herr, E. L., & Johnson, E. (1989). General employability skills for youths and adults: goals for guidance and Counseling programs. *Guidance and Counseling, 4,* 4.

Herr, E. L. (1989). *Counseling in a Dynamic Society. Opportunities and Challenges.* Alexandria, VA: AACD Press.

Herr, E. L. (1990). Employment counseling in a global economy. *Journal of Employment Counseling, 27,* 147-159.

Herr, E. L. (1991). Multiple agendas in a changing society: Policy challenges confronting career guidance in the U.S.A. *British Journal of Guidance and Counseling, 19*(3), 267-282.

Herr, E. L., & Cramer, S. H. (1992). *Career Guidance and Counseling Through the Lifespan. Systematic Approaches.* New York: Harper Collins.

Herr, E. L. (Ed.) and Associates (1992). *The School Counselor and Comprehensive Programs for Work-Bound Youth. A Position Paper.* Alexandria, VA: The American Counseling Association.

Herr, E. L. (Ed.) (1993). *The School Counselor and Comprehensive Programs to Work-Bound Youth. An American Counseling Association (ACA) Position Paper.* Alexandria, VA: American Counseling Association.

Herr, E. L., & Niles, S. G. (1994). Multicultural career guidance in the schools. Chapter 9 in *Multicultural Counseling in Schools* (177-194). Edited by Paul Pedersen and John C. Carey. Boston: Allyn and Bacon.

Hershenson, D. (1992). Personal Communication.

Herzog, A., & Bachman, J. (1982). *Sex Role Attitudes Among High School Students.* Ann Arbor, MI: University of Michigan Survey Research Center, Institute for Social Research.

Hilton, Margaret (1991, March). Shared training: Learning from Germany. *Monthly Labor Review, 114*(3), 33-37.

Hoerner, J. L. (1991). Tech-prep: A viable solution for the forgotten half. *American Technical Education Association Journal,* April-May, 18-20.

Holland, J. L. (1966). *The Psychology of Vocational Choice.* Waltham, MA: Blaisdell.

Holland, J. L. (1973). *Making Vocational Choices: A Theory of Careers.* Englewood Cliffs, NJ: Prentice-Hall.

Holland, J. L., Magoon, T. M., & Spokane, A. R. (1981). Counseling psychology: Career interventions, research and theory. *Annual Review of Psychology, 32,* 279-300.

Holland, J. L. (1982). *Some Implications of Career Theory for Adult Development and Aging.* Paper presented at the American Psychological Association Convention, Washington, D.C.

Holland, J. L. (1985). *Making Vocational Choices: A Theory of Vocational Personalities and Work Environments, 2nd Ed.* Englewood Cliffs., NJ: Prentice-Hall.

Hotchkiss, L., & Borow, H. (1990). Sociological perspectives on work and career development. In D. Brown & L. Brooks (Eds.). *Career Choice and Development. Applying Contemporary Theories to Practice* (pp. 262-307). San Francisco: Jossey Bass.

Hoyt, K. B. (1965). High school guidance and the speciality oriented student research program. *Vocational Guidance Quarterly, 13,* 229-236.

Hoyt, K. B. (1980). *Evaluation of K-12 Career Education: A Status Report*. Washington, D.C.: Office of Career Education.

Hoyt, K. B. (1994). A proposal for making transition from schooling to employment an important component of educational reform. Chapter 17 in *High School to Employment Transition: Contemporary Issues* (pp. 189-200). Edited by A. J. Paulter, Jr., Ann Arbor, MI: Prakken Publications, Inc.

Hudson Institute (1987). *Workforce 2000; Work and Workers for the 21st Century*. Indianapolis, IN. The Author.

Hull, D. M., & Pedrotti, L. S. (1983). Meeting the high-tech challenge. *VOCED, 58*, (3), 28-31.

Hulsart, R. (1983). *Employability Skills Study*. Denver, CO: Colorado Department of Education.

Human, J., & Wasen, C. (1991). Rural mental health in America. *American Psychologist, 46*, 232-239.

Jepsen, D. A. (1974). Vocational decision-making strategy-types: An exploratory study. *Vocational Guidance Quarterly, 23*(2), 17-23.

Jepsen, D. A. (1989). Adolescent career decision processes as coping responses for the social environment. In R. Hanson (Ed.) *Career Development: Preparing for the 21st Century*, (Chap. 6) (pp. 67-82). Knoxville, TN: The University of Tennessee, Department of Technological and Adult Education.

Johnson, H. (1980). A free enterprise elementary career education project. *The School Counselor, 27*, 325-317.

Johnson, W. L. (1981). Groups that help minorities find jobs. Career World: *The Continuing Guide to Careers, 9*, 28-29.

Johnston, W. L., & Packer, A. H. (1987). *Workforce 2000: Work and Workers for the Twenty-First Century*. Indianapolis, IN: Hudson Institute.

Jones, S. (1987). Youth and work: Outreach, assessment, preparation. *Perspectives, 3,* 117-121.

Kazanas, H. C. (1978). *Affective Work Competencies for Vocational Education.* Columbus, OH: National Center for Research in Vocational Education, Ohio State University.

Katzman, S. E. (1989). A response to the challenge of the year 2000. In R. Hanson (Ed.), *Career Development Preparing for the 21st Century.* Knoxville, TN: University of Tennessee, Department of Technological and Adult Education.

Katzman, S. E. (1991). A response to the challenges of the year 2000. In *Career Development in the 21st Century* (pp. 15-22). Edited by Robert Hanson, Ann Arbor, MI: ERIC Counseling and Personnel Services.

Kauffman, J., Schaefer, C., Lewis, M. V., Steven, D. W., & House, E. W. (1967). *The Role of the Secondary School in the Preparation of Youth for Employment.* University Park, PA: Institute for Human Resources.

Keeley, (1990).

Kinnier, R. T., Brigman, S. L., & Noble, F. C. (1990). Career indecision and family enmeshment. *Journal of Counseling and Development, 68,* 309-312.

Kirsch, J., Jungeblut, A., & Campbell, A. (1992). *Beyond the School Doors: The Literacy Needs of Job Seekers Served by the U.S. Department of Labor.* Washington, DC: U. S. Department of Labor, Employment and Training Administration.

Klerman, J. A., & Karoly, L. A. (1994). Young men and the transition to stable employment. *Monthly Labor Review, 117*(8), 31-48.

Knowles, M. (1977). The adult learner becomes less neglected. *Training, 14*(9), 16-18.

Kohn, M. L. (1977). *Class and Conformity: A Study in Values, 2nd Ed.* Chicago: University of Chicago Press.

Krumboltz, J. D. (1983). *Private Rules in Career Decision Making.* Columbus, OH: Ohio State University, National Center for Research in Vocational Education.

Kutscher, R. (1987). Projections 2000: Overview and implications of the projections to 2000. *Monthly Labor Review, 110*(9), September, 12-20.

Kuttner, Robert (1990). A toast to the cold war's end—with a shot of reality. *Business Week,* 3140 (January 8), 21.

Law, G. F. (1969). Vocational curriculum: A regular place for guidance. *American Vocational Journal, 44,* 27-28, 60.

Leibowitz, Z. B., Farren, C., & Kaye, B. L. (1986). *Designing Career Development Systems.* San Francisco: Jossy-Bass.

Leonard, G. E. (1972). Career guidance in the elementary school. *Elementary School Guidance and Counseling, 6,* 283-286.

Leong, F. T. (1985). Career development of Asian Americans. *Journal of College Student Personnel, 26,* 539-546.

Lichter, D. (1988). Race, employment hardship and inequality in American non-metropolitan south. *American Sociological Review, 54,* 436-446.

Liem, R., & Rayman, P. (1982). Health and social costs of unemployment. *American Psychologist, 37,* 1116-1123.

Lynch, R. L. (1991). Teaching in the 21st century. *Vocational Journal, 66*(1), p. 29.

Lyons, C. (1994). Think globally, act locally. *Vocational Education Journal, 69*(7), 6.

Maccoby, M., & Terzi, K. (1981). What happened to the work ethic? In J. O'Toole, J. L. Scheiber, & L. C. Woods (Eds.), *Working, Changes and Choices*, (pp. 162-171). New York: Human Science Press.

Mackin, R. K., & Hansen, L. S. (1981). A theory-based career development course: A plant in the garden. *The School Counselor, 28*(5), 325-334.

Mangum, G. T. (1988). *Youth Transition from Adolesence to the World of Work*. Paper prepared for youth and America's Future: The William T. Grant Foundation Commission on work, family and citizenship. Washington, D.C.: The William T. Grant Foundation Commission.

Marshall, R., & Tucker, M. (1992, November 9-15). The best imports from Japan and Germany. *Washington Post National Weekly Edition*, p. 24.

Martin, J. (1992). Your new global work force. *Fortune, 126*(13), December 14, 52-68.

Massachusetts Institute of Technology, Quality Education for Minorities Project (1990). *Education That Works: An Action Plan for the Education of Minorities*. Cambridge, MA: The Author.

Matthay, E. R., & Linder, R. (1982). A team effort in planning for the academically disadvantaged. *The School Counselor, 29*(3), 226-231.

McIntire, W. G., Marion, S. F., & Quaglia, R. (1990). Rural school counselors: Their communities and schools. *The School Counselor, 37*, 166-172.

Meyer, R. H., & Wise, D. A. (1982). High school preparation and early labor force experience. In *The Youth Labor Market Problem: Its Nature, Causes, and Consequences* (pp. 277-339). Chicago: University of Chicago Press.

Miller, C. H. (1973). Historical and recent perspectives on work and vocational guidance. In *Career Guidance for a New Age*, edited by Henry Borow. Boston: Houghton Mifflin.

Minshall, C. (1984). High technology occupational trends. Columbus, OH: National Center for Research in Vocational Education. The Ohio State University.

Morgan, M. A. (1980). *Managing Career Development*. New York: Van Nostrand, Reinhold.

Munson, W. W. (1992). Self-esteem, vocational identity, and career salience in high school students. *Career Development Quarterly, 40*, 361-368.

Murphy, G. (1984). *Personality: A Biosocial Approach to Origins and Structure*. New York: Harper & Row.

Murray, J. D., & Keller, P. A. (1991). Psychology and rural America: Current status and future directions. *American Psychologist, 46*, 220-231.

National Alliance of Business and the National Advisory Committee on Vocational Education (1984). *A Nation at Work: Education and the Private Sector*. Washington, D.C.: The Author.

National Assessment of Vocational Education, United States Department of Education (1989). *Final Report. Volume 1. Summary of Findings and Recommendations*. July, Washington, D.C.: The Author.

National Career Development Association (1985). Consumer guidelines for selecting a career counselor. *Career Development, 1*(2), 1-2.

National Career Development Association (1991). Career counseling competencies. Position paper adopted by the Board of Directors.

National Center for Educational Statistics, U. S. Department of Education (1992). *Vocational Education in the United States*. Washington, D.C.: The Author.

National Commission on Secondary Vocational Education (1985). *The Unfinished Agenda. The Role of Vocational Education in the High School*. Columbus, OH: The National Center for Research in Vocational Education, Ohio State University.

National Education Association (1988). *Student Dropouts/ Pushouts*. Washington, D.C.: The Author.

National Employment Counselor Association (1975). Role of the employment counselor. *Journal of Employment Counseling, 12*, 148-153.

National Occupational Information Coordinating Committee (1988). *The National Career Counseling and Development Guidelines*. Washington, D.C.: The Author.

NTSC (1993). Preparing the work force of the future. *NTSC Bulletin*, Fall, p. 3.

National Vocational Guidance Association (1981). *Vocational/ Career Counseling Competencies Approved by the Board of Directors*. September, Falls Church, VA.

Nevo, O. (1987). Irrational expectations in career counseling and their confronting arguments. *Career Development Quarterly, 35*, 239-250.

Nijkamp, P., Bouman, H., & Verhoef, B. (1990). High-tech employment—Place and competence. *Applied Psychology: An International Review, 39*(2), 207-222.

Nussbaum, B. (1988). Needed: human capital, Special report. *Business Week*, 3070, (September 19) 100-102.

Office of Technology Assessment, U. S. Congress (1988). *Technology and the American Transition: Choices for the Future.* Washington, D.C.: U. S. Government Printing Office.

Oinonen, C. M. (1984). *Business and Education Survey: Employer and Employee Perceptions of School-to-Work Preparation.* Madison, WI: The Wisconsin Department of Public Instruction/The Parker Fund of the Janesville Foundation.

Oliver, L. W., & Spokane, A. R. (1988). Career-intervention outcome: What contributes to client gain? *Journal of Counseling Psychology, 35,* 447-462.

Olson, C., McWhirter, E., & Horan, J. J. (1989). A decision-making model applied to career counseling. *Journal of Career Development, 16,* pp. 107-117.

O'Reilly, B. (1992). Your new global work force. *Fortune, 126*(13), December 14, 52-66.

Osterman, P. (1989). The job market for adolescents. In D. Stern & D. Eichorn (Eds.). *Adolescence in Work: Influences of Social Structure, Labor Markets, and Culture* (pp. 235-258). Hillsdale, NJ: Laurence Erlbaum Associates.

Palmo, A. J., & DeVantier, J. (1976). An examination of the counseling needs of voc-tech students. *Vocational Guidance Quarterly, 25,* 170-176.

Panel on Adolescent Pregnancy and Childbearing. Washington, D.C., The National Research Council.

Parsons, F. (1909). *Choosing a Vocation.* Boston: Houghton Mifflin.

Peabody, D. (1985). *National Characteristics.* New York: Cambridge University Press.

Perkins, Carl D. (1984). Vocational Education Act of 1984. PL 98-524, U.S. Congress.

Perkins, Carl D. (1989). Vocational Education Act of 1989, Title III, Part D of PL 98-524.

Perry, N. S., & Schwallie-Giddis, P. (1993). The counselor and reform in tomorrow's schools. *Counseling and Human Development, 25*(7), 1-8.

Perry, N. S. (1993). School counseling. Chapter 4 in *Counselor Efficacy: Assessing and Using Counseling Outcomes Research*, p 37-50. Edited by G. R. Walz and J. C. Blewer. Ann Arbor, MI: The University of Michigan, ERIC Counseling and Personnel Services Clearinghouse.

Policy Information Center, Educational Testing Service (1990). *From School to Work.*

Pratzner, F. C., & Ashley, W. L. (1985). Occupational and adaptability and transferable skills: Preparing today's adults for tomorrow's careers. In *Adults and the Changing Workplace.* 1985 Yearbook of the American Vocational Association. Washington, D.C.: American Vocational Association.

Prediger, D., & Sawyer, R. L. (1985). Ten years of career development: A nationwide study of high school students.

Preparing the work force of the future. (1993). *NTSC Bulletin*, Fall, 3.

Raelin, J. A. (1980). *Building a Career: The Effect of Initial Job Experiences and Related Work Aptitudes on Later Employment.* Kalamazoo, MI: The W. E. Upjohn Institute for Employment Research.

Research and Policy Committee, the Committee for Economic Development (1985). *Investing in Our Children, Business and the Public Schools.* New York: The Committee.

Reich, Robert B. (1991). *The Work of Nations Preparing Ourselves for 21st Century Capitalism.* New York: Alfred E. Lenopf.

Richman, L. S. (1994). The new worker elite. *Fortune, 130*(4), August, 22, 56-59, 62, 64, 66.

Rogers, C. (1961). *On Becoming a Person.* Boston: Houghton Mifflin.

Rounds, J. B., & Tinsley, H. E. (1984). Diagnosis and treatment of vocational problems. In S. Brown & R. Lent (Eds.) *Handbook of Counseling Psychology,* (pp. 137-177). New York: Wiley.

Royston, W., Jr. (1970). Forsyth County Vocational High: An investment in youth. *American Vocational Journal, 45,* 58-61.

Sarkes-Wircenski, M., & Wircenski, J. L. (1994). Transition programming for individuals from special populations. *High school to Employment Transitions: Contemporary Issues,* (pp. 139-150). Edited by Albert L. Pautfer, Jr., Ann Arbor, MI: Prakken Publications, Inc.

Schlosstein, S. (1989). *The End of the American Century.* New York: Congdon & Weed.

Schulenberg, J. E., Vondracek, F. W., & Crouter, A. C. (1984). The influence of family on vocational development. *Journal of Marriage and the Family, 46,* 129-143.

Sears, S. J. (1991). Secondary school of the future. Unpublished paper.

Sewell, W. H., & Hauser, R. M. (1975). *Education, Occupation, and Earnings.* New York: Academic Press.

Silberman, H. F. (1974). Job satisfaction among students in work education programs. *Journal of Vocational Behavior, 5,* 261-268.

Silberman, H. F. (1994). Research review of school-to-employment experience. In *High School to Employment Transition: Contemporary Issues* (pp. 61-72). Edited by A. J. Pautler, Jr. Ann Arbor, MI: Prakken Publications, Inc.

Silvestri, G. T. (1993). Occupational employment: Wide variations in growth. *Monthly Labor Review, 116*(11), 58-86.

Simon, R. I. (with Bottom, G.) (1990). What did I learn in the 1980's? A poorly educated labor force may cost the U.S. dearly. *Forbes, 145*(1), January 8, 103-104.

Simon, R. I., Dippo, D., & Schenke, A. (1991). *Learning Work. A Critical Pedagogy of Work Education.* New York: Bergin & Garvey.

Smith, E. J. (1975). Profile of the black individual in vocational literature. *Journal of Vocational Behavior, 6*, 41-59.

Spokane, A. (1991). *Career Intervention.* Englewood Cliffs, NJ: Prentice-Hall.

Stephens, D. B., Watt, J. T., & Hobbes, W. S. (1979). Employer preferences for the form and substance of employment application cover letters. *Journal of Employment Counseling, 16*(4), 238-243.

Stephens, W. R. (1970). *Social Reform and the Origins of Vocational Guidance.* Washington, D.C.: National Vocational Guidance Association.

Stern, B. E. (1977). *Toward a Federal Policy on Education and Work.* Washington, D.C.: U.S. Department of Health, Education, and Welfare.

Stern, D., & Nakata, Y. (1989). Characteristics of high school students' paid job, and employment experience after graduation. Chapter 8 in *Adolescence and Work: Influences of Social Structure, Labor Markets and Culture* (pp. 189-234). Edited by David Stern and Dorothy Eichorn, Hillsdale, NJ: Lawrence Erlbaum Associate Publishers.

Stern, D., McMillan, M., Hopkins, C., & Stone, J. R., III (1990). Work experience for students in high school and college. *Youth and Society, 21*(3), 355-389.

Stevenson, W. (1978). The transition from school-to-work. In A. Adams and G. L. Mangum (Eds.). *The Lingering Crisis of Youth Unemployment* (pp. 65-90). Kalamazoo, MI: The W. E. Upjohn Institute for Employment Research.

Sue, D. W. (1981). *Counseling the Culturally Different.* New York: Wiley.

Sue, S., & Morishima, J. K. (1982). *The Mental Health of Asian Americans,* San Francisco: Jossey Bass.

Super, D. E. (1951). Vocational adjustment: Implementing a self-concept. *Occupations, 30,* 88-92.

Super, D. E. (1957). *The Psychology of Careers.* New York: Harper & Row.

Super, D. E., Starishevsky, R., Matlin, N., & Jordaan, J. P. (1963). *Career Development: Self-Concept Theory.* New York: College Entrance Examination Board.

Super, D. E., & Associates (1974). *Measuring Vocational Maturity for Counseling and Evaluation.* Washington, D.C.: National Vocational Guidance Association.

Super, D. E. (1977). Vocational maturity in mid-career. *Vocational Guidance Quarterly, 25*(4), 294-302.

Super, D. E. (1980). Life-span, life-space approach to career development, *Journal of Vocational Behavior, 24,* pp. 282-298, pp. 295, Orlando, FL: Academic Press.

Super, D. E. (1984). Career and life development. In D. Brown & L. Brooks (Ed.). *Career Choice and Development: Applying Contemporary Approaches to Practice.* San Francisco: Jossey-Bass.

Super, D. E. (1985). *New Dimensions in Adult Vocational and Career Counseling*. Occasional paper No. 106. Columbus, OH: The National Center for Research in Vocational Education.

Super, D. E., & Nevill, D. (1986). *The Values Scale: Theory, Applications, and Research Manual*, Research Edition, Palo Alto, CA: Counsulting Psychologist Press.

Super, D. E. (1990). A life-span life-space approach to career development. In. D. Brown & L. Brooks (Eds.). *Career Choice and Development: Applying Contemporary Theories to Practice*. San Francisco: Jossey-Bass.

Swift, D. (1988). Preparing rural students for an urban environment. Ann Arbor, MI: ERIC/CAPS Digest.

Tennyson, W. W., Hansen, L. S., Klaurens, M. K., & Antholz, M. S. (1975). *Educating for Career Development*. St. Paul, MN: Minnesota Department of Education (Revised 1988, National Vocational Guidance Association).

Tiedeman, D. V. (1961). Decision and vocational development: A paradigm and its implications. *Personnel and Guidance Journal, 40,* 15-20.

The Commission on Precollege Guidance and Counseling, The College Board (1986).

The Council of Chief State School Officers (1991). *European Lessons from School and the Workplace*. Washington, D.C.: The Author.

The Economist (1994). Training for jobs. 330, March 12, (7584), 19-20,2 6.

The Research Policy Committee, the Committee for Economic Development (1985).

Toffler, A. (1980). *Powershift, Knowledge, Wealth, and Violence at the Edge of the 21st Century*. New York: Bantam Books.

Toffler, A. (1980). *The Third Wave*. New York: Morrow.

Thompson, A. S. (1954). A rationale for vocational guidance. *Personnel and Guidance Journal, 32,* 535.

United States Bureau of Labor Statistics (1988). Projections reported in *Monthly Labor Review. 111*(3), 25.

United State Bureau of Labor, Bureau of Labor Statistics (1994-95). *Occupational Outlook Handbook, 1994-95 Edition.* Washington D.C.: U. S. Government Printing Office.

United States Congress (1984). The Carl D. Perkins Vocational Education Act. Public Law 98-524.

United States Department of Labor/U.S. Department of Education (1988). *The Bottom Line: Basic Skills in the Workplace*. Washington, D.C.: U.S. Government Printing Office.

United States Department of Labor, Employment and Training Administration (1989). *Work-Based Learning: Training America's Workers.* November. Washington, DC: The Author.

United States Department of Labor (1989). *Occupational Employment, Occupational Outlook Quarterly, 33*(3), 28-37.

United States Department of Labor Secretary's Commission on Achieving Necessary Skills (1991). What work requires of schools: A SCANS Report for America 2000. Washington, D.C.: The Author.

United States Department of Education (1988). *The Bottom Line: Basic Skills in the Workplace*. Washington, D.C.: U. S. Department of Labor.

United States Department of Education (1991). *Combining School and Work: Options in High Schools and Two-year Colleges*. Washington, D.C.: The Author.

United States Department of Labor (1991-92). Apprenticeship. *Occupational Outlook Quarterly, 36*(1), Winter, 27-40.

United States Department of Labor, Employment and Training Administration (1993). *Finding One's Way: Career Guidance for Disadvantaged Youth.* Research and Evaluation Report Series 93-D. Washington, D.C.

United States Employment and Training Administration, U.S. Department of Labor (1993).

United States House of Representatives (1975). Introduction. The career guidance and counseling act of 1975. Washington, D.C.: The Committee on Elementary, Secondary and Vocational Education.

Veum, J. R., & Weiss, A. B. (1993). Education and the work histories of young adults. *Monthly Labor Review, 116*(4), 11-20.

Walton, L. E. (1957). The scope and function of vocational guidance. *Educational Outlook, 31*, No. 4, May, 119-28.

Wander, H. (1987). Population, labor supply, and employment in developing countries. in Unemployment: A global challenge. Edited by Bertram Gross and Albert & Pfaller. *The Annals of the American Academy of Policy and Social Science, 492,*69-79.

Warnat, W. L. (1991). Preparing a world-class work force. *VOCED, 66*, (5), 26-29.

Watts, A. G. (1981). Introduction. In Watts, A. G., Super, D. E., & Kidd, J. M. (Eds.). *Career Development in Britain* (pp. 1-8). Cambridge, England: Hobson's Press.

Watts, A. G. (1986). *Work Shadowing.* Report prepared for the School Curriculum Industry Partnership. York, England: Longman.

Watts, A. G., Dartois, C., & Plant, P. (1988). *Educational and Vocational Guidance Services for the 14-25 Age Group in the European Community.*

Watts, A. G. (1992). Careers guidance services in a changing Europe. *International Journal for the Advancement of Counseling, 15,* 201-208.

Watts, A. G., Guichard, J. Plant, P., & Rodriguez, M. L. (1993). *Educational and Vocational Guidance in the European Community.* Brussels: Commission of the European Communities.

Wegmann, R. G. (1979). Jobs search assistance: A review. *Journal of Employment Counseling, 16,* 197-226.

Weinrach, S. G. (1984). Determinants of vocational choice: Holland's theory. In D. Brown & L. Brooks (Eds.). *Career Choice and Development.* San Francisco: Jossey-Bass.

White, R. M. (1990). Technology and the independence of nations. In *Engineering and Human Development,* (pp. 5-11). Edited by Heidy E. Sladovich. Washington, D.C.: National Academy of Engineering.

Whitman, D. (1989). The forgotten half. *U.S. News and World Report, 106,* 25, June, 44-49, 53.

Williamson, E. G. (1964, May). An historical perspective of the vocational guidance movement. *Personnel and Guidance Journal, 52,* 854-59.

Wirth, A. G. (1993). Education and work: The choices we face. *Phi Delta Kappan, 74*(5), 360-366.

Wirt, A. G., Muraskin, L., Goodwin, D., & Meyer, R. (1989). *Final Report: Volume 1—Summary of Findings and Recommendations.* National Assessment of Vocational Education. Washington, D.C.: U. S. Department of Education.

Wilson, J., & Daniel, R. (1981). The effects of a career-options workshop on social and vocational stereotypes. *Vocational Guidance Quarterly, 30*(4), 341-349.

W. T. Grant Commission on Work, Family, and Citizenship (1988). *The Forgotten Half: Non-College Youth in America. An Interim Report on the School-to-Work Transition.* January, Washington, D.C.: The Author.

Wolfe, J. (1993). The Pennsylvania Youth Apprenticeship Program Model. Paper presented at the Govenor's Conference on Workforce Development. Lancaster, Pennsylvania. May 27-28.

Wood, S. (1990). Tacit skills, the Japanese management model and new technology. *Applied Technology: An International Review, 39*(2), 169-190. *World Press Review* (May, 1988).